W9-AKT-731

Planning
for the
Unplanned

Planning for the Unplanned

Recovering from Crises in Megacities

ASEEM INAM

Taylor & Francis Group

NEW YORK AND LONDON

Published in 2005 by
Routledge
Taylor & Francis Group
270 Madison Avenue
New York, NY 10016

Published in Great Britain by
Routledge
Taylor & Francis Group
2 Park Square
Milton Park, Abingdon
Oxon OX14 4RN

© 2005 by Taylor & Francis Group, LLC
Routledge is an imprint of Taylor & Francis Group

Printed in the United States of America on acid-free paper
10 9 8 7 6 5 4 3 2 1

International Standard Book Number-10: 0-415-95129-1 (Hardcover) 0-415-95130-5 (Softcover)
International Standard Book Number-13: 978-0-415-95129-6 (Hardcover) 978-0-415-95130-2 (Softcover)
Library of Congress Card Number 2004021713

No part of this book may be reprinted, reproduced, transmitted, or utilized in any form by any electronic, mechanical, or other means, now known or hereafter invented, including photocopying, microfilming, and recording, or in any information storage or retrieval system, without written permission from the publishers.

Trademark Notice: Product or corporate names may be trademarks or registered trademarks, and are used only for identification and explanation without intent to infringe.

Library of Congress Cataloging-in-Publication Data

Inam, Aseem.
   Planning for the unplanned : recovering from crises in megacities / Aseem Inam.
     p. cm.
   Includes bibliographical references and index.
   ISBN 0-415-95129-1 (hc : alk. paper) -- ISBN 0-415-95130-5 (pb : alk. paper)
   1. Emergency management--Planning. 2. Cities and towns--Safety measures. 3. Disasters--Mexico--Mexico City. 4. Disasters--California--Los Angeles. 5. September 11 Terrorist Attacks, 2001. 6. Disaster relief. I. Title.

HV553.I49 2005
363.34'525--dc22

2004021713

Taylor & Francis Group
is the Academic Division of T&F Informa plc.

Visit the Taylor & Francis Web site at
http://www.taylorandfrancis.com

and the Routledge Web site at
http://www.routledge-ny.com

To
my parents
Inam Rahman and Mira Rahman
for their extraordinary love and devotion
and to
my brother
Amar Inam
(1958–2003)
for his life of infectious passion and compassion

Contents

List of Principal Acronyms

BANOBRAS	Banco National de Obras (National Bank for Public Works)
CDBG	Community Development Block Grant program
DF	Distrito Federal (Federal District)
DDF	Departamento del Distrito Federal (Department of the Federal District)
FEMA	Federal Emergency Management Agency
FONHAPO	Fondo Nacional de Habitaciónes Populares (National Fund for Popular Housing)
FOVISSSTE	Fondo de Vivienda del Instituto de Seguridad y Servicios Sociales del los Trabajadores al Servicio del Estado (Housing Fund for State Workers)
HNC	Hoy No Circula (No Driving Today)
HUD	U.S. Department of Housing and Urban Development
INFONAVIT	Instituto Nacional del Fondo de Vivienda para los Trabajadores (National Institute of the Fund for Workers' Housing)
LAHD	Los Angeles Housing Development (Formerly Housing Preservation and Production Department)
LMDC	Lower Manhattan Development Corporation
PRI	Partido Revolucionario Popular (Renovation of Social Housing)
RLA	Rebuild Los Angeles
SBA	Small Business Administration
SEDUE	Secretaria de la Desarrollo Urbano y Ecologia (Ministry of Urban Development and Ecology)
WTC	World Trade Center

Preface

IN THE EARLY 1990s, after several years of working as a professional architect, urban designer, and planner, I noted a disconnect between the focus on the individual in academic training on the one hand and an emphasis on institutional culture in professional practice on the other. I wondered: How does the institutional behavior of planning agencies influence the evolution of cities?

At the time, I was living in Los Angeles, a supposed embodiment of much that is wrong with urban planning: a poor transportation system, deteriorating environmental quality, a lack of affordable housing, and an expansive physical spread of the city, commonly known as "sprawl." Yet, if the city was so poorly planned and managed, how did it continue to attract thousands of new residents each year? A third set of questions arose when I visited Mexico during the same period. Professional and academic urban planners tend to disparage the quality of cities in developing countries such as Mexico while these countries struggle with years of colonial exploitation, scarce resources, and continued dependency. Why do we choose to not pay greater attention to Mexico's rich history of building cities and of its contemporary resourcefulness?

This book lies at the intersection of these questions. The major theoretical thrust comes from the work of James March, who captures the seemingly illogical and messy world of institutions that I had experienced firsthand as a professional. March, along with Johan Olsen, paints intricate pictures of public institutions that ring true. "Information is gathered, policy alternatives are defined, and cost-benefit analyses are pursued, but they seem more intended to reassure observers of the appropriateness of actions being taken than to influence the actions" (March and Olsen 1989, 48). Similarly, the bureaucratic behavior of public institutions is driven by routines, which make them often appear to be rigid and insensitive. However, routines also embody collective values, create predictability, and create major capabilities for institutions through rule-bound behavior (March and Olsen 1989, 24). The nature of bureaucracy, for example in municipal planning agencies, is a hindrance but also a powerful tool for effective action. Crises are unexpected opportunities for testing the effectiveness of such action, especially of bureaucratic institutions not designed to deal with sudden crises in the first place.

Theoretical propositions should be tested through empirical evidence. My field research in Los Angeles was inspired by a remarkable editorial in the January 22, 1994 issue of the highly respected magazine, *The Economist*, just days after the earthquake that left sixty-one people dead and thousands injured or homeless. The editorial listed a number of recent crises suffered by Angelinos, including riots, fires, recessions, and now, an earthquake. Yet, the city survived, and in some cases thrived, because of a spirit of persistence, innovation, and cosmopolitanism. The editorial concluded, "At its best, looking forward, there is no more inspiring city in America." I was in Los Angeles at the time of the earthquake, and witnessed the extraordinary pace of the city's rebuilding efforts, which was indeed inspiring.

My personal experience of Mexico City is similar. Like Los Angeles, Mexico City is rife with crises and potential crises. The city is crowded, dirty, and expensive, yet it is also full of people who survive through ingenuity and persistence. The city's planning institutions barely manage with few resources and often fail to achieve their own goals. In this context, I was surprised to find fleeting references in various books to a successful housing program following the 1985 Mexico City earthquake. The program was praised for granting secure property titles to low-income residents, constructing large amounts of well-designed housing, and working with existing community groups. Yet, no mention was made as to why this unique program was so successful. My field research in Mexico City was intended to find the answers.

A few years later, I was in the process of revising the book manuscript when the terrible tragedy of September 11, 2001 occurred. I was horrified, and watched closely as the rescue, clean up, and recovery efforts took place. The physical, psychological, and symbolic devastation to New York City was immense, but very quickly there was talk of a rebuilding project which would exceed all expectations. All kinds of plans were proposed for the site where the World Trade Center once stood and design competitions were launched. I wondered: how would the intersection of institutions, crises, and routines in urban planning play out in New York? I proceeded to find out, and as I describe in the postscript chapter, it is a nuanced and cautionary tale.

What do I hope to achieve with this book? I present one view on what works in planning, and why. This view focuses on often-maligned public sector planning institutions in often-maligned megacities. I hope students and scholars of policy, urban planning, and public administration will understand that local governments and planning agencies do not necessarily have to follow the fashion of becoming more like private businesses in order to be effective. Instead, planning agencies possess a great repertoire of specialized routines that can be deployed in appropriately modified ways and quickly implemented under circumstances of crisis. In other words, one very highly successful response to sudden shocks in cities is routine planning. Seen in this light, the book could be considered a celebration of bureaucracy in times of upheaval.

The research project that led to its fruition in this book was nurtured by the expert guidance of Edward Blakely, Martin Krieger, and Phil Ethington at the University of Southern California in Los Angeles. Martin Krieger's towering intellect and love for learning has been singular in the evolution of this book. I also benefited from the comments of professors Tridib Banerjee, Jeffrey Nugent, Harry Richardson, and Shui Yan Tang, and the engagement of good friends Deepak Bahl, Sukumar Ganapati, Jeff McLaughlin, Judy Steele, and Ashwani Vasishth. At the University of Cincinnati, Ohio, the collegiality and input of Johanna Looye and Michael Romanos helped further sharpen the research.

The book project received considerable impetus at the University of Michigan in Ann Arbor. The Rackham Graduate School awarded a Faculty Research Grant as well as funding from the Dean's Discretionary Fund, the Office of Vice President for Research provided a Publication Subvention Grant, and the Taubman College of Architecture and Urban Planning awarded a Faculty Fellowship that enabled me to work on the book. Margaret Dewar, the formidable Chair of the Urban and Regional Planning Program, was instrumental in her moral and material support. A number of urban planning graduate students ably assisted at one point in time or another: Heather Bacon, Francisco Lara, Ethan Solomon, Simon Van Leeuwen, and Sanjeev Vidyarthi.

Finally, this book would not have been possible without the active participation of those in Los Angeles and Mexico City who gave of their time, their effort, and their knowledge: Marva Smith Battle-Bey, Hal Bernson, Brian Betel, Priscilla Connolly, Xavier Cortes, Maya Dunne, Roberto Eibenschutz, Jorge Gamboa, Boris Graizbord, Fernando Greene, Wendy Gruel, Con Howe, German Hurtado, José Luis Lezama, Alma Rosa Lopez, Clyde Oden, Jossie Portillo, Lupita Sanchez, Greig Smith, Noemi Stolarski, and Barbara Zeidman. These are some of the citizens and professionals who make Los Angeles and Mexico City work.

Chapter 1

Planning for the Unplanned

THE GREAT HANSHIN EARTHQUAKE of January 17, 1995 was a signal event in the history of urban crises. Not only was it Japan's most deadly and destructive natural disaster in over seventy years, it also raised disturbing questions about existing hazard management and post-recovery planning that had been regarded as among the most effective in the world. Despite decades of attention to the goals of hazard reduction by Japanese governments, industries, and citizens' organizations, over 6,000 residents of the country's second-largest metropolitan area were killed, about 60,000 were injured, and large parts of the Kobe-Osaka urban region experienced heavy damage and disruption. Fires took hold rapidly and burned out of control, structures and lifelines that had been designed and built to hazard-resistant standards gave way, emergency management operations failed to live up to expectations, and recovery programs dragged on well beyond their anticipated termination dates (Mitchell 1999, 1).

How do cities plan for the unplanned? Do we plan for recovery from every possible sudden shock? Do we prepare earthquake recovery plans, hurricane recovery plans, and flood recovery plans? What about plans for recovery from severe air pollution or from the destruction of riots? How does one prepare a plan for the recovery after a horrible and entirely unexpected tragedy, such as the terrorist attacks on New York City on September 11, 2001?

I come to these critical questions through a convoluted journey. In 1993, while conducting research on infrastructure in Mexico, I became familiar with the almost relentless accounts of the failure of planning in Mexico City. The accounts included the often-justified and now familiar litany of urban sprawl, traffic congestion, air pollution, high crime rates, poor economic conditions, and lack of affordable housing. What appears most often—implicitly if not explicitly—is the apparent inability or incompetence of planning institutions to address these critical urban issues.

Thus, it was startling to discover distinguished scholars such as Alan Gilbert, Peter Ward, and Priscilla Connolly actually hailing a planning effort as a success in Mexico City (Gilbert 1993, Ward 1990a, and Connolly 1990). My curiosity led me to find out more about this allegedly successful planning intervention, the Renovación Habitacional Popular (RHP) housing recovery program following the 1985 Mexico City earthquake.

A year later, while living in Los Angeles, I experienced the effects of the Northridge earthquake and its tremendous destruction. Buildings collapsed and many lives were lost, but I was struck by an uncharacteristic composure in the city. This clarity and determination toward recovery permeated successful planning efforts emerging in the earthquake's wake. One, which was widely reported, was the extremely rapid and efficient rebuilding of the city's highways. On a smaller scale, was the less widely-reported Ghost Town housing recovery program, which rebuilt pockets of concentrated residential damage and multi-family housing in Los Angeles. As in Mexico City, public officials in local communities and the media praised the effectiveness of the Ghost Town program (Bernson 1996; Gordon 1995; Markman 1995). I was surprised to find this rare success in a city known more for poor planning, the perceived reason for its unfettered and haphazard growth.

How did these planning institutions succeed in such difficult circumstances? Several explanations are possible. Some institutions utilize their resources more efficiently; others simply have greater resources to begin with. A few planning institutions exert great power due to the support of local politicians or business interests. Charismatic and determined leaders drive institutions to accomplish their goals of urban revitalization, or social equity. Planning institutions succeed due to the confluence of forces in history, such as an increasing social awareness of the affordable housing problem combined with the election of a former housing advocate as mayor. All of these answers are plausible. However, in my research, I began to discover *systematic* features that contributed to the success of the planning institutions. In cities filled with uncertainty and complexity, these planning institutions effectively tackled unexpected and sudden *change* by relying on the old and the familiar, rather than the new and the innovative.

In this study, I look at two megacities, Los Angeles and Mexico City, which are presumed examples of poor planning, such as haphazard growth, physical dispersion, traffic congestion, air pollution, severe economic disparities, natural disasters, and humanly created crises. I do so to assess how and why some planning institutions work better than others in such difficult conditions. I focus on institutional culture, using crises as a test of an institution's strengths and weakness. How did planning institutions respond to the 1985 earthquake in Mexico City and the 1994 earthquake in Los Angeles?

Both housing recovery programs were successful, rebuilding housing in a remarkably short time, leveraging large amounts of resources, coordinating among a wide range of organizations, reaching out to communities, and not only restoring normalcy, but actually improving upon pre-earthquake conditions.

Most people assume that one needs to be flexible in times of crises and not encumbered be by the bureaucratic. I argue, on the contrary, that both planning programs were successful because they were bureaucratic. Both relied on standardized routines, rigorous sets of established regimes, familiar programs, and institutionalized hierarchies. Also contrary to popular perception, I found that neither the leaders at the top of the institutions nor those workers at the grassroots level were the most important in the implementation of routines. The key actors were middle managers in these planning institutions because they knew the institutional structures inside out and also knew what the routines were and how to use them. They knew exactly what procedures to use and who to contact—they were successful go-betweens between national government and the grassroots community groups. They could take shortcuts, such as appropriately modifying routines, due to the urgent nature of the crises.

To test these ideas further, I then look at two negative examples of planning after the 1989 air pollution crisis in Mexico City and the 1992 Rodney King riots in Los Angeles. Both programs failed because the government tried to be inventive instead of effectively using workable precedents and existing systems. In Mexico City, the government tried to innovate by copying strategies from other countries that had introduced programs many years prior and had adapted them gradually to their own contexts. In Los Angeles after the riots, the municipal government brought in a successful businessman from the distant suburbs to rebuild communities rather than link into existing community groups and networks.

The last case study is of the recovery efforts after the terrorist attacks of September 11, 2001 on New York City. The rebuilding effort is a much more complex example because parts of it failed, while others succeeded. The example also shows a more complicated view of routines, in that it is not simply a question of whether or not to use routines for effective planning. The question is also which routines to use and in what ways. The New York example is also complicated because it is of real consequence not only to local residents and to the psychological recovery of the whole country, but of symbolic significance to the global community of cities. The rebuilding of Lower Manhattan will be a litmus test of how vulnerable megacities will practice successful planning in the future.

REVEALING INSIGHTS

This study is of interest to scholars in urban studies—including sociology and political science—and urban planning, students of public policy and planning, and professional practitioners of planning, policy, and public administration. Readers will find several useful and revealing insights.

One insight of this study is that institutional routines are used for effective response to novel situations, such as urban crises. Novelty is not as much the property of a situation as it is of our reaction to it, and the most standard institutional response to novelty is to find a set of familiar routines that can be used to address it. In this manner, successful planning institutions in Mexico City and Los Angeles relied on housing routines that could be adapted and implemented quickly because they were already legitimate in the eyes of the community, specialized for the task, and fit the situation. On the other hand, a lack of workable routines contributed significantly to the failure of the air pollution and economic development programs in those two cities.

A second insight is that institutional routines were similar in the two cities, but for different political-economic reasons. For example, both the RHP and Ghost Town programs were based on top-down, centralized planning, but due to differing rationales. In Mexico, this is due to a centralized administrative structure whereby the Mayor of Mexico City was appointed directly by the President of the country, and the ruling Partido Revolucionario Institucional party relied on an authoritarian structure to keep its members in line at the national, regional, and local levels. In the United States, crisis management, such as during natural disasters, has been traditionally the responsibility of the federal government due to its ability to pool risks as well as resources, and due to the political sensitivity of local constituencies to national politicians. Thus, planning institutions behave remarkably similarly in different contexts, but for different reasons.

A third insight is that planning institutions impact urban development through a dance between standard routines and adaptation to variances. On the one hand, an institution's specialization and identity often rest on a repertoire of standardized routines. On the other hand, processes of urban development are highly uncertain and fluctuating. Effective planning institutions are those that manage to navigate successfully between the two. Thus, the RHP program in Mexico City responded to the demands of the residents to be rehoused in their original neighborhoods, and subsequently adapted existing low-income housing finance strategies to suit the economic needs of the affected communities. Similarly, the Ghost Town program in Los Angeles was developed out of a mix of existing institutional relationships and housing finance mechanisms, and a new knowledge and mapping of housing conditions following the earthquake.

The four case studies from Mexico City and Los Angeles and a fifth one from New York City offer a more general insight. They provide a deeper understanding of urban planning processes. First, the case studies reveal that explicit and systematic institutional analysis helps us understand what works in planning, and why. Second, the case studies demonstrate the manner in which institutional routines serve as powerful and effective tools for addressing novel situations. Thus, much of the supposed novelty and innovation of successful earthquake recovery programs in Mexico City and Los Angeles could in fact be attributed to previous experience and existing programs. The successful planning efforts show us that "[n]ew government programs are rarely new. They usually depend for inspiration and legitimacy on programs previously established. New programs build on the old by layering new purposes on old programs and by altering their scope" (Herson and Bolland 1991, 298).

A valuable methodological insight is in the comparative nature of analysis. We make implicit comparisons regularly, as we make decisions based on comparisons among choices, for example among courses of actions. Most scholarly analysis also involves comparisons. The principal reason for making a comparison in a global context is to shed light on how some common process produces different kinds of results in different places, or to examine why different processes produce similar results: looking first at what the case studies have in common, then at the major differences among them, and, finally, at the common processes which have led to the wide and very real differences which we now find. This book examines the benefits of global comparison through five localized case studies in completely different political-economic and cultural contexts.

However, even in such apparently different contexts, the critical question is *how* we compare rather than *what* we compare. In this book, the analytical framework for comparison is based on the following elements:

- Institutional theory to understand the nature of planning agency behavior
- Crisis situations as occasions for policy analysis and test cases for institutional effectiveness
- Comparative case study and narrative research methodologies
- "How"? and "Why"? questions about the five planning efforts

Furthermore, this comparative analysis was guided by a number of principles such as the notion of functional equivalence and the articulation and aggregation of interests. Functional equivalence implies that one should not be mislead by superficial data and labels and suggests that instead one ask questions such as: by what institutional structures are particular types of planning policies transmitted? How much autonomy is enjoyed by the public sector planning institutions? Such questions warn us of situations in which the same role may be played by different institutions in various countries. For example, in Mexico political actors and considerations largely influence urban planning decisions and policies, while in the United States private sector actors and considerations largely influence urban planning decisions.

This theoretical approach and research methodology is applied primarily to the four case studies in Mexico City and Los Angeles, and yielded valuable, often unexpected, insights into urban planning strategies in different political-economic contexts. Given that the United States is widely considered to be a highly decentralized and community-based democracy, it was surprising that the adopted housing reconstruction strategy in Los Angeles was the opposite: highly centralized and with a lack of community initiative. The Mexico City RHP case study highlights a delicate, and surprisingly successful, *dance* between an extremely centralized political structure and massive community mobilization at the local level. Finally, the study reveals different urban planning motives—i.e., political co-optation in Mexico City and neighborhood revitalization in Los Angeles—for similar housing reconstruction strategies. These insights suggest that urban planning strategies at a global level are neither all the same nor all different; rather, effective urban planning strategies are similar in certain ways and different in others. The key is to understand what works under what conditions, and global comparisons—such as the one outlined in this study—are one of the most effective ways of doing so.

FRAMING THE ANALYSIS

I have conducted this research through the search for a plot in urban planning by way of analysis of theory, institutional literature, and empirical evidence from the field. The plot of a story is a structure of relationships by which the events contained in the account are endowed with a meaning as parts of an integrated whole. We discover plots in urban planning through theoretical analysis, institutional literature, and, of course, empirical evidence from the field. Two conventional and opposing types of plots dominate the theories and literature on public institutions. An understanding of these plots allows us to better understand why institutions behave the way they do.

The first conventional plot is about administrative efficiency as a way of characterizing institutional action (i.e., policy formulation and implementation). This type of plot sees administration as the neutral instrument of public policies with the dual objectives of economic efficiency and domineering control. The ideal in this case is strong managerial leadership, clear lines of authority and responsibility, manageable spans of control, meritocratic personnel procedures, and the utilization of modern techniques for management.

The second conventional plot is about political struggle among contending interests as a way of characterizing institutional action. In this plot, fundamental political interests, within public institutions and without, seek access, representation, control, and policy benefits. Institutional forms reflect victorious interests and establish a mechanism for future dominance.

I propose a third plot in order to examine the role of public institutions in urban planning. This view proposes that the very organization of political life makes a difference, and that institutions affect the flow of history. Without denying the importance of both the social context of politics and the motives of individual actors however, this type of institutional analysis proposes a more autonomous role for public institutions. In this story, the actors are not so much individuals or interest groups, but public institutions such as a municipal planning agency. The politics of urban planning, therefore, depends not only on economic and social conditions, but also on the design of public institutions. In order to develop this plot, I draw from a wide range of literature on urban planning and socio-economic development, including the work of Albert Hirschman and James March.

Institutional literature, particularly the work of James March and Johan Olsen (March and Olsen 1984, 1988, 1989) has been devoted to understanding how public institutions behave, and then showing how these institutions behave in a decidedly non-rational manner, in terms of the rationality defined by the rational choice literature. For example, institutional theory suggests the *process* of decision-making is often more critical to its participants that the actual *outcome*. Such explanations offer insights into the frequent mismatch between institutional intentions and procedures on the one hand, and end results on the other. To further this literature, this study develops an analytical framework of recovery from crisis situations as a concise and clear example of institutional action and as a test of institutional effectiveness.

For the purposes of this research, institutional literature and planning theory are considered to be neither systems with presupposed outcomes, nor methods that provide incontestable answers. Rather, conceptual frameworks are utilized here as an interrogative process of critical thinking into the conduct of institutional actors within particular political-economic contexts. Theory, in this context, is a means for interpreting institutional actions and decisions grounded in specific contexts, in the sense that

> to interpret an event is to seek an understanding of how it fits into a pattern of perception or motivation, history or culture. The focus is on an emergent unity or coherence—capitalism as a social order; modernism as a cultural phenomenon; a distinctive form of legal ordering.[1]

Through personal interviews, site visits, analyses of official documents and newspaper accounts, and data analysis from Mexico City and Los Angeles, the study develops empirical findings and contributes to theory. The case studies demonstrate a more general principle (the usefulness of institutional analysis in urban planning) and more specific insight (the importance of routines in planning institutions' actions).

The overall analytical framework of the study is summarized, along with the relevant case study findings in Table 1.1. Table 1.1 also serves as a guide to the analytical framework and its component parts, which are arrayed in three tiers.

The first tier of the framework identifies a number of short-term outputs, such as rapid action, massive funding, community outreach, institutional coordination, and improved conditions, which characterize the successful actions of planning institutions that deliver housing services in Mexico City and Los Angeles. The second tier identifies the explanatory factors that were, to a large extent, responsible for the successful outputs of the planning institutions. These explanatory factors are institutional routines, such as established arrangements, policies, programs, and practices that were utilized in the formulation and implementation of the successful outputs. The third tier identifies, in turn, the principal reasons such institutional routines are effective; that is, appropriate to the task at hand and emerging from the specific political-economic context. These reasons include institutional legitimacy, institutional specialization, and institutional fit.

PLANNING FOR MEGACITIES: MEXICO CITY AND LOS ANGELES

Why are Mexico City and Los Angeles appropriate contexts to study the effectiveness of planning institutions? Both Mexico City and Los Angeles are large metropolitan areas confronting complex challenges that are shared by other cities around the world, such as New York City, São Paulo, London, Paris, Istanbul, Mumbai, Bangkok, and Tokyo. These common challenges include sheltering and transporting of large populations, as well as the continual threat of crises, whether natural disasters or humanly created ones. The ability to tackle crises—unwelcome, unexpected and sudden change—is a critical, yet often overlooked, measure of planning institution effectiveness.

The housing programs following the earthquakes in Mexico City and Los Angeles were selected for study because public officials, members of the affected communities, the media, planning consultants, and academic scholars considered them successful. Both the programs are of a similar time period, the 1980s and the 1990s. This study of successful urban planning

Table 1.1 Overview of Analytical Framework as Applied to Successful Case Studies

Analytical Framework	Case Studies	
Institutional Elements	Renovación Habitacional Popular, Mexico City	Ghost Town Program, Los Angeles
Successful Outputs of Institutional Programs		
Rapid action	Over 48,000 units built or repaired in 2 years	Over 7,000 housing units repaired in 2 years
Massive funding	$392 million committed for total program costs	$200 million committed for housing loans only
Improved conditions	Tenure shift to ownership, larger units, sensitive designs	Neighborhood safety, stability, and revitalization
Community outreach	Negotiated agreement with earthquake victims, community groups, universities, consultants	Community partnerships at individual homeowner, neighborhood association, and institutional levels
Institutional coordination	Vertical integration in housing sector with international agencies, local and national government, community groups, private sector contractors	Horizontal integration with different local institutions in housing, public works, general services, police, and city administration sectors
Institutional Routines Utilized for Successful Outputs		
Arrangements	Local/federal/international relationships between DDF, FONHAPO, and World Bank	Local/federal relationships between City Council, LAHD, HUD, and U.S. Government
Policies	Centralized policy making (top-down)	Federal crisis management (top-down)
Programs	Existing focus on low-income housing and community participation programs	Existing focus on low-interest housing financial programs
Practices	Housing as political co-optation—buying off political support of constituencies	Housing as neighborhood revitalization—private sector and community involvement
Effectiveness of Institutional Routines		
Institutional legitimacy	Agreement used to establish programs and political legitimacy (i.e., corporatism)	Site visits by leaders conveyed political concern and legitimacy (i.e., due process)
Institutional specialization	Repertoire of low-income housing funding procedures, programs, design strategies	Repertoire of housing finance mechanisms, programs, disaster relief
Institutional fit	Supply-side strategies: trial and error process based on previous FONHAPO experience	Demand-side strategies: extensive knowledge and database of current housing conditions

Source: Aseem Inam.

programs in Mexico City and Los Angeles is also a means of delving into stereotypical images of "unsuccessful" or detrimental planning that these two cities appear to evoke. Studying successful actions by planning institutions in different political-economic contexts provides a basis for understanding the similarities and differences in strategies. These two case studies were also selected because I have a personal knowledge and experience of both these large and complex cities. Furthermore, the case studies present a unique opportunity for comparing planning practices in a developing versus a developed country context.

The secondary case studies, the Hoy No Circula (No Driving Today) program started in Mexico City in 1989 during a crisis situation sparked by a dramatic rise in the levels of air pollution, and the Rebuild Los Angeles program started in 1992 during the crisis of the Rodney King riots, serve as contradistinctions to the primary case studies mentioned above. The main purpose, then, of the secondary case studies is to examine unsuccessful planning programs that failed as measured by a lack of outputs such as rapid action or community outreach, as well as a lack of institutional routines. Furthermore, the air pollution and riots crises serve as examples of humanly created shocks (as opposed to the conventional notion of natural disasters embedded in the perception of earthquakes), but in the same political–economic contexts of the United States and Mexico.[2]

Megacities such as Mexico City and Los Angeles are those greater metropolitan regions that, according to United Nations projections, were expected to have over ten million inhabitants by the beginning of the new millennium (Linden 1993). Three basic assumptions accompany this definition: that there is a set of physical and managerial problems common to these enormous urban agglomerations; that the urban problems which planning institutions deal with are not necessarily exclusive to megacities, but appear in more exaggerated form in those cities; and that megacities also provide the loci for research, innovation, and dissemination of new technologies, including successful institutional action.

The dominant view of the megacity seems to be that of a place riven by problems. Crises, such as natural disasters, are usually fitted all too readily into these problem sets. However, the ambiguity of living in a megacity emerges from a simultaneous exposure to the constant threat of crises as well as to the centers of opportunity. The two contrasting characterizations of the megacity are freighted with policy implications for the reduction of, and recovery from, crises. A pathological perspective on cities is readily paired with an emphasis on disaster vulnerability; a more optimistic perspective underscores the potential for resilience. An emphasis on vulnerability tends to narrow the scope for individual or group actions by at-risk populations since they are regarded as passive victims in need of protection. Conversely, an emphasis on resilience suggests that individuals and institutions are often capable of acting in an effective manner, for example by finding ways of being both accommodating as well as resilient in the face of crises (Mitchell 1999).

Megacities tend to evoke images of despair in the popular imagination, whether they are located in Mexico or in the United States:

> A newcomer today [to Mexico City] is more apt to arrive by air, and before he [*sic*] even glimpses the dried up bed of Lake Texcoco, now edged with miles of slum hovels, the first thing he sees is an almost perpetual blanket of smog that shrouds the entire city. It is an ugly graying brown. There is something strangely sinister about it—a cloud of poison. The pilot orders the seat belts tightened and announces an imminent descent into the murk and filth,[3]

and

> [a]s one of the world's largest cities and capital of one of Latin America's most industrialized and prosperous nations, Mexico City hardly looks the part . . . Street vendors vie with cars, buses, hand-driven carts, and pedestrians for right-of-way on narrow streets still barely wide enough.[4]

Mexico City experiences problems common to the megacities of developing countries, including budgetary stress, high levels of unemployment and poverty, urban service gaps, air pollution, and transportation problems (Wirth 1997). Similarly, in Los Angeles, the

> ethos of growth, sprawl, and possibility was continuing unchecked, or so it appeared, in the Southland. The subdivisions snaked south, down the coast to northern San Diego County. They had moved north, past the Ventura County line, until they were licking at the edges of suburban Santa Barbara County, eighty miles away,[5]

and

> [d]ecades of systematic under-investment in housing and urban infrastructure, combined with grotesque subsidies for speculators, permissive zoning for commercial development, the absence of effective regional planning, and ludicrously low property taxes for the wealthy have ensured an erosion of the quality of life for the middle classes in older suburbs as well as for the inner-city poor.[6]

Many issues are so linked with city size and institutional capacity that in several ways, Mexico City and Los Angeles have more in common with each other than with smaller cities in their own countries. These common issues include the sheer size of their populations and the challenges confronted by their respective planning institutions in sheltering and moving so many people in highly dense areas. Other issues include the outdated technology of infrastructure based on systems developed a century ago. There are economic issues of increasing demands on limited city budgets and the polarization of income levels between rich and poor communities in each city. An increasing awareness of environmental issues has brought problems of large amounts of air, water and land pollution, and other deterioration to the forefront. The urban policies formulated to address these common issues often manifest themselves as isolated initiatives among sectors, and the institutional frameworks for planning have been severely criticized for bureaucratic rigidity and inefficiency.

The extremely rapid growth of megacities' populations in the twentieth century has strained the resources, leadership, infrastructure, and institutions of already overburdened countries. Question marks hang in the polluted air over megacities like Mexico City and Los Angeles. Many cities of the developed world are also coping with waves of poor newcomers at a time when their tax base is eroding as companies and well-to-do citizens move out, driven away by high costs, crime, and a deteriorating quality of life. Planning scholars buttress such negative scenarios by statements such as:

> towards the twentieth century's end, [Mexico City] is the ultimate world city: ultimate in size, ultimate in threat of paralysis and disintegration, ultimate in the problems it presents for its politicians and planners. And these problems are of interest not merely to the people who live and work in the Valley of Mexico, but also to the whole of the world. For if by some miracle Mexico City's growth can be controlled and serviced and planned, then perhaps any other city on earth has hope too.[7]

The vulnerability of megacities such as Los Angeles is clearly highlighted by the destructive February 1992, January 1993, and January 1995 floods (a total of $500 million in damages), the October–November 1993 firestorms ($1 billion in damages), and the January 1994 earthquake ($42 billion in damages), all in a period of less than a decade. When damage accounting was completed in 1997, the Los Angeles (or Northridge) earthquake emerged at the time as the costliest disaster in United States history; more destructive than the combined impacts of the Midwest floods, Hurricane Andrew, the Loma Prieta earthquake of San Francisco, and South Carolina's Hurricane Hugo (Davis 1998, 7).

Megacities are also, however, as Lewis Mumford put it, a "symbol of the possible," and this is true in the developing world no less than the developed. Cities are where entrepreneurs create their schemes and find the markets and financing to bring those plans to fruition, where the elites of technology, industry, and the arts meet to brainstorm, and where deep shifts in culture and politics might begin with an unexpected encounter. Megacities such as Mexico City and Los Angeles also possess the often-overlooked examples of institutional effectiveness in planning, especially in the public sector, as the case studies will demonstrate.

Peter Hall also points out a number of important similarities in the physical layout of Mexico City and Los Angeles:

> In significant respects, Los Angeles is more and more conforming to the notions of Kevin Lynch: it may cease to be a full motorization city and instead become the prototype for a new type of polycentric city region tied together partly by freeways, partly by different kinds of mass transit connecting its centers along high-density corridors. And this may be a model not merely for the cities of the developed world, but also—as the plans for Mexico City have shown—for the sprawling cities of the still-developing world . . . In developing such a model, planners in the world cities will find that they still have open to them a wide range of options . . . If . . . the [Central Business District] is relatively weak and the highway system follows a grid pattern, then equally planners can develop se-lected lines for high-intensity development, with improved public trans-port, connecting selected sub centers which would be encouraged to expand: the pattern now being followed in Los Angeles and Mexico City.[8]

Los Angeles and Mexico City thus share a number of critical similarities: They both exhibit characteristics of developing and developed countries (e.g. disparities of wealth and poverty, large populations of migrants and immigrants); they are both highly complex and seemingly overwhelming cities with similar problems of transportation, pollution, migration and in-frastructure; and they are both managed, or as some claim, mis-managed, and planned by what appears to be a bewildering and often times confusing institutional framework. Most importantly, perhaps, they are both cities of the future: large, diffuse, and dealing in the present with problems that many cities will face in the future.

There are also important differences between the two cities. First, at the national level, the political systems are different: Mexico has been historically dominated by a single party, the Partido Revolucionario Institucional, while the United States is considered to be much more of a pluralistic democracy.

Planning for the Unplanned

Table 1.2 Comparative Profiles of Megacities: Mexico City and Los Angeles

Census Data	Mexico City			Los Angeles		
	1980	1990	2000	1980	1990	2000
Central city population	6.87 million	8.23 million	8.61 million	2.97 million	3.49 million	3.69 million
Central city population as percentage of metropolitan area population	53%	57%	48%	37%	39%	39%
Metropolitan area population	13.00 million	15.05 million	17.79 million	7.48 million	8.86 million	9.52 million
Metropolitan area average annual population growth rate	1970–1980: 5.2%	1980–1990: 1.27%	1990–2000: 1.82%	1970–1980: 0.06%	1980–1990: 1.84%	1990–2000: 0.07%
Number of housing units In metropolitan area	2.59 million	3.12 million	4.22 million	2.85 million	3.16 million	3.27 million

Source: James Pick and Edgar Butler, *Mexico Megacity* (Boulder, CO: Westview Press, 1997), 40; Instituto Nacional de Estadistica, Geografica e Informatica, Ciudad de Mexico (Area Metropolitana): Resultados Definitivos: Tabulados Basicos: XI Censo General de Poblacion y Vivienda, 1990. (Aguascalientes: Instituto Nacional de Estadistica, Geografia e Informatica, 1992a), 2, 89; Instituto Nacional de Estadistica, Geografica e Informatica, Anuario Estadistico de los Estados Mexicanos: Edicion 1991, (Aguascalientes: Instituto Nacional de Estadistica, Geografia e Informatica, 1992b), 6, 208; and U.S. Department of Commerce, Bureau of the Census, 1990 Census of Population and Housing: Summary Social, Economic, and Housing Characteristics: United States (Washington DC: U.S. Government Printing Office, 1990), 387, 627; Luisa Molina and Marion Molina, *Air Quality in the Mexico Megacity*, (Doldrecht: Kluwer Academic Publishers, 2002), 62, 68; Consejo Nacional de Poblacion, Escenarios Demograficos y Urbanos de la Zona Metropolitana de la Ciudad de Mexico, 1990–2010 (Mexico City: http://www.conapo.gob.mx/distribucion_tp/zmcm/zmcm004/004.ht28.gif (accessed December 4, 2003).

These differences in political regime mean that different combinations of populism and intervention have been used locally to influence the population. Second, the two countries show important economic differences. Inflation and unemployment rates are lower in the United States, while a prolonged recession in Mexico, following the currency devaluation in 1994, devastated segments of the lower-income groups. Third, the two cities also display some intriguing physical and demographic differences, such as different population growth rates. The growth rate of Mexico City has slowed, while Los Angeles continues to be one of the fastest-growing metropolitan regions in the United States. As a result, there is a clear difference in the structure of the population. In Mexico City a majority of the adult population are migrants from within the country, while Los Angeles contains a large foreign-born population. Apart from a common shortage of water, in both cities growth has been able to spread at low densities. The problem in these cities has been how best to service consequent patterns of urban growth over extremely large areas of land. Fourth and finally, there is a different attitude in each city towards public intervention in specific planning issues such as housing. Although both cities in the past built public housing on a large scale, the 1980s saw major changes in terms of the policy toward subsidies. In Mexico City, they were available only to victims of the 1985 earthquake, and in Los Angeles, the approach has been largely demand-side, through rental subsidy vouchers, for example. Table 1.2, provides a comparative profile of the population and housing conditions in the two cities.

The same-scale maps of Mexico City and Los Angeles, in Figures 1.1 and 1.2, demonstrate the similarly enormous physical spread of the two metropolitan areas.

ORGANIZATION OF BOOK

The book is organized around the analytical framework, four case studies, analytical insights, and a postscript on the planning response to the September 11, 2001 tragedy in New York City. Chapter 2 presents the theoretical basis for analysis in this study, and a background for the case studies. The chapter contains an outline of the analytical framework derived from institutional literature, an argument for considering crises as opportunities for policy analysis and as tests of institutional effectiveness, and a description of the institutional framework for housing in Mexico City and Los Angeles. The analytical framework of institutional routines in the process of crisis recovery are heuristic devices for organizing insights into planning processes, as gleaned from economics, political science, sociology, and other social sciences to make previously overlooked models available to urban planners and planning institutions.

Chapter 3 presents the first case study, an analysis of the successful RHP housing recovery program in Mexico City following the 1985 earthquake. The second case study, described in Chapter 4, examines another successful planning effort, the Ghost Town housing recovery program following the Los Angeles earthquake of 1994. The analytical framework and measures of institutional effectiveness (as successful outputs of institutional actions) are applied to both case studies in this part of the study. Chapter 5 provides a counterpoint to the case studies of successful planning efforts by examining the institutional factors responsible for the failure of two programs in the same cities. The programs are the Hoy No Circula air pollution mitigation program in Mexico City begun in 1989, and the Rebuild Los Angeles economic development program started in 1992 in Los Angeles. The case studies are not expected to fully convey the kaleidoscopic complexity and material reality of the urban planning process. Rather, the focus is on successful outputs and institutional routines, which were at the heart of the crisis

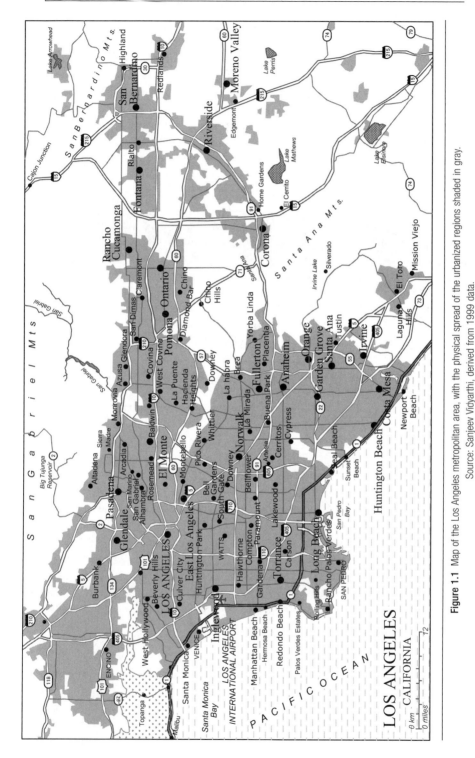

Figure 1.1 Map of the Los Angeles metropolitan area, with the physical spread of the urbanized regions shaded in gray.

Source: Sanjeev Vidyarthi, derived from 1999 data.

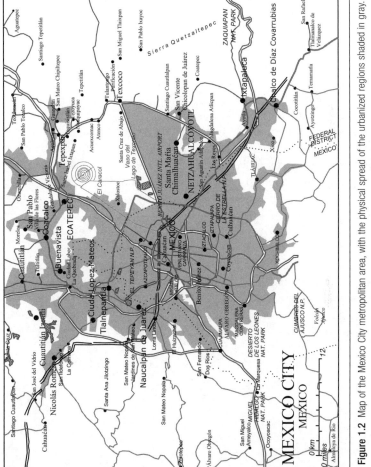
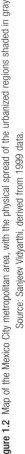

Figure 1.2 Map of the Mexico City metropolitan area, with the physical spread of the urbanized regions shaded in gray.
Source: Sanjeev Vidyarthi, derived from 1999 data.

recovery processes and organic determinants of the course of future urban development in Mexico City and Los Angeles.

Chapter 6 provides a discussion of the study's empirical and theoretical findings. These include institutional routines as plot in urban planning, similar successes in different political-economic and planning contexts, and limitations of the study, alternative explanations, and larger lessons for urban planning. The postscript on New York City turns the lens of the institutions/routines/crises analytical framework on a planning effort of global significance, and finds more nuanced variations of the insights from the other case studies. Those who are interested in the methodological approach (e.g., sequence of case study fieldwork) and specific tools (e.g., interview questions in Los Angeles and Mexico City) should consult Appendix A, which discusses the manner in which issues and concerns raised in the previous chapters were investigated utilizing a combination of case study, narrative, and comparative research methodologies.

The scope of this comparative analysis entails sacrifices of depth and exhaustiveness, rendering it guilty of omission, reductivism, and overreliance on government sources. These sacrifices, however, are made in pursuit of achieving a synthetic interpretation of institutional theory, to better understand the nature of urban planning processes, and ultimately, to generate policies for more effective planning institutions. A hazard of writing about such issues as crisis recovery is the daily outpouring of new crises and new research even as this book goes to press. Nonetheless, the fundamental principles of planning institutions using old and familiar routines to effectively address new and unexpected crises remain valid. Arising from these foundations, a new kind of perception of planning institutions, crises, and megacities will emerge in an ever-changing landscape. In other words, crises in megacities are normal, and planning is a powerful tool for recovery.

Chapter 2

Opportunity Strikes

URBAN PLANNING IS UNDERTAKEN BY A HOST OF ACTORS—businesspeople, politicians, bureaucrats, citizens, and, of course, planners. In this complex and sometimes confusing process, the exact nature, role and potential of planning institutions are often underestimated or misunderstood. Planning institutions, especially public sector organizations, wield considerable influence on planning outcomes. While most of the literature focuses on the manner in which planning is carried out by *individual* actors such as planners, it is also necessary to examine the role of *institutional* actors, particularly public sector organizations. Public sector planning, in particular, is an important function of the institutional apparatus, mediating between private interests and social choices (Sager 1999b, 130). Thus, an institutional perspective on planning is highly significant.

One intention of this chapter is to underscore the important and necessary role that institutions play in urban planning outcomes. A second intention is to establish the usefulness and relevance of institutional analysis in better understanding complex urban planning processes. Institutional actors in planning require appropriate knowledge, skills, and perspectives to equip themselves for effective participation in such multi-institutional policy formulation and implementation. Moreover, planners require insights into the nature of institutions and politics, especially when policy formulation and implementation is based on differing rationalities and multiple authorities. The chapter also explores how planning institutions conceptualize crises, and how an institution's response to crises is a test of its effectiveness. A planning institution—such as a transportation department or a redevelopment agency—will find it difficult to determine its crisis recovery strategies unless it establishes its concept (i.e., perception) of what a crisis is and what role the institution must play in its recovery. Finally, the chapter establishes a context within which planning institutions are affected by, and responded to, crises. Megacities are those cities with over 10 million people in their metropolitan regions. Megacities such as Mexico City and Los Angeles are prone to crises whether they are natural disasters such as earthquakes and floods, or humanly-created ones such as severe air pollution and riots. Thus, an increasingly critical issue in planning is how institutions respond to the unexpected and sudden shock of a crisis in extremely large cities marked by complexity and uncertainty.

The chapter begins by identifying major viewpoints in the discussion over institutions, and frames the discussion in terms of its usefulness to urban planning as means (as a lens through which to understand urban planning) and ends (as a way to study planning institutions and their decisions themselves). In this discussion of institutions, I emphasize public sector institutions, because they act as sources of legitimization and power, provide the means for coordinating and distributing resources at different levels of governance, and serve as mechanisms for the establishment of agreed-upon standards, rules and strategies of intervention. An institutional framework for analysis provides a perspective whereby institutional context and design serve as constraints as well as opportunities for effective action in urban planning, especially in response to crises.

INSTITUTIONAL ANALYSIS AND URBAN PLANNING: MEANS OR ENDS?

An institutional analysis of urban planning is a useful and valuable tool in two ways: first, in terms of institutional analysis as *means* (e.g., analyzing the outcomes of planning actions by multiple actors); and second, in terms of institutional analysis, as *ends* (e.g., analyzing the actions of one public sector organization). Institutional analysis as means utilizes institutional frameworks of analysis to examine the nature (e.g., source of institutional authority) and purpose (e.g., role within larger institutional network) of the principal actors to explain specific outcomes in urban planning. For example, local master plans are often formulated with great effort, resources, and time, but with little implementation and impact. Why is that such a common occurrence? To gain insight, we would analyze uneven power relations between local institutions (e.g., a chamber of commerce with undue influence on local development), and investigate the distinct role that each institution plays within the larger process (e.g., planning agencies as tools for consolidating a mayor's political legitimacy, rather than as technocratic entities).

Institutional analysis as ends utilizes institutional theory to understand why planning institutions act the way they do, especially when such actions appear to be irrational. For example, in order to understand why a planning agency undertakes community participation without much faith in the usefulness of such exercises, we might analyze the institutional precedents and factors that have led to such actions, including ways of establishing institutional legitimacy through established procedures, consultative decision making and an appearance of appropriateness. Many planners would prefer not to engage in the time-consuming, energy-draining, and complicated process of community participation because it slows the down the planning process and often gives rise to increased community resistance to planning proposals. However, agencies continue to engage in community participation because it has become an institutionalized expectation in a democratic society, in the guise of formal mandates, funding criteria, and legal regulations.

NATURE OF INSTITUTIONS

The term "institution" is derived from the Latin word *instituere*, which means to set up or to establish (Ethington and McDonagh 1995b, 468). Definitions of institutions tend to vary widely, but an institution is generally understood to be a significant rule (e.g., property rights), a practice (e.g., democratic decision making), an arrangement (e.g., different levels of government), or an organization (e.g., housing institution) in a society. Thus, an institution is a set of interconnected and more or less formalized rules shaping the interaction of different actors. Administrative routines, organizational structures, and political practices can all make up such a set of rules. All of these phenomena are institutions, because they are complexes of norms and behaviors that persist over time by serving collectively valued purposes (Uphoff 1986, 9).

The more usual definitions emphasize the rules and constraints aspect of institutions, which are considered as precedents for the evolution of behavioral norms. For example, "institutions are rules, enforcement characteristics of rules, and norms of behavior that structure repeated human interaction" (North 1986, 86). In a similar vein, "institutions are the rules of a society or of organizations that facilitate coordination among people by helping them form expectations which each person can reasonably hold in dealing with others" (Ruttan and Hayami 1984, 204). The most commonly used examples of institutions as rules and constraints are property rights and contracts that lay down rules to govern specified activities involving different parties. Likewise, markets, be they stock exchanges, labor markets, credit markets, wholesale markets, or traditional bazaars, are institutions because they embody rules and regulations, formal and informal, which govern their operation. From this perspective, an institution is a valued and persistent set of rules that shapes patterns of human behavior and relationships. Thus, an institution is a "legitimized social grouping," an entity that possesses a legitimating authority such as the power of an elected state

(Douglas 1986, 46). Cultural rules and codes of conduct are institutions in so far as they, too, can constrain the arrangements, or relationships, between different individuals and/or groups, and often refer to legitimating authorities.

Three characteristics are basic to the concept of an institution. First, the rules and constraints of all institutions are prescriptions commonly known and used by a set of participants to order repetitive, interdependent relationships. Prescriptions dictate which actions are required, prohibited or permitted (Ostrom 1986, 5). Second is the ability of their rules and constraints to govern the relations among individuals and groups. Whether they are voluntarily accepted through custom or tradition, or are reinforced and policed through an external authority and a coercive incentive system, these rules and constraints must apply to social relations in order to serve an institutional role. Third, institutions allow for predictability. The rules and constraints have to be understood, at least in principle, as being applicable in repeated and future situations. Rules and constraints should have some degree of stability; otherwise, they would not have an institutional character.

Institutions form and change in a world that is constantly in the process of becoming (Bolan 1996). They change in time through a dialectic process. Humans are both the producers and the products of their social worlds. The product acts back upon the producer. With this dialectical process, Anthony Giddens (1984) reconciles the traditional agency-versus-structure dichotomy by suggesting that active agency (e.g., a decision-making actor) interacts with constraining structuring dynamics (e.g., a set of institutional arrangements). This is a key insight in the agency-versus-structure debate, for it suggests that autonomous actors behave in an institutionally structured world, and that the power of influence runs both ways.

The most tangible types of institutions are formal institutions; that is, structures of recognized and accepted roles that have acquired special status and legitimacy for having satisfied people's functional and normative needs. Organizations are task-systems, systems of roles and rules within which individuals serve as agents to realize organizational values, missions, policies, and strategies of action. Individual members, such as planners, contribute to the accumulation of organizational reservoirs of knowledge about the environment, strategies of action, and experiences that sometimes become exemplars for future action. Individuals' contributions enter into organizational memories, maps, and programs, on which other individuals draw as they enact roles. The lives of professionals in society are bound up with the lives of the formal bureaucratic organizations through which work is done (Schön 1983). For planners, bureaucracies are the institutional settings of professional practice, and for such institutions as local governments, real estate development firms, and nonprofit groups, professional practitioners are necessary to the performance of organizational work.

Not all organizations are necessarily institutions. "A 'pure' organization is . . . a rational instrument engineered to do a job, a lean, no-nonsense system of consciously coordinated activities," (Selznick 1992, 233) while "to institutionalize" is "to infuse with value beyond the technical requirements of the task at hand." A familiar example of this process is the way individuals invest their churches, schools, firms, and military units with high levels of loyalty and commitment . . . "Infusion with value" . . . takes place in other ways as well: for example . . . by the many commitments to persons and groups (e.g., a constituency) made in the course of implementing a policy or protecting a going concern.[1] In the context of urban development, an example of an organization would be a developer whose principal existence is to build housing projects purely for purposes of profit, while an institution would be a community development corporation that also builds housing projects, but with the purpose of long-term commitment to the community, including shelter provision, tenure security, live/work opportunities, and neighborhood investment—all of which are valued over and above its purely technical task of constructing buildings.

INSTITUTIONAL APPROACHES

New Institutional Economics

One school of thought is based on the notion of rational choice in decision making, and is known as the New Institutional Economics (NIE). The NIE adds a healthy dose of realism to the standard assumptions of microeconomic theory. Individuals attempt to maximize their actions over stable and consistent preference orderings, but they do so in the face of cognitive limits, incomplete information, and difficulties in monitoring and enforcing agreements (North 1990; Eggertsson 1990). Institutions arise and persist when they confer benefits greater than the transaction costs (that is, the costs of negotiation, execution, and enforcement) incurred in creating and sustaining them (DiMaggio and Powell 1991, 3–4).

Why, according to the NIE, are institutions indispensable? Since institutions are rules governing behavioral relations among individuals, it is the functions that the rules perform which make institutions matter (Lin and Nugent 1995, 2307–2308). The most basic function is to economize, that is, to allow one or more of the agents to improve their welfare without making others worse off, or to allow them to attain a higher level of their objectives within their constraints. One means of achieving this basic economizing function of institutions is by taking advantage of potential economies of scale, specialization, and/or external economies. Another means of improving welfare is to prevent individuals and groups from making mistakes, by collecting more and better information.

Such rational choice approaches to institutional analysis, which are the foundation of the NIE, combine a focus on formal institutions (i.e., institutions as ends) and use of highly formal methods of analysis (i.e., institutions as means). Rational choice theorists understand political behavior as proceeding within institutional and historical settings that set parameters of choice (Ostrom 1986; North 1990; Eggertsson 1990). This leads them to focus on three components of behavior: (1) the feasible set of actions available to actors within the logical, physical, and economic constraints of their context, (2) the set of actors' rational beliefs about what constitutes the causal structure determining what actions will result in what outcomes, and (3) the subjective ranking of the feasible alternatives by an actor. Acting rationally implies choosing the highest ranked element in the feasible set. Based on such assumptions, the major elements that make up the rational choice paradigm in the NIE include the contractual nature of institutions, markets versus hierarchies, transaction costs, rationality of structure, individualistic explanation, and economic methods of analysis.

The NIE's concern with institutions lies in rule and governance systems that develop to manage economic exchanges. These systems occur at many levels, including institutions governing an entire economy and those exercising control over a specific industry as well as the structures of individual institutions. A key concept is that of transaction costs, which are the costs of economic exchange, including the time, effort, and monetary value of negotiation and implementation of business agreements.

Rational choice analysts in the NIE school of thought have been correct to stress that key actors must be specified, and that there must be room for strategic choices and maneuvering in explanatory arguments. Unfortunately, rational choice theorists too often presume that actors must be individuals, rather than looking for groups or institutions that in some ways act together. Moreover, some rational choice analysts are often so taken with formal deductive modeling that they necessarily avoid messy historical changes and real-life political processes, aspects of institutional complexity that are often addressed by scholars of the New Institutionalism, described below.

New Institutionalism in Sociology and Political Science

The New Institutionalism in organizational theory and sociology comprises a rejection of rational-actor models, an interest in institutions as independent variables, a turn toward cognitive and cultural explanations, and an interest in properties of supra-individual units of analysis that cannot be reduced to aggregations or direct consequences of individuals' attributes or motives. In sociology, institutionalization is both a "phenomenological process by which certain social relationships and actions come to be taken for granted and a state of affairs in which shared cognitions define what has meaning and what actions are possible" (Zucker 1983, 2). Whereas economists and public-choice theorists often consider "institution" and "convention" to be synonyms, sociologists and organization theorists restrict the former term to those conventions that, far from being perceived as mere conveniences, "take on a rule-like status in social thought and action" (DiMaggio and Powell 1991, 8–9).

The New Institutionalism embraces the view of institutions as complexes of cultural rules that are being increasingly rationalized through the actions of the professions, nation-states, and the mass media and that hence supported the development of more types of organizations. Organizations are not simply the product of increasing technical sophistication, but also are the result of the increasing rationalization of cultural rules. Important mechanisms, such as coercive, mimetic, and normative, diffuse institutional effects through a field of organizations, and they emphasize structural isomorphism (i.e., similarity) as an important consequence of both competitive and institutional processes (DiMaggio and Powell 1991).

The New Institutionalism promotes a shift from a focus on individual behavior to a focus on institutional structures. The structures defining the state are such entities as administrative agencies, interest groups, political parties, and voluntary associations. New Institutionalists typically seek to assess the capacity for state action and the degree to which the state can be seen as an autonomous actor distinct from the society in which it is located. New Institutionalism portrays institutions as semi-autonomous actors within socio-historical processes. It recognizes the reality of inefficiency, contingency, and accident in history, and the relative autonomy of ideas and symbolic action in historical development (Ethington and McDonagh 1995b; March and Olsen 1984).

In political science, James March and Johan Olsen (1984, 1989) have done pioneering work in understanding the unusual logic of American political systems:

> First, we see the logic of appropriateness as a fundamental logic of political action. Actions are fitted to situations by their appropriateness within a conception of identity. Second, we see action—including action in politically important and novel situations—as institutionalized through structures of rules and routines. Third, we see rules as reflecting historical experience in a way that ordinarily makes the rules, but not the experience, accessible to individuals who have not themselves lived through the experience . . . Fourth, although rules bring order, we see

sets of rules as potentially rich in conflict, contradiction, and ambiguity, and thus producing deviation as well as conformity, variability as well as standardization. Fifth, we see the network of rules and rule-bound relations as sustained by trust, a confidence that appropriate behavior can be expected most of the time.[2]

The institutionalist approach in political science emphasizes that political institutions are not entirely derivative from other social structures, such as class, but have independent effects on social phenomena (Scott 1995). In addition, social arrangements are not primarily the result of aggregating individual choices and actions; and many structures and outcomes are not those planned or intended, but are the consequence of unanticipated and constrained choice (March and Olsen 1984).

The value of these varied institutional approaches for urban planning is multi-fold, but can be most usefully organized as institutional analysis as means versus ends.

INSTITUTIONAL ANALYSIS AS MEANS
FOR UNDERSTANDING PLANNING PROCESSES

Urban planning processes are complex and plural, marked by conflict, cross-purpose, and bargaining the outcomes of which seem often uncontrollable and unintended (Lynch 1981). In such complex processes, understanding the precise impact of planning institutions can be greatly assisted by a convergence in the understanding of institutions in the social sciences. Increasingly, institutionalists acknowledge the importance of historical contingency and the ongoing influence of historical formations. The New Institutional Economics has seen the development of path-dependency theories and revisions of transaction cost analysis that take institutional norms into account (North 1990). Historical institutionalists are more likely to trace sequences of outcomes over time and show how earlier outcomes change the parameters for subsequent developments. Historical institutionalists are also interested in conjunctures of separately located processes or conflicts, an approach that is of great value for analyses of planning.

Kevin Lynch, in writing about processes of city-building, observes that the principal determinants of change are the shifts in people's motives and values, and in their political and social *institutions*, and not in any iron laws of economics or in some glacial inevitability of technological development (Lynch 1990, 536). Patsy Healey suggests that both the sociological New Institutionalism and the Communicative Planning Theory recognize the significance of cultural assumptions and relational processes of governance in shaping social, political, and economic relations and that both recognize the role of deliberative processes in their interactive dimensions, in transforming the way governance works (Healey 1999, 118–119). Healey also suggests that some political cultures provide much more fertile ground for collaborative approaches in planning because their institutional histories have allowed a store of institutional capital to build up which encourages horizontal consensus seeking and fosters awareness of spatial issues (Healey 1998, 14). Shlay focuses on the fact that reducing space-based inequality requires a firmer understanding of the role of large and powerful institutions in perpetuating these patterns (Shlay 1993). For example, more can be learned about urban spatial dynamics by studying the routines and regulations that govern urban space such as institutional regulations that control the urban land market, tax policies of the federal government, or property investment criteria of large financial institutions.

There are three levels of analysis suggested by the New Institutional Economics, depending on which variables are treated as endogenous (Eggertsson 1990; Lane 1993). Applying these levels of institutional analysis to planning institutions yields the following results: Level I analysis would focus on an output such as a typical planning practice and the processes leading to it, Level II analysis would focus on the character of a planning institution and the stakeholders who influence it, and Level III analysis would focus on the large planning institution system and the actors who shape it (Christensen 1993). The three levels of institutional analysis are summarized in Table 2.1.

At the first level, the emphasis is on how outputs are determined by the institutional structure and individuals' preferences. Institutions are exogenous in this analysis. Economic outputs depend on the structure of property rights and the organization of exchange in society, in addition to preferences. Outputs from political bodies, for example a municipal legislature, depend on the established rules and norms of the legislature as well as on the representatives' preferences. The output would be a decision or policy. Determining factors include political rules combined with the interests of politicians and bureaucrats. Applied to planning, at Level I, one would questions such as: Why did the output (e.g., a housing program) turn out the way it did? The variables examined would include institutional mandate, decision making processes, and budget priorities.

At Level II, institutions (formal, valued organizations) become the focus of analysis. The structure of the institutions emerges as the outcome of interaction between individuals or groups pursuing their interests. At this level, the analysis deals with the explanation of the institutional structure, and not the effect of that structure on outputs. In short, institutions are endogenous. The theory of the firm and the different ways of organizing exchange within a given structure of property rights and political rules is found at this level (Coase 1937: Alchian and Demsetz 1972: Williamson

Table 2.1 Three Levels of Institutional Analysis

Level of Analysis	Focus	Elements of Analysis	Sources of Data
Level 1	Output (e.g., a particular decision, policy, program, or project, such as the Ghost Town housing recovery program following Los Angeles earthquake of 1994)	– Institutional arrangements – Institutional structure – Institutional rules and policies – Institutional norms and values – Interests of actors	– Interviews with officials – First-hand observations of institutional behavior – Analysis of institutional documents (e.g., policy documents, official documents, etc.) – Secondary sources (e.g., newspaper accounts, journal articles, etc.)
Level II	Structure of institution (e.g., a government or a practice such as public hearings, such as the Los Angeles Housing Department)	– Nature of interaction between different groups – Nature of legal and political rules	– Questionnaires – Interviews with officials – Analysis of official documents – Secondary sources – Study of historical archives
Level III	Institutional system (e.g., political, economic and legal institutions such as property rights of the nature of the state, such as the institutional framework for housing in the United States)	– International relations (e.g., trade, military conflict, political negotiation, etc.) – Cultural evolution of society	– Analysis of official documents – Secondary sources such as similar studies – Study of historical archives

Sources: Derived from Thrainn Eggertsson, Economic Behavior and Institutions (New York: Cambridge University Press, 1990); Jan-Erik Lane, The Public Sector: Concepts, Models and Approaches (London: Sage Publications, 1993); and W. Richard Scott, Institutions and Organizations (Thousand Oaks, CA: Sage Publications, 1995).

1975). The analysis is concerned with how actors regulate the mechanisms of transactions between themselves, but without making an attempt to change the basic political and economic rules in society. The models of economic organization can be extended to government organizations involved in defining, deciding, and enforcing the formal rules of society (Moe 1984). Other examples of institutional analyses at this level include examining the way procedural requirements became infused with value in the Tennessee Valley Authority, and a market and state framework to explain the emergence of organizational forms to reduce the costs of economic transactions.

Planning scholars such as Andreas Faludi have recognized that differences in institutional structure make for certain predictable differences in performance; that is, institutional structure will bias policy-making toward some outcomes and away from others (Faludi 1970). Thus, at a Level II analysis of planning, one would ask: Why does the institution usually act the way it does? Generic institutional variables in the public sector planning environment include a wide range of actors, such as bondholders, investors, taxpayers, regulatory agencies, institutions in a different branch (e.g., legislature or courts), interest groups, employees' unions, and suppliers of resources (e.g., funding, staff, or materials).

At the third level, the analysis explains the system of property rights, and the state and public institutions, including the rules for authority, agenda control, and decision making. North divides these formal rules into three categories: political rules (e.g., authority, agenda control, and decision), economic rules (e.g., property rights), and individual contracts (North 1990). The study of political and economic rules takes place on this third level of analysis, where studying economic rules requires a model of the state, the basic political rules in action, and the interests involved. Other examples of institutional analyses at this level include examining differences in value systems and normative frameworks at the societal level and their consequences for institutions; and examining differences in the organization and operation of the state as it affected the course of political change in the United States versus China.

The question for planning analysis at Level III would be: Why does the planning system behave the way it does? This level reflects the dynamic environment of planning, where the cast of institutional and individual actors and the policy formulation and implementation arena change according to the particular issue. The level activates the planning institution by delineating the particular issue's variables: actors, interests, resources, participation, influence, and action channels. Actors are participating stakeholders with concerns that motivate them to participate; that is, their stakes in potential resolution of the issue. Resources include not only finances but also power and knowledge. This level helps planners assess participation: who is likely to participate in the issue's resolution, and to what degree? Participation and resources calculate influence. The action channel is the policy formulation and implementation structure, which may be formally prescribed (e.g., budget cycles), generally structured (e.g., the environmental impact assessment process), or relatively informal (e.g., the process of getting endorsements before elections).

The key underlying dimension in these three levels of institutional analysis is the scope of the phenomena encompassed (whether measured in terms of space, time, or number of persons affected), and the focus (such as an output, like a decision or a policy, or the structure of an institution, or the nature of an entire institutional system).

Institutional frameworks, as seen in Table 2.1, serve at a fundamental level as checklists, and prompt us to discover knowledge corresponding to a particular situation. They refer to large fields of theory and practice in code-like simplifications, pointing toward possibilities. The framework's simple code word or phrase, such as characteristic arrangements or typical policies or systematic processes (e.g., "public-private partnerships," "neighborhood revitalization," "community participation") present variables, which then present immediate questions, such as: What are the typical policies that characterize this particular planning institution? The prompt reminds users to ask larger questions (e.g., drawn from institutional theory and case studies) that probe more deeply and in a more focused manner. For example, when the framework prompts practices, it refers not only to the institution's specific practices, but also asks about purpose-related issues such as the legitimacy and fit of such a practice to a particular set of circumstances. Similarly, a stakeholder framework, or template, helps planners identify stakeholders in new and changing practice settings. A strategy-development template helps already-situated planners develop strategies for specific planning issues (Christensen 1993, 209).

Such a framework would be useful in examining, for example, the sometimes bewildering metropolitan patchwork characterized by a large variety of urban planning and services institutions at the local, state and federal levels (Herson and Bolland 1990). For example, some local governments are becoming more resourceful in areas of service provision and management, often looking to private entities (e.g., contracting with private firms for garbage collection) and neighboring governments (e.g., provision of ambulance services by a large municipality). Special districts have become a particularly favored planning and service-provision tool since, unlike local governments; the districts do not need to adhere to state debt and revenue-raising restrictions. There are metropolitan districts to handle public transit, sewage and water supply, and airport services. In fact, special districts rose to prominence to administer federal programs in public housing, community development, and natural resources (Goldfield 1988, 312). As such institutions multiply; concerns have risen regarding reduced political legitimacy and fiscal accountability, which could be examined through institutional frameworks of analysis.

INSTITUTIONAL ANALYSIS AS ENDS
FOR UNDERSTANDING A POLICY OR PLANNING AGENCY

Institutions are also seen as ends, or objects of analysis. A basic theme of institutional literature is that institutions do matter, and that institutions are not neutral in relation to the policies they host. March and Olsen claim that we cannot separate the set of individual interests from the set of institutions, and that institutions come before interests in all kinds of social interaction

(March and Olsen 1984). For example, the Not-In-My-Backyard (NIMBY) anti-development movement exists in the United States because property rights tend to favor individual interests rather than collective ones. Institutional actions have distinctive criteria. Different institutions may give more or less play to individual interest, but the distinctive criteria of institutional action are official duty and legitimate authority. Institutions do not simply constrain or channel the actions of self-interested individuals; they prescribe actions, construct motives, and assert legitimacy. Giddens points out that individual actors draw on rules, resources, and relations to create action, which subsequently recreate the structures (i.e., rules, resources, relations) that permitted the action in the first place (Giddens 1979).

Institutions integrate the actions of the polity, to coordinate its interests, and to make it cohere as an organized system. Institutions bond otherwise atomistic and self-interested individuals together in an organized society. They promote cooperation and resolve otherwise irreconcilable conflicts through rules and routines (Skowronek 1995). In this manner,

> institutions provide numerous social benefits. For example, they allow social actors to produce, by acting with others, benefits that they would fail to achieve by acting alone. In some contexts, these benefits are called gains from trade; in others, gains from cooperation; in still others, advantages of coordination. The stability of these institutions and the knowledge of that stability shared by the members of a group or community enable the types of behavior necessary to achieve these benefits.[3]

The social context of politics and the motives of individual actors are of immense significance, but institutional analysis posits a more independent role for public institutions. The state is not only affected by society but also affects it. Political democracy depends not only on economic and social conditions but also on the design of public institutions. Group conflicts among groups are mitigated by institutional mechanisms for the resolution of political disputes; that is, by the courts, the voting booth, and the bargaining table. Bureaucratic agencies such as planning institutions, legislative committees, and appellate courts are arenas for contending social forces, but they are also collections of routines (i.e., standard operating procedures and structures) that define and defend values, norms, interests, identities, and beliefs. Most institutionalized organizations exist in the nonprofit and public sectors, because these sectors deal most directly with issues of social and public significance. Table 2.2 visualizes the spectrum of types of organizations and institutions that exist in the private, nonprofit, and public sectors.

Public sector institutional behavior theory often begins by assuming that self-interest is the basis of all political action This narrow assumption

Table 2.2 Spectrum of Institutions by Three Sectors

Private Sector Produces benefits for persons outside the organizations		Nonprofit Sector Serves interests of members through collective action		Public Sector Has force of the law and resources of state behind it	
Private Businesses:	Service Organizations:	Membership Organizations:	Cooperatives:	Administration:	Government:
Service, trade, and manufacture enterprises	Formed to help persons other than members	Self-help associations for specific tasks	Organizations pooling members' economic resources	Bureaucratic agencies	Elected or appointed bodies
Example: Real estate development corporation	*Example:* Homeless shelters	*Example:* Neighborhood associations	*Example:* Housing cooperatives	*Example:* City housing departments	*Example:* City councils
Profit-oriented Organizations	Organizations and institutions based on the principle of membership direction and control			Bureaucratic institutions	Political institutions

Sources: Derived from Norman Uphoff, Local Institutional Development: An Analytical Sourcebook with Cases (West Hartford, CT: Kumarian Press, 1986), 4–7.

leads to pessimistic conclusions about the potential for change and policy makers' and citizens' ability to conceptualize and act upon some broader vision of the public interest. If policy makers and public managers are seen as motivated only by the desire to remain in power, little can be expected of them in terms of leadership or the management of change (Krueger 1974; Buchanan 1980). If all political action is assumed to emanate from a desire to capture the state for personal benefit, then there is little basis for anticipating reasoned dialogue about the content of public policy (Tullock 1965; Niskanen 1971).

An alternative and broader view of public institutions is based on a logic of role-, rule-, and process-driven action and is thus different from reductionist, self-interest driven, or efficiency-bound evaluations. In this view, observers of processes of institutional policy formulation and implementation regularly discern features that are hard to relate to an outcome-oriented conception of collective choice. Information is gathered, policy alternatives are defined, and cost-benefit analyses are pursued, but this research seems intended to reassure observers of the appropriateness of actions being taken than to influence the actions (Selznick 1992). Furthermore,

> potential participants seem to care as much for the right to participate as for the fact of participation; participants recall features of the process more easily and vividly than they do outcomes; heated argument leads to decision without concern about its implementation; information rel-

evant to a decision is requested but not considered; authority is demanded but not exercised.[4]

This helps explain the paradox of community participation, where the *process* is more significant than the *results*. Such a conception of institutional action helps us gain an improved understanding of the dynamics of planning institutions, as described in the next section.

A planning institution contributes to sustained improvement in the quality of life, productivity, incomes or built environment at the neighborhood, local, or regional levels. A planning agency or organization becomes a planning institution when its services become highly valued for the continuing development of its particular community. John Friedmann most succinctly describes the value of such planning institutions when he states that

> [w]hen planning is used, it is meant to serve a public or general purpose, such as ensuring the stability and growth of the economy; undertaking selected public investments and, in the absence of private sector interest, inducing desired actions on part of the private sector through various forms of subsidy; restraining private sector actions to safeguard the well-being of the population at large; redistributing income on grounds of equity; protecting individuals and businesses against the uncertainties of the market; and so forth.[5]

Activities or outputs of the institution must be objectively valuable for urban planning (e.g., improved housing conditions or more convenient transportation), and they must be perceived as valuable to the people involved if the institution itself is to become and remain valued by the community.

The most obvious planning institutions are those that formulate regional or urban plans or deal directly with land-use issues. Planning institutions are also involved in housing and community development, transportation, and economic development. Urban planning is also characterized by institutional arrangements (e.g., relationships between different government agencies), institutional policies (e.g., building codes), institutional programs (e.g., low-income housing), and institutional practices (e.g., community participation as a ritual of democratic decision making). Many planning institutions are part of the public sector, and as such constitute part of the framework of governance of society because they provide the means for distributing resources, and are powerful and legitimizing sources of authority.

Mandelbaum recognizes the role of institutionalized routines in urban planning when he argues that planning processes are those repeated forms of cognition and interaction through which individuals and groups develop, and from which they choose from their repertoire of behavior (Mandelbaum

Table 2.3 Hypothetical Institutional Framework of Analysis in Housing

Institutional Actor	Characteristic Arrangements	Characteristic Policies	Characteristic Programs	Characteristic Practices
International aid agency	Deals primarily with national governments	Encourages market-based interventions	Provides housing loans with attached policy conditions	International experts transfer Western models to developing countries
National housing ministry	Under the influence of national executive and finance ministry	Housing as means for attaining political objectives	Low-income programs for targeted groups with subsidies	Internationally trained technocrats involved in top-down process
Regional planning authority	Plays advisory role only, under authority of national government	Broad-based policies incorporating social, economic, and political factors	Few housing programs with teeth or any implemented	Preparation of studies and plan that attempt to balance different interests
City council	Fragmented body with limited resources	Short-term policies to respond to urgent needs	Programs consist of allocating received funds	Dominated by particular council members
City housing department	Operates under legal authority of city council and funds from national housing ministry	Policies focused on self-help, low rental, and subsidized low-income housing	Programs involve private financial institutions and builders	Encourages community participation through public hearings
Private financial instituitions	Funds from financial markets	Policies based on credit worthy families	Programs for middle- and upper-income families	Economic criteria are primary
Local home builders	Dependent on financial institutions and housing markets	Housing is for profit only	Programs where market exists or can be created	Housing is a commodity to be marketed
Neighborhood associations	Small-scale grassroots group	Protecting property values	Increasing awareness through petitions	Fragmented efforts focused on specific issues

Source: Aseem Inam.

1985, 5). Bolan notes that while planners are usually called upon to solve problems that seem to require only building a new road, developing a subsidy package for attracting new businesses, or modifying an existing low-income housing program, these conventional products of the planner's craft are increasingly ineffective without new or redesigned institutions (Bolan 1995, 510).

Christensen makes a strong claim for an institutional understanding of planning, and offers possible tools to do so (Christensen 1993). Christensen suggests that planners' positions in power relations, inter-governmental arrangements, and interactive decision-making processes require institutional and political savvy. She provides a number of templates that enable planners to gain insights into the institutional settings and dynamics of planning. Table 2.3 shows a hypothetical example of an institutional framework for planning, as represented by the housing sector. The table is inspired by a combination of Christensen's templates, and could be the basis for further articulation in particular contexts and specific case studies.

The recognition of the significance of institutions as ends has been heightened in recent times. For example, the World Bank's policy paper (World Bank 1992) on housing sectors identifies seven enabling instruments that governments can use to enhance housing sector operations: three that address demand-side constraints (i.e., mortgage finance, rationalization of subsidies, and development of property rights), three that address supply-side constraints (i.e., cost-benefit analyses of regulations, provision of infrastructure, and organization of the building industry), and one that improves the management of the housing sector as a whole: the institutional framework (see Table 2.4). The six other enabling instruments are to be supported and guided by the development of an institutional framework for managing the housing sector, strengthening institutions that can oversee and manage the performance of the sector as a whole, bringing together all the major public

Table 2.4 Seven Enabling Instruments for an Effective Housing Sector

1. **Overall Mechanism:** Strengthening Institutional Framework of Housing	
Supply-Side Mechanisms	**Demand-Side Mechanisms**
2. Organization of Building Industry	5. Development of Property Rights
3. Provision of Infrastructure	6. Rationalization of Subsidies
4. Cost-Benefit Analyses of Land Use/Housing Regulations	7. Mortgage Finance

Source: World Bank, 1992.

institutions as well as key private sector and nonprofit sector institutional actors, and ensuring that policies, programs, and practices actually benefit those who possess housing exigencies.

ANALYTICAL FRAMEWORK FOR ASSESSING INSTITUTIONAL EFFECTIVENESS

Institutional analysis is significant in urban planning for three reasons: as means—that is, as a vehicle of analysis; and as ends—that is, as object of analysis; and as design—that is, as phenomena to be reformed. Social explanations of institutional action and change help us understand the history of contemporary events (i.e., institutions as means). Critically, an understanding of institutional evolution allows us to determine whether our existing institutions further those goals by which they are usually justified (i.e., institutions as ends). Normatively, an understanding of how institutions evolve influences our ability to reform them (i.e., institutions as design). Recognizing the significance of institutions enables an institutional analysis of fields such as urban planning in order to discover what works, and why. Institutional analysis highlights systematic mechanisms like institutional arrangements, policies, programs, and practices that encourage success or failure.

The institutional framework for analysis systematizes thinking about how context influences particular situations, how circumstances shape options, how options are adapted to particular situations, and how routine characteristics affect policy in the introduction of action. Analytically, these are important sets of relationships to map out. Such a mapping can also be a way of thinking strategically about introducing and sustaining modifications in institutional design. Systematic thinking about interrelationships and consequences of context, circumstance, and policy characteristics therefore provides both an analytic tool for understanding the process of institutional action and a first cut at developing strategies for introducing and sustaining design for institutional effectiveness.

In the institutional perspective adopted in this book, institutional actors are driven by institutional duties and roles and/or in calculated self-interest; and policy is organized around the construction and interpretation of meaning and/or the making of choices. Furthermore, routines, rules, and forms evolve through history-dependent processes that do not reliably and quickly reach unique equilibria. Finally, the institutions of planning are not simple echoes of social forces, and the planning system is something different from, or more than, an arena for competition among rival interests.

From the various aspects of institutional analysis described above, this book proceeds from the following principles:

- institutional context and action serve as opportunities as well as constraints for effective action (i.e., institutional structures directly affect planning outcomes)
- the rules and constraints, arrangements, and predictability of institutions all have in common routines (i.e., established courses of procedures)
- level of institutional analysis focuses on outputs (i.e., a planning program)
- object of institutional analysis is public institutions (i.e., administrative agency of the state)
- mapping the institutional framework of planning (e.g., in the housing sector) in order to understand the institutional routines that contributed to a planning institution's outputs

The above-mentioned elements constitute the primary focus of the analytical framework. The secondary focus of the analytical framework is the policy and institutional dimensions of crises.

Applying this framework to several case studies, I examine the successful outputs of public sector planning institutions during crisis situations by emphasizing the role of institutional routines. Routines consist of structured activities in the form of habitualized behavior; they are patterned actions that reflect the tacit knowledge of institutions and actors (Scott 1995). A set of routines or standards defines appropriate action under a variety of circumstances. The routines, by and large, operate to eliminate conflict of interest by defining what the community can expect from planning institutions. Routines also give a framework for organizing activities by limiting demands and allowing the community to judge the planning institution's performance (North 1990, 38). Thus, routines do not solve all problems; however, they do simplify life—especially during crisis situations, as we shall see in the following sections.

CRISES AND PLANNING: ADVERSITY OR OPPORTUNITY?

What is the relationship between crises and planning? The standard planning response to a crisis is to prepare a plan for the next crisis. However, several authors have criticized the narrow, bureaucratic, and technical nature of such plans (Cuny 1983; Karetz and Lindell 1990; Hamza and Zetter 1998). Planning institutions cannot predict every conceivable life-, health-, or property-threatening event that cities face, and examples abound of disaster plans failing to facilitate effective crisis recovery (Allen 1994). Fundamentally, the concept of a crisis as just a unique event requiring immediate response and material aid ignores the critical relationships between the crisis and other issues, such as the ability of planning institutions to adapt, learn and enhance their effectiveness in the urban development process.

A crisis situation is an unstable condition, as in political, social, or economic affairs, involving an abrupt or decisive change. It is necessary to distinguish between the commonly used and often confusing terms of "hazard," "disaster," and "crisis." A hazard is a possible source of danger and a chance of being harmed. A disaster is an occurrence causing widespread destruction and distress, including grave misfortunes and total failures of human actions. Crisis is the most relevant term for our purposes, for it refers to a crucial or decisive turning point, whether it is a natural disaster or a set of human actions. Furthermore, we are more concerned with studying the consequences of crises and their aftermaths than with analyzing their origins or exact nature.

Crises are increasingly urban issues, with such megacities as Tokyo, Sao Paolo, New York, Mexico City, and Los Angeles being constantly confronted by either natural or human crises. A crisis situation in an urbanized region is a large, sudden shock and disturbance to the existing urban system. Examples include environmental crises like a severe pollution alert or a natural disaster such as an earthquake or flood; social crises like large-scale urban riots; and economic crises such as labor-union strikes that cause major disruption of essential services such as transportation. Wars have frequently caused large-scale destruction of urban areas, especially in the twentieth century, when armed conflict devastated cities such as Dresden, Hiroshima, Phnom Penh, Kabul, and Baghdad. Political terrorism and crime are also potent agents of urban destruction, as are hazardous industrial technologies, as seen in the tragedy of Bhopal in India in 1984, when an industrial leak from a Union Carbide plant led to the death of two thousand residents, mostly in the informal settlements surrounding the factory. Urban areas are not necessarily crisis prone by nature, but become prone because of structural processes creating rapid urbanization, population movements, and concentration (Hamza and Zetter 1998, 292). For example, residents of cities often settle on unsafe areas (e.g., flood plains, landslide-prone foothills), or create a crisis (e.g., air pollution, slum fires). Some crises are created intentionally, such as those caused by arson or terrorism, such as the horrific attacks on New York City on September 11, 2001.

A crisis should be defined primarily on the basis of its consequences rather than the phenomenon that caused it (Cuny 1983, 13). While natural phenomena such as earthquakes, hurricanes, and floods can occur worldwide, their potential for widespread disaster is more a function of the ability of settlements and communities to cope with these events than of the phenomena themselves. For example, an 8.2 magnitude earthquake in an unpopulated area may provide ample data for geologists, but it is not considered a crisis (Comerio 1998, 4). However, when an earthquake of such magnitude occurs in a densely populated city, the results can be catastrophic.

The frequency of such events in cities such as Mexico City and Los Angeles has increased in recent years; thus, the vulnerability of their residents has increased as well. For the purposes of this study, then, a crisis is a situation in which decision-makers within vital institutions perceive one to exist; that there is a general consensus among them that the situation of a crisis is real and threatening; and that they believe that failure to act will lead to even more serious economic and political consequences, especially within urban contexts (Grindle and Thomas 1991, 160).

Crises and Urban Planning

The perception of risk from crisis situations is crucial to setting the public agenda in urban planning. Key decision-makers must perceive a disparity between what is and what ought to be. The chances of a problem being given high priority in urban planning forums are markedly enhanced if the problem is perceived to involve catastrophic loss of life and property as well as dangerous long-term political and economic impacts. Problems associated with low-probability/high-consequence events are often not made evident by indicators such as employment, crime, and population growth rates. They need a push to get attention. The push in the case of natural hazards is provided by a disaster event that calls for immediate action. Such an event moves key actors, including urban planning institutions, from general awareness to action-oriented decision making (Berke and Beatley 1992, 35). For example, the 1995 Kobe earthquake was not only the worst urban disaster to hit Japan since the Tokyo earthquake of 1923, but also seriously disrupted the nation's economy, costing an estimated $200 billion or about 5 percent of Japan's gross domestic product (Whittow 1995, 81). In the aftermath of the earthquake, the Japanese government learned that in their heavily urbanized and crisis-prone country, the built environment remains at risk despite recent advances made in earthquake engineering. The country would not only have to replace the seriously damaged or destroyed structures, but it would also have to re-examine and re-design the entire stock of vulnerable structures.

Opportunity windows are occasions during which a problem becomes pressing, creating an opportunity for leaders to push their proposals as solutions. In crisis recovery, these windows are opened by a disastrous event, and if proposals are ready (e.g., neighborhood revitalization programs), the disaster provides an opportunity to argue for enactment. Once the window opens, however, it does not stay open long. The disaster that prompted the opening quickly passes from the scene. By its nature, a crisis event is of short-lived; thus, the necessity for rapid action. People can stay excited only for so long. Planning proposals, such as those in the form of institutionalized programs, must be developed well in advance of the time when the window opens. Without earlier consideration (e.g., formulated as institutional routines), decision makers cannot take advantage of the opportunity window, where if solutions are not modified appropriately and enacted quickly, the window closes.

Crises are thus opportunities for institutionalizing and strengthening planning, through resource allocation and innovative thinking. For example, during the housing crisis provoked by massive immigration of refugees into Israel during the early 1990s, planners convinced elected leaders to allocate budgets and to provide active support for innovative approaches to mid-range and long-range planning that significantly surpassed anything the country had seen for decades (Alterman 1995, 171–173). Indeed, planners there played a much more important role in this crisis than they did in non-crisis times. They performed a wide spectrum of roles drawn from the planner's repertoire, and did so with more leeway for action and innovation than before the crisis. Crisis situations, due to their heightened complexity, uncertainty, and change and their propensity to provoke sharpened responses, serve as examples of institutional decision making for policy analysis and as test cases for judging institutional effectiveness.

Crisis Recovery

The time between the occurrence of a crisis and the point at which normal activities are re-established is the period of recovery. The first stage of emergency response in the form of putting out fires, conducting searches, rescuing victims, and providing temporary food and shelter is followed by the longer-term recovery efforts of repairing buildings and infrastructure, providing financial assistance, and attempting to return to normalcy; that is, to pre-crisis conditions. Total recovery from a crisis can be measured according to the emotional recovery of the victims; economic recovery, including replacement of lost income, restoration of jobs and production, and re-establishment of markets; and replacement of physical losses, including land, housing, and personal belongings (Cuny 1983).

Crisis is often invoked as a reason for adopting major changes in public policy (Grindle and Thomas 1991). In class analytic models, theorists argue that a crisis allows the state to take on more autonomy from societal actors and to introduce measures that may infringe on the power and interests of dominant social classes. In public choice theory, a crisis offers a unique opportunity to break through the hold of rent-seeking behavior to consider larger issues such as the national interest. In a bureaucratic politics approach, crisis is the condition that often sets off bureaucratic games, defining the stakes and presenting opportunities for personal and bureaucratic competition and bargaining. In a state interests approach, a crisis is an opportunity for state elites to define new strategies for addressing major problems of development and to take an active role in putting together supportive coalitions for reform. In all these approaches, then, crisis presents a moment or an opportunity for bringing about significant changes in public policy.

Such a scenario followed the large Mexico City earthquake of 1985. A former senior official of the post-earthquake housing recovery program, Renovación Habitacional Popular (RHP), described the situation:

> In the government, there was also a strong debate occurring, which has not been documented. This had to do with the office of the Presidency and the process of transition. Such events, such as the earthquake, tend to provoke struggles amongst various groups in the government, especially those associated with the office of the Presidency, such that certain groups gain ground while others lose. The Mayors of dominant cities with a major political presence, such as Mexico City . . . are always strong candidates for the Presidency. The Ministries, for example, of the Interior, also have considerable power in such situations, especially because they have control over resources and budgets. So, within the first 10 or 15 days, there was a struggle within the Government for control of the emergency, involving the Army, the Ministry of Interior, and the city government, amongst others. Finally, the control was accorded to the city, whose Mayor was Ramon Aguillera, because the Army would make the situation more complicated and would present too harsh a response.[6]

Due to their heightened intensity, crisis situations like that in Mexico City also provide occasions to observe the policy space afforded for institutional policy formulation and implementation.

Research by Grindle and Thomas demonstrates that the options available to institutions are not fully determined by the interests of social classes, organized groups, international actors, international economic conditions, or by the hold of history or culture on policy choices (Grindle and Thomas 1991). These factors clearly determine the outer boundaries of choice; however, institutions also have room to maneuver and the capacity to influence the content, timing, and sequence of policies. This room for maneuvering and influence defines a policy space for any given issue, a space that is determined by the ability of an institution and its leadership to introduce and pursue a reform measure without precipitating an institutional or leadership change or major upheaval and violence in the society, or without being forced to abandon the initiative.

In such ideas of adaptive institutions, it is usually assumed that institutions adapt to their given policy space; that is, the room afforded by a combination of political groups, economic conditions, and cultural tradition, among others. This assumption permits us to see the process of adaptation as mechanisms for matching appropriate institutions with exogenously created policy spaces. In reality, institutions at least partially create their own policy spaces, and the resulting complications of such an influence are significant. For example, much of the richness of ecological theories of politics stems from the way in which actions of each participant are part of the policy space of the others. The policy space of each institutional actor is, therefore, partly self determined as each reacts to the other (March and Olsen 1989). Moreover, there is a tendency for large, powerful institutions to be able to specify their policy space, thus forcing other actors to adapt to them. This is a fairly standard characterization of the position of dominant ethnic or gender groups, of persons in authority in totalitarian regimes, or of leading firms in a concentrated industry.

The tendency of institutions to influence their environment can be observed through the phenomenon of routines, a set of familiar and well-established arrangements, policies, programs, and practices that characterize particular institutions. Routines are the vehicles by which institutions fulfill their reason for existing because they are the link between precept and action. Such routines are designed for ordinary situations in which standard operating procedures are utilized for repetitive and uncomplicated tasks. However, a repertoire of routines is also the basis from which institutions—such as those in urban planning—approach novel situations (e.g., crises). In the end, novelty is not a property of a situation so much as it is of our reaction to it, and the most standard institutional response to novelty is to find a set of routines that can be used. Rules and routines are shaped by a changing experience, and the process by which routines come to encode the novelties they encounter into new routines is vital to understanding the role of routines in urban planning. Thus, routines can be tested, analyzed, and modified during crisis situations as a deliberative experimentation of possibilities.

Rachelle Alterman's study of the response of planners and policy-makers in the Israeli central government to the immigration waves and crisis in 1990–1992 is one such example of routinizing novelty in planning (Alterman 1995). Planners attempted to rely on established modes by arguing that existing institutional arrangements and policies would be able to meet the challenge if only given greater budgets and leeway for action. The Ministry of Housing cited a potential housing stock of 10,000 units at hand in vacant housing units, and the Lands Administration announced that it had enough land reserves for potential release, only if the approval process were made more speedy and legal solutions found for vested rights. Thus, in order for decision-makers to pass from a state of shock (as an initial response to crisis) to action (as part of the recovery from crisis), someone had to translate the crisis into a routine problem that could be conceptualized and managed through normal public policy.

In urban planning, sometimes the crisis is based on an almost violent citizen opposition to a proposed change, such as the demolition of a building or the construction of a highway through a neighborhood. The crises take many forms, but all appear to have the ability to focus opinion and effort to response. Furthermore, in a crisis, a system must handle a situation for which existing resources, institutional structures, rules, and procedures are supposedly inadequate. Such dilemmas in planning take on a sharpened edge. Crises therefore encapsulate important lessons for everyday urban planning.

The Coates House Hotel fire on Quality Hill in Kansas City is an example of a planning response to an urban crisis (Schneekloth and Shibley 1995, 154–155). The fire was serious, and the building, once just one among many eyesores, was now a health hazard that needed to be demolished before it endangered more lives. The Historic Kansas City Foundation, however, brought a great deal of public pressure to bear on saving the structure by starting a carefully conceived and well-publicized cleanup program at the site of the fire. The fire and the resulting "Save the Coates House" campaign brought new hopes for a renovated Quality Hill neighborhood, which included, but was not just limited to, the restoration of Coates House. McCormick Barron, developers from St. Louis, added to the pressure by defining the crisis as more than preservation and safety, and by reinforcing growing concerns that no new middle-class housing had been built in Kansas City in decades and that the downtown was dying. The energy gathered by such multiple interpretations of crisis conditions transformed into collective action, leading to the dramatic improvement of Quality Hill. Such examples provide lessons for judging the effectiveness of planning institutions, as we will see in the next section.

A number of criteria have been suggested for judging the effectiveness of public institutions that deal specifically with urban planning and socio-economic development activities (Lane 1993; Ostrom et al. 1993; Eggertsson 1990; Self 1982). Aaron Wildavsky (Wildavsky 1979, 226–227) enumerates several performance criteria for public sector institutions, which are relevant to urban planning as well. These include "price (a specified objective accomplished at a lower cost), quality (better policies for the same money), quantity (more produced at the same cost), maintenance (we can fix things when they go wrong), experience (see our proven record), values (our values will embody your preferences) and talent (when it comes down to it, you are buying our cleverness and we are superior)."

Most normative ways of judging institutions derive from ideal conceptualizations, such as the rational model (Mitroff 1983; Corwin 1987; Harrison

1994). The rational model portrays institutions as goal-directed instruments, wherein the institutional structure is a tool for achieving clearly defined goals. The important aspects of this model are clear goals, administrative control, specialized expertise, efficient functioning, and the capacity to integrate the different components. The rational model is utopian because it assumes that good institutions are essentially static and are in a state of harmonious equilibrium with society where consensus is desirable.

One alternative to the rational model—the organic model, which is more pertinent to crisis response—assumes that institutions are driven by their need to adapt and survive, not by official goals. Goals are regarded as rationalizations intended to legitimate the institution's activities and justify its claims to resources. For an institution to survive, it must adapt to changing realities through bargains which are required to meet the competition, to satisfy political pressures, to comply with changing laws, and to acquire needed resources.

The organic model emphasizes the importance of institutional response and adaptation. Responding to constant change and a number of crises in urban areas has become increasingly critical for planning institutions. Perhaps the most important institutional goal of crisis recovery is return to normalcy as quickly as possible. This is because crisis situations lead to rapid changes, and our "appetite for rapid change is strictly limited. People cannot bear to have their cherished beliefs challenged or their lives altered continuously. Anxiety is induced because they cannot get their bearings, and have trouble knowing exactly what they should be doing" (Wildavsky 1979, 224). Furthermore, when crisis situations directly impact the built environment and give rise to urban planning issues, such as the devastation of housing, "protracted emergency periods, particularly where victims are in temporary mass shelters for extended periods, have the greatest potential for conflict to emerge over relief programs, temporary housing, and recovery" (Bolin and Stanford 1991, 32). Thus, critical measures of institutional effectiveness are the rapid action, massive funding, and community outreach that planning institutions undertake in order to return to normalcy and provide stability in the affected neighborhoods. These measures of institutional effectiveness will be discussed further in the final section of the chapter on how crises help planning institutions become more effective.

Crisis situations in urban planning can lead not only to normalcy, but to improved conditions (another measure of institutional effectiveness) as well. In this manner, crisis is also an opportunity for policy-makers and planning institutions to redefine strategies for addressing major problems of urban development, to take an active role in putting together supportive coalitions for change, and to experiment with programs that may not be possible under ordinary circumstances. How well these actions are carried out can be a test of a planning institution's effectiveness.

The Selection Committees of the Rudy Bruner Award for Excellence in the Urban Environment, sponsored by the Bruner Foundation in New York, have over the years tended to select projects that took full advantage of crisis situations (Schneekloth and Shibley 1995). For example, the Southwest Corridor project the 1980s in Boston used the crisis of a proposed highway scheme and its attendant "stop-the-highway" movement to address an immediate threat to neighborhood preservation, as well as to argue for better public transit and the need for regional economic development. The immediate crisis for three neighborhoods was a proposed highway cutting through their neighborhoods, which brought people together to fight against it. The slogan was "People before highways!" For others—such as businesses— interested in the regional economics of the area, the crisis was defined instead as a lack of access between the suburbs and the downtown. Ultimately, mass transit replaced the elevated highway plan and satisfied the needs of business interests, while the transit corridor was decked over in several places to create a linear park linking the neighborhoods. The process of transforming a crisis into positive action in Boston required the contribution of community organizers who initially worked to stop the highway and then became involved in the transit project for fifteen years. The transformation process also occurred due to institutional structures, such as an elaborate system of committees and organizations; for example, a small task force appointed by the Governor through which neighborhood and business interests worked collaboratively.

CRISIS RECOVERY AS ANALYTICAL FRAMEWORK

There are phases or stages of institutional action during and following a crisis situation. Actions taken in the first hours or days after the crisis—the period of emergency—include assessing priorities for immediate action, removing dead and injured people, shoring up precarious structures, and clearing roads. The period of emergency gradually gives way to the period of reconstruction, during which detours may be marked, roads repaired or rebuilt, and housing demolished, repaired, or rebuilt. Finally comes the period of recovery, when the transportation system or housing services may resume normal functioning, and efforts focus on recovering economic losses and analyzing the experience with the aim of improving the pre-disaster phase of future disasters (Wachs and Kamel 1996).

The significance and constant threat of crises in urban areas cannot be underestimated, especially for the planning institutions which attempt to help recover from their huge impacts. For example, in January 1995, "a middling-sized shock of M6.9 on the Richter scale laid waste to whole sections of Kobe, killing 5,470 people, injuring a further 33,000 and leaving 310,000 local residents homeless. The city's port, Japan's largest container facility, [was] expected to be out of action for a year or two" (Valery 1995, 3). Furthermore, as the world economies expand into increasingly complex technology, it is inevitable that both people and cities will face increasing risk from accidents in industry, as the release of toxic gases in Bhopal, the nuclear accident of Chernobyl, and the plane crash into apartments in Amsterdam have demonstrated.

Crises are also opportunities in urban planning, if properly understood as such. Crisis situations tend to magnify pre-crisis social trends, particularly those relating to the levels of inequality in the society. "An earthquake like this," U.S. Secretary of Housing and Urban Development Henry Cisneros said following the 1994 Los Angeles earthquake, "bares the truth" (cited in Stanfield 1994, 392). Two truths in particular disturbed Cisneros that day: the large number of poor people whose long-standing housing problems came to light only because their homes were destroyed by the quake, and the broad extent of housing discrimination that had gone undetected but appeared to have resurfaced in the aftermath of the disaster. Similarly, the widespread discussions and debates about the 1985 Mexico City earthquake's long-term impact heightened public consciousness that the city is ecologically highly vulnerable not only to another devastating earthquake, but also to crises brought on by water shortages and worsening pollution (Kandell 1988, 574). In such cases, crises may be seized upon as opportunities to reorder social priorities and the distribution of resources. Crises such as a political assassination, sharp economic downturn, or severe drought also bring to the fore concern for the collective interest that is central to progressive thinking (Sanyal 1996).

Furthermore, spillover of broader issues is promoted when leaders and institutions are persistent in their efforts and use their expertise to develop linkages. For example, people may easily move from one issue, such as the adverse environmental impact of rapid urbanization, to the next, such as the impact of new development on hurricane evacuation times, because they are linked to the common concern about urban growth. Spillover also occurs in terms of better preparations for future crises; for example, building codes generally get upgraded following major disasters like the Mexico City and Los Angeles earthquakes. The stricter codes that quickly followed the Sylmar, California earthquake of 1971 get some of the credit for keeping buildings from collapsing in the 1994 Los Angeles earthquake.

Crises as Opportunities

Crisis situations can help planning institutions become more effective. Often, however, planning institutions will fixate on one particular strategy and will develop an entire plan around one standard approach. Instead, I would like to highlight three different aspects of a beneficial relationship between crises and planning: the "hiding hand" which masks crisis adversity but also institutional potential; the advantages of complex interactions and loose coupling that characterize public sector planning institutions; and a few appropriate measures of institutional effectiveness for crisis recovery.

Albert Hirschman's concept of the "hiding hand" has subtle and far-reaching implications for urban planning as well as for institutional development (Hirschman 1967). In undertaking new programs, such as during crisis situations, institutions tend to underestimate the difficulties to be overcome, but also underestimate their own ability to overcome them. For the most part, this is a good thing. If the problems were fully appreciated at the outset, people would probably never begin, since they would be even less capable of visualizing conceivable remedies. The hiding hand also disguises the risky and innovative aspects of a program in the idea that success merely requires the application of a model previously shown to be effective in different but parallel situations.

Hirschman describes three features of a process for discovering appropriate programs under normal conditions and subsequently during crisis situations. First, avoid early, rigid specification of performance characteristics. There may be many routes to success, not all of which can be foreseen at the outset. Second, during the early stages of program development there should be no firm stipulation of the way in which different program elements may be fitted together and accommodated to each other. That can come later, after each team has had sufficient opportunity to innovate. Third, it is unwise to determine in advance which program design is likely to be best. In urban planning, it may be more effective to develop a number of programs in order to let these virtues and problems reveal themselves before committing to any one in the heat of a crisis situation.

Charles Perrow's notions of complex systems and loose coupling are particularly relevant to crisis situations and planning institutions (Perrow 1984). Perrow characterizes multiple-goal agencies such as welfare departments, the Department of Energy, and the Office of Management and Budget—which are similar to many public sector planning departments in their goals and operations—as possessing complex systems and loose coupling; that is, these institutions are characterized by personnel specialization which limits awareness of interdependencies, unintended feedback loops, inferential information sources, and the availability of alternative methods as well as buffers and redundancies.

Critics decry such characteristics in public sector institutions claiming it is wasteful, for example when more than one planning institution is responsible for developing low-income housing programs. However, these types of redundancies are exactly what is needed in times of crises, when a planning institution might be limited by physical damage or lack of re-sources, or when another planning institution might have expertise which is more appropriate to a particular crisis, such as funding a rapid, top-down, large-scale housing recovery program, or a grassroots, bottom-up, scattered-sites program, depending on the what the crisis recovery calls for. The nature of response depends not only on the nature of the crisis but also on the type of expertise a planning institution has to offer.

In order to utilize more effectively the characteristics of complex interactions and loose coupling, Perrow suggests that institutions strengthen their crisis recovery abilities through decentralization. Decentralization enables personnel closest to the crisis situation to analyze the disturbance and formulate indigenous substitutions and alternative paths to recovery, which may very well be modifications and adaptations of established institutional programs.

Finally, I would like to suggest five outputs of institutional action, and explain why these criteria are appropriate measures of a planning institution's effectiveness during crisis situations. These outputs emerge not only from scholarly research (e.g., Cuny 1983, Lynch and Hack 1984, Comerio 1998), but also through repeated analysis of empirical evidence in the four case studies I conducted in Mexico City and Los Angeles. The five outputs are rapid action, massive funding, improved conditions, community outreach, and institutional coordination.

The first successful output is rapid action, because response time is important for crisis situations and emergency services, such as those required for housing reconstruction, including building demolition or stabilization. One way of judging this is to examine the speed of actual institutional performance as compared to regular procedures for accomplishing the same task. This is crucial for a speedy recovery to the psychological comfort of normal conditions, because the main objective among private decision makers is to return to normalcy as quickly as possible (SCEPP 1991, 65). According to studies on crisis recovery by Mary Comerio, repairs and rebuilding should ideally occur within two years (Comerio 1998, 26–27).

The second successful output is massive funding, because an infusion of resources is a critical variable in the implementation of any planning program, especially those that occur during periods of political, economic, or social upheaval. The initial lack of familiarity with the crisis situation and a sense of urgency dictate an allocation of resources in proportion to the gravity of the upheaval. The allocation of substantial resources by planning institutions is also seen as a symbol of concern and action.

The third successful output, improved conditions, refers to both the physical and the socio-economic conditions of affected neighborhoods after crises. For example, given the efficiencies of scale and the organization of the construction industry, it may appear to be cheaper to clear a site, discard all the old structures, and rebuild on a regular pattern than it is to patch and revise piecemeal. But this financial calculation fails to take into account resource depletion, social loss, personal anguish, or political resistance. Reuse in a settled region is supported by a web of services already in place, not only of urban infrastructure and public facilities, but the network of human relations and activities whose disruption and replacement are such a serious cost in any new settlement. Moreover, the environment finally resulting is likely to be richer and more inviting (Lynch and Hack 1984, 347). Improved conditions also imply not only complete physical and social recovery, but also better architectural designs, more disaster-resistant structures, and greater sensitivity to the contemporary urban fabric. Furthermore, planning institutions' long-term recovery programs can help develop local leadership, contribute to building community organizations, and help to improve local skills (Cuny 1983, 159).

The fourth successful output, community outreach, is based on the belief that planning institutions that communicate well with their community about their policies and programs are more effective. Outreach lets the community know that the planning institution is interested in their views and in responding to their problems. Outreach helps the institution react quickly to specific issues identified by the community and helps to assess community attitudes about proposed policies and programs. In crisis recovery, the degree and type of community outreach helps determine whether the institution is simply an agent of relief or a participant in larger community processes, for example of the long-term improvement of the neighborhood.

The fifth successful output, institutional coordination, reflects the degree to which planning and other relevant institutions are vertically and horizontally integrated (Wachs and Kamel 1996). Vertical integration is the degree of connection among local organizations and state and federal agencies. Horizontal integration is the degree to which different agencies at a single level of government—for example, municipal government—are linked through the flow of information, communication, shared resources, and similarity of practices. The 1987 Whittier earthquake in California dramatically highlighted the crucial role institutional partnerships play: the recovery process was led by the city, but was significantly assisted by outside resources.

Frequently, crisis situations give rise to such institutional coordination, which not only ensures smoother operations but also enables the creation of ideas and programs that may not have been considered under normal circumstances. For example, Alterman describes the crisis of housing for the massive waves of immigrants into Israel in the early 1990s (Alterman 1995, 162). The Chief Engineer of the Ministry of Housing assembled an ad hoc forum that included private developers, development professionals, central and local government representatives, and two members from academia. For a time, this new forum functioned as a national think tank of sorts; all participants volunteered their time, and the sense of a joint, important mission united them, thus enabling more effective institutional action.

The five successful outputs describe above offer some measures of effective institutional action in urban planning. They are best considered in combination with each other, rather than in isolation. These criteria are tested in the case studies in this book so as to examine just how such successful outputs manifested themselves, and to understand the factors that contributed to their success or failure.

The standard planning response to a crisis is to prepare a plan for the next crisis. Such a simplistic and bureaucratic response, while commendable for its contribution to crisis preparedness, is nonetheless too shortsighted and narrow-minded a strategy. Disaster plans tend to promote a technically oriented and overly localized strategy that rarely takes into account a broader array of community goals, involving a larger number of citizens, and linkages with greater patterns of development (Burby et al. 1999). Formal disaster plans have been adopted by over 80 percent of U.S. localities, yet an assessment by the International City Management Association concluded that local governments continue to be surprised when the procedures in their lengthy plans prove irrelevant in crises (Karetz and Lindell 1990, 5). Different critics have attributed such failures to various factors, including a failure to learn from experience and doing the wrong kind of planning.

From the aspects of crisis situations described in the preceding sections of this chapter, I focus on the following elements as part of the analytical framework of this study: crisis as a situation in an urban area marked by heightened complexity, uncertainty, and change; crisis as an opportunity for policy analysis in terms of policy changes, policy spaces, and institutional adaptation; and crisis as a test of institutional effectiveness in terms of the institution's ability to promote a return to normalcy, or even to attain improved conditions. While the decision-making impetus for institutions during crisis situations is exceptional (e.g., a sense of urgency), the actual formulation of policies, programs, and practices to respond to such an exceptional situation is often based on institutional routines (e.g., existing procedures). The advantage of translating institutional routines into plans and policy measures for crisis recovery is that they are largely accepted, have already been tried, and are thus quite feasible. Before applying this analytical approach to the primary case studies of successful planning in Mexico City and Los Angeles, it would be pertinent to provide a background with an outline of the institutional frameworks of housing in the two cities.

INSTITUTIONAL FRAMEWORKS OF HOUSING

One of the purposes of a comparative analysis of the two primary case studies between Mexico City and Los Angeles is to study the effects of different housing institutions on different contexts; that is, to understand what works institutionally under what conditions in urban planning generally, and in housing specifically. Housing institutions in the two cities are, in theory, distinct, because they are part of national housing systems established through enactment of national legislation, establishment of national and local institutions, formulation of national policies implemented at the local level, application of national resources, and implementation of national programs which are particular to each political-economic context and set of specific urban conditions.

Housing development activities in Mexico City cover a wide range of possibilities: on one side of the spectrum is the formal housing sector based primarily on single-family residential units and property ownership; on the other side is the informal housing sector based primarily on illegal land acquisitions such as land invasions and squatter settlements, and informal means of construction such as self-help strategies. In order to understand the housing process functions at various points of this spectrum, housing activity may be divided into three categories: private sector housing involving credit from private banks, popular housing built by the informal and non-profit sectors, and finally, public sector housing built or promoted by state agencies with federal or state funds.

The private sector in Mexico City includes both formal and informal systems of housing supply. Given the limited extent to which demand has been met through the state sector, housing production is largely private. Middle-income and upper-middle-income groups seek housing through formal and legal supply systems, while the poor acquire land illegally and self-build. Private housing supply has moved from a predominantly multi-family rental housing market for middle- and low-income groups to a predominantly single-family ownership housing market for upper-middle and high-income groups. Furthermore, in recent decades there has been an increase in ownership housing and a decrease in rental housing, along with a change in the geographical distribution of private housing towards suburban locations (i.e., municipalities in the surrounding State of Mexico).

The popular or informal housing sector has been the fastest-growing housing sector, constituting about 65 percent of total housing stock in Mexico City (Dowall and Wilk 1989). The popular housing sector represents a viable means to many urban residents who cannot otherwise access the formal land and housing market. Although the settlement pattern is still characterized by illegal land acquisition (either through land invasions or illegal sales of property titles) and self-help construction, there have been changes in the types of residents and scale of settlements. While the popular settlements in the 1970s started with massive land invasion involving new residents from the countryside, the popular settlements in more recent years take place more gradually and involve residents that have had to move from other locations in Mexico City. Furthermore, the struggle for land regularization of illegal settlements is a common practice in Mexico City, and the strategies of community institutions in charge are becoming so systematic and widespread that they now operate on a national scale.

Irregular settlements in Mexico City comprise squatter settlements where households capture land through well-orchestrated invasions that involve large numbers of families. Although in Mexico City several famous invasion settlements exist in the south of the city, this mode of acquisition tends to be the exception rather than the rule. Illegal subdivisions of land for sale—by landlords, real estate companies, or *ejidatarios* (i.e., shareholders in common land) —is a much safer, if more expensive, means to acquire a plot than invading it. They are illegal because servicing norms are not met, or because authorization of sale and transfer of title is not forthcoming or sought by the developers.

Rapid expansion of these neighborhoods occurred during the 1950s and 1960s; since then the pace of formation has slowed. An estimated 50 to 60 percent of Mexico City's population lives in settlements that began through one or other of these land alienation processes, although post hoc legislation and servicing combined with on-site dwelling consolidation and improvement have often changed the legal and physical status of the neighborhood (Ward 1990b).

Intervention by public sector housing institutions has changed in nature and has increased dramatically in recent years. Both qualitatively and quantitatively, housing intervention has become responsive to different sets of needs and income groups. Three principal branches of the public sector housing supply have acquired importance in Mexico over the years.

First, selected groups are assisted by social security or welfare agencies such as the Mexican Social Security Institute (Instituto Mexicano de Seguro Social, or IMSS) and the Civil Pensions and Retirement Directorate for State Employees (Instituto de Seguridad y Servicios Sociales de los Trabajadores al Servicio del Estado, or ISSSTE). Second, the social membership housing funds are specifically designed to accelerate the supply of housing to blue-collar registered workers (Instituto Nacional del Fondo de Vivienda par los Trabajadores, or INFONAVIT) or to state employees (Fondo de Vivienda del Instituto de Seguridad y Servicios Sociales de los Trabajadores al Servicio del Estado, or FOVISSSITE). Third, agencies have been specifically established to attend to housing needs of lower-income groups; these agencies include the National Housing Institute (Instituto Nacional de Vivienda, or INV), the National Public Works Bank (Banco Nacional de Obras, or BANOBRAS), and their more recent offshoots, Instituto Nacional de Desarrollo de la Comunidad (INDECO) and Fideicomiso Fondo de Habitaciones Populares (FONHAPO).

Since 1980, public sector housing production expanded with a public housing agency (FONHAPO) beginning to make a significant contribution for the first time. FONHAPO was created in 1981 and strengthened from 1983 onward as a popular housing fund for low-earning self-employed workers and those in the informal sector. FONHAPO's housing actions included sites and services, core units, support programs to assist self-builders improve their dwellings, upgrading programs that include credit for land regularization, acquisition of apartments by renters, and the construction of small completed homes. FONHAPO has been one of the rare planning institutions in Mexico able to claim any success in its housing programs; it was also one of the leading institutional actors for success of the RHP program described in the next chapter.

The economic crash of 1982 and the subsequent period of austerity offer insights into housing policy in Mexico at a time of intense hardship. Faced with a sharp rise in unemployment and underemployment, a decline in real wages, and reduction or removal of subsidies on subsistence items, social welfare policy—especially housing—became a critical ingredient in Mexico's ability to dig in through the recession and offset social unrest. Within a period of four months the old Human Settlements Ministry had been recast, and the new Ecology and Urban Development Ministry (SEDUE) unveiled a Program of Immediate Housing Action (Programa de Vivienda de Accion Inmediata, or PVAI) designed as a response to the housing problem. In general, it aimed at controlling land speculation, developing federal reserves, promoting community participation in urban service installation and in self-help and sites-and-services, and regrouping the financial systems to cover the least protected social groups. The RHP program was based on a number of these routines that are typical of Mexico City's institutional framework of housing. The existing arrangements for housing provision in Mexico City are summarized in Table 2.5.

In contrast to Mexico, housing finance and production in the United States is overwhelmingly the responsibility of the private sector. Still, all levels of the U.S. government play roles of varying importance in determining housing supply and demand. In some cases, local governments build, own, and manage housing using resources provided by the federal government. The financing of new construction and of mortgage obligations has been greatly influenced by the regulations and credit guarantees of the federal

Table 2.5 Institutional Framework for Housing in Mexico City

Sector/Level	Private Sector	Nonprofit Sector	Public Sector
International level	International financial markets	International charities such as the Red Cross	World Bank*
National level	Home builders		SEDUE (Ministry of Urban Development And Ecology)
			BANOBRAS (National Public Works Bank)
			FOVISSSTE (National Fund of the Institute of Social Services and Security for State Workers)
			INDECO (National Institute for Community Development)
			INFONAVIT (National Fund of Housing for Workers)
			FONHAPO (National Fund for Popular Housing)*
Regional level			
Local level	Financial institutions	Self-help housing groups	DDF (Department of the Federal District)
	Real estate developers	Illegal squatter settlement groups	

Source: Aseem Inam.
Note: * denotes a key institutional actor in the Renovación Habitacional Popular program.

government. The availability of land for housing and for other urban development is quite heavily regulated at the local level. Moreover, the attractiveness of housing and residential construction is greatly influenced by tax policies adopted by the federal government and by the systems of taxation used by local governments.

Most federal and state housing policies in the United States operate through tax and capital markets to increase the demand for housing or the supply of capital to the housing sector. Simultaneously, the regulation of public health, safety, and welfare is undertaken by the fifty states and by the many counties, cities, and towns within them. These regulations may include the establishment of standards for construction and maintenance of dwellings and even the regulation of rents. Legal power to regulate land use lies with the states and has been delegated by the states to the municipalities for various purposes (e.g., zoning).

The dominant institutional actor at the federal level in the institutional framework for housing in Los Angeles, and in the Ghost Town housing recovery program case study, is the U.S. Department of Housing and Urban Development (HUD). Created in 1965, HUD administers the Community Development Block Grant (CDBG) program, the Section 8 Housing voucher program, the HOME housing block grant program, and renovation and tenant assistant funds for the nation's local public housing authorities. Prior to 1973, most HUD programs were supply-side programs. That is, construction and mortgage interest subsidies were paid to developers for the purposes of building and operating low-income housing. In 1974, HUD switched course and enacted the Section 8 program, a demand-side approach that pays qualified households an allowance equal to the difference between local apartment rents and 30 percent of their income. Section 8 funds are authorized by Congress and administered by local public housing authorities.

With the shift from a supply-side to demand-side orientation, and the phase-out of public housing construction, HUD's responsibilities for housing construction and renovation were substantially reduced. Under the Reagan and first Bush administrations, HUD's budget was also reduced. In more recent years, HUD has seen some of its funding base restored, beginning with the McKinney Act in 1989 (providing for the awarding of homeless relief funds) and then the HOME block grant program in 1990. HUD does not administer any emergency disaster relief programs. The one action the agency can undertake is to reallocate excess Section 8 vouchers where available, and facilitate rehabilitation funds to the impacted area (Comerio, Landis, and Rofe 1994, 31).

State government roles in housing exist in three areas. First, states create basic legislation-setting standards, and in a few cases, provide administrative mechanisms for the regulation of building and housing at the local level. Examples include state building codes, eviction provisions, environmental standards, and labor regulations. Second, states have in the past twenty years provided some assistance to low- and even moderate-income housing development, largely by helping finance below-market-rate loans or loan guarantees. They have been effected through state-level housing finance agencies, which have the power to issue bonds for housing purposes. Third, states have often pioneered in developing programs of support for housing that have then been adopted at the federal level. Although such experimental programs have never amounted to much quantitatively, they have provided a laboratory for innovation. Thus states often serve as pioneers in developing new housing programs, and their efforts have proven useful in stimulating later innovation at the federal level.

State-level planning institutions generally have little influence over urban planning at the local level, because their laws defer to the power of local government. One example is California's Department of Housing and Community Development (HCD). By law, all municipal and county governments must submit a draft of the housing element or section of their general plan to HCD for review and comment. However, HCD has no legal authority to require improvements in the housing elements and local governments are not even required to give HCD a copy of the final version, though most do so anyway. Furthermore, there is no administrative procedure for penalizing local governments if their housing plans are inappropriate in some manner. The HCD can, with the state Attorney General's assistance, file lawsuits against local governments in California in the hope of making them comply with the intent of the law (Fulton 1991, 30).

Local actions have in many ways more impact on the shape of housing in the United States than do federal or state ones. Local governments, such as that of the City of Los Angeles, are empowered to regulate existing housing and the conditions under which new housing is constructed. Even when new housing construction is funded directly by higher levels of government, it is carried out at the local level. The important point is that while many levels and agencies of government participate in the process that leads to the provision of housing, no single agency in the United States has comprehensive responsibility for the growth of the housing supply.

Property taxes collected at the local level are the major source of revenue for most municipal, county, and special district governments. Innovative approaches in housing by local governments range from rehabilitation and management of city-owned and tax-foreclosed housing, to below-market-rate loans (such as those used in the Ghost Town program), to technical assistance and coordination of private housing activities, and assistance to self-help groups. Public-private partnership is the term used to designate the various mechanisms used to combine limited public sector funds with private sector profit-motivated activities in the hope of lowering the total costs of housing below those that private sector would otherwise produce.

The Housing Authority of the City of Los Angeles operates the city's public housing program. Regulatory functions are located in the Building and Safety Department, and planning functions are carried out by the Planning Department. One of the major institutional actors and producers of housing has been the Community Redevelopment Agency, much of it financed by a California law which mandates that 20 percent of the revenues generated in tax increment districts be allocated to affordable housing.

In 1980, Los Angeles' housing functions were nominally set in the Community Development Department, which implemented the city's CDBG program. At the beginning of the 1980s, the city typically spent around 50 percent of its federal block grant on housing functions (Goetz 1993, 141).

The CDBG program was to play a major role in the success of the Ghost Town housing recovery program after the Los Angeles earthquake of 1994.

The turning point for local housing policy in Los Angeles came in 1988, when the Mayor's Blue Ribbon Committee on Affordable Housing released its report (Goetz 1993). The Committee found that there was no citywide housing policy document, no formalized process to monitor the housing market, and no procedures for evaluating the housing assistance delivery system. The City Council unanimously endorsed the Committee's recommendations, and went forward in 1990 with the creation of the Los Angeles Housing Department (LAHD) and the Affordable Housing Commission. The Housing Department was established to run the city's rehabilitation and new construction programs, as well as to take over the city's rent control program and housing planning functions. The Housing Department clearly took the lead in the city's earthquake recovery program for the Ghost Town program (which is analyzed in a subsequent chapter), shaping policy and coordinating with neighborhood, city, state, and federal institutions. The institutional framework for housing in Los Angeles is summarized in Table 2.6.

HOUSING RECOVERY: RENOVACIÓN HABITACIONAL POPULAR AND GHOST TOWN PROGRAMS

The two case studies in the following chapters, the RHP and Ghost Town housing recovery programs in Mexico City and Los Angeles respectively, were acclaimed for their uniquely successful institutional actions. Both programs dealt with areas of concentrated residential devastation, and represented a relatively large scale of effort and intervention by public sector planning institutions. Furthermore, both programs emerged during difficult crisis situations, and contained five successful outputs that were present to different degrees and in different forms—rapid action, massive funding, improved conditions, community outreach, and institutional coordination—thus enabling me to explore similarities and differences between the institutions' actions. These five successful outputs emerged from repeated analyses of the documentation (e.g., studies, reports, and interviews) on the two programs. The comments of Mexico City community leader, German Hurtado, are typical in their evocation of successful outputs:

> it [the RHP program] was effective because it had money [i.e. massive funding]. Moreover, it was effective because the cost of the housing was low for the residents . . . Moreover, [it was effective because] there was an agreement with the social organizations which allowed such development [i.e., community outreach] . . . The success was that in a short time it was able to attain its objectives [i.e., rapid action].[7]

Table 2.6 Institutional Framework for Housing in Los Angeles

Sector/Level	Private Sector	Nonprofit Sector	Public Sector
International level	International financial markets		
National level	Fannie Mae (Federal National Mortgage Association)		U.S. Congress*
	Freddie Mac (Federal Home Loan Mortgage Corporation)		HUD* (U.S. Department of Housing and Urban Development)
Regional level		Southern California Association of Non-Profit Housing	California Department of Housing and Community Development
			California Housing Finance Agency
			SCAG (Southern California Association of Governments)
			Housing Authority of the County of Los Angeles
Local level	Financial institutions	Habitat for Humanity*	Los Angeles City Council*
	Real estate developers	San Fernando Valley Legal Services	Housing Authority of the City of Los Angeles
		Homeowners' associations	LAHD* (Los Angeles Housing Department)
		Churches	CRA (Community Redevelopment Agency)

Source: Aseem Inam.
Note: * denotes a key institutional actor in the Ghost Town program case study.

The next chapters analyze the successful outputs of the two programs, and their respective institutional routines in more detail. We will see exactly how such successful outputs manifested themselves in the housing recovery programs, in terms of the amount of time spent in accomplishing program objectives, the number of housing units built or repaired, the amount of funds harnessed, the degree of physical improvement in the affected neighborhoods, the extent of community involvement, and the nature of coordination among the large number and variety of institutions that contributed to the success of each program.

Chapter **3**

Successful Planning in Mexico City

*There were about 3,000 residents in the block-long, thirteen-story
Nuevo León [housing project], and almost half of them were trapped,
dead or alive. As soon as the temblor ceased, hundreds of people
from the adjoining buildings began a desperate search through the
ruins for survivors. "There was so much dust that we had to cover our
faces with handkerchiefs, and bystanders were shouting that there
would be an explosion because of all the gas in the air," said Tito
Montalbán, a nineteen-year-old Politécnico student. "But the screams
and cries from the people buried under the rubble were too much to
bear. We just kept digging until our hands bled without giving a thought
about whether we would be blown up."[1]*

THE RENOVACIÓN HABITACIONAL POPULAR housing recovery program following the Mexico City earthquake of September 1985 is remarkable for
both its massive scale and its unexpected success. Part of one of the
largest reconstruction projects since World War II, RHP constructed, rehabilitated, and repaired 48,749 housing units within two years. Even
more importantly, the RHP program won enthusiastic praise from members of the affected community, professionals, and scholars in a country
where most housing programs initiated by planning institutions are considered failures:

The [RHP] program did what it was supposed to do—it reached its
objectives—which is achieved with great difficulty by [normal] housing programs. The program achieved a magnificent relationship with
the community, which was very difficult in the beginning. Little by
little, the relationship became very cooperative.[2]

Members of the affected community were obviously pleased with
the size, quality, and tenure arrangements of the RHP housing units.

"Oh, our life is improving now," said Mrs. Pablo Montoya, as she showed a visitor around the new RHP apartment complex (cited in Stockton 1986, 13). "Things are getting so much better." Professional architects, engineers, and planners—many of whom were invited to participate in the RHP program—were impressed as well. "The problems of building in the same areas are enormous," said Eduardo Terrazas, a prominent Mexican architect, "but I'd say that nowhere has so much been done in such a short time after a natural disaster" (cited in Riding 1986, 5). The RHP program was also accorded international design recognition when the International Union of Architects gave it an award of excellence for low-income housing (see Figures 3.1 and 3.2).

Most striking, however, is the praise of scholars such as Peter Ward, Alan Gilbert, and Priscilla Connolly, who have an intimate knowledge of Mexican housing programs and their frequent lack of success. For example, Peter Ward wrote that when the RHP program's construction began, "the housing 'solution' was most impressive" (Ward 1990a, 195). Priscilla Connolly suggested that the RHP program was "an achievement which merits special comment, not only because of its scope but more importantly as a case of urban renewal" (Connolly 1990, 27). Specifically, according to Connolly, the RHP "program was able in most cases to house the families in their

Figure 3.1 Façade of an old tenement building at 100 Calle de Peru in the historic district (Colonia Centro) renovated by the RHP program in Mexico City.
Source: Aseem Inam, August 1996.

Figure 3.2 Low-income housing by RHP integrated with economic activity
at 121 Calle Sastreria in the Colonia Morelos of central Mexico City.
Source: Aseem Inam, August 1996.

original plots, i.e., with the same neighbors, and the program was administered on a plot-by-plot basis This effectively went a long way to preserving
the community spirit of the population, most of whom had lived and worked
in the area for more than one generation" (Connolly 1990, 28). Alan Gilbert,
yet another distinguished scholar of Mexican housing, suggested that "the
[Mexican] government launched an enormously effective program to produce
low-cost homes in the central area [of Mexico City]" (Gilbert 1993, 28).
Following the earthquake, "the new [RHP] agency had achieved remarkable
success in allocating new property titles, constructing new housing, and
working with existing urban social movements that had used the earthquake
to rally popular support" (Davis 1994, 283).

This unusual success can be traced to several elements of the housing
and planning program. "Traditional components of Mexican architecture
(e.g., strong vivid colors, central patios, large common entrance archways,
and window surrounds) were incorporated very successfully into these
designs" (Ward 1990a, 195). The units also offered a good value: "The result,
therefore, was a high standard dwelling, with an exchange value of around
(then) 6 million pesos, yet each dwelling cost little more than 3 million
pesos to be paid over an eight year period" (Ward 1990a, 195). Furthermore,
the new dwellings were not just a short term solution, but rather had a
long-term impact: "The brightly colored and reasonably sensitively designed

apartment blocks are what people through Mexico now claim they want: completed housing (rather than self-help), and bold bright colors" (Ward 1990a, 196). The program also prevented displacement and improved tenure: "Overall . . . the earthquakes, and the government's subsequent response, had managed to prevent the displacement of low-income households. At the same time, the shift from renting to ownership had accelerated" (Gilbert 1993, 29). Finally, the program completed its massive task with impressive speed and skill: "In a highly efficient program, nearly 50,000 new units were constructed. Most of the protesters [or inhabitants] were delighted at receiving such well-designed new homes in the central area, especially as they got them at highly subsidized prices" (Gilbert 1994, 139). This chapter focuses on the major mechanisms, such as institutional routines, that helped obtain such extraordinary housing and planning success during a crisis situation in Mexico City.

CRISIS SITUATION: 1985 EARTHQUAKE

The first earthquake, registering 8.1 on the Richter scale, hit Mexico City at 7:19 a.m. on Thursday, September 19, 1985. The second quake followed the next afternoon, registering 7.5 on the Richter scale. The earthquakes had toppled over more than 250 buildings, and severely damaged between 3,000 and 4,000 others. The official death toll was 4,287 (Riding 1986, 5) but most estimates placed the number of people dead at around 10,000.

The historic central area suffered terrible damage. While most of the historic buildings remained upright, a large number of famous local landmarks did not, including hospitals, federal ministries, and hotels. The large public housing complex at Tlatelolco was severely damaged. Overall, around 100,000 housing units were damaged in Mexico City, some 30,000 of which had to be demolished (Rohter 1987; Gilbert 1994). The estimated property damage was US$4 billion (Comerio 1998, 130). As in Los Angeles, the earthquake constituted a housing crisis, since residential structures comprised the major loss.

The loss of life and the physical destruction were notably severe due to the high density of the population, buildings, and economic activity in the area. The land under the central area of Mexico City is a dried out, filled-in lake bed underlain by roughly 130 feet of clays of various densities. A noteworthy proportion of the structures damaged during the earthquake were located in the lake zone. Because of this unique geological location— a city resting on a surface of highly compressible clay—Mexico City reacted like a bowl of jelly during the 1985 earthquake.

The damaged housing units were concentrated in the central *delegaciones* (districts, or boroughs) of the Federal District (Distrito Federal, or DF): 60

percent in Cuahtemoc, 34 percent in Venustiano Carranza, and 6 percent in Gustavo Madero—which included the *colonias* (neighborhoods) of Centro, Morelos, Valle Gómez, Guerrero, Doctores, Obrera, and Roma—all of which covered an area of nineteen square miles (see Figure 3.3). The area is located in the central part of Mexico City, and is characterized by its high density, mixed land use, and a large number of decaying buildings. The highest proportions of low- and controlled-rent housing units in the city are located here, and the income level of the residents is moderate to low. Most of the dwellings were in *vecindades*, residential tenement structures built around a courtyard. Many of the damaged structures were protected by the laws of the National Institutes of Anthropology and History, and of Fine Arts, for their architectural and historical value.

Initially, the Mexican government was caught off guard by the earthquake. In fact, President Miguel de la Madrid admitted that the administration had failed to coordinate rescue efforts adequately. Instead, self-organized groups in affected communities took the initiative. Non-governmental organizations such the Red Cross, the Salvation Army, Catholic Relief Services, and numerous rescue teams from other countries such as France, West Germany, and Switzerland also provided assistance. With virtually no operational contingency plan in case of a crisis situation, the Mexican military moved in and cordoned off the devastated neighborhoods. Public institutional actors jockeyed for power, and struggles ensued between the Ministry of Interior, the Department of the Federal District, the Military, and the President's Office. President de la Madrid eventually took control of the situation and announced the creation of two crisis committees; one focused on the devastation to the Federal District (DF), and another focused on all other devastated areas. Members of committees included the Department of the Federal District, the Geophysics Institute of the National University, the Laboratory of Soil Mechanics of the Polytechnic Institute, the Engineers Association, the Architects Association, and the Mexican Association of Seismic Engineering. Committee members worked in their respective jurisdictions to assess the damage to buildings and determine which were safe for inhabitation.

Estimates vary as to the number of Mexico City families rendered homeless; the final official figure was around 100,000. The residential areas most affected housed large numbers of tenants. Many had lived for generations in the center of the city and had long been protected by rent controls. Tens of thousands instantly became homeless; many more continued to live in buildings that were badly damaged. Within two weeks of the tragedy, the affected population—many of whom were camping on the streets—had organized sufficiently to create massive mobilizations articulating concrete demands for government action.

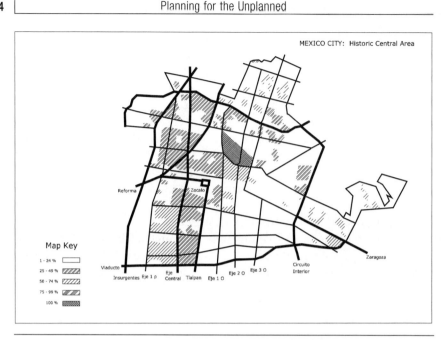

Figure 3.3 Map of RHP operation area—bounded by major streets—in central Mexico City, indicating degree of progress on projects as of December 31, 1986, just one year after the earthquake.
Source: Renovación Habitacional Popular, Renovación Habitacional Popular en el Distrito Federal: Programma operativa (Mexico City: Renovación Habitacional Popular), 120.

SUCCESSFUL INSTITUTIONAL ACTION: RENOVACIÓN HABITACIONAL POPULAR (RHP)

Initially sluggish and erratic, the government's reaction grew more clear and articulate in response to local and international pressure. The Mexican government established a National Reconstruction Fund the day after the earthquake, and announced an emergency housing program on September 30, 1985. By October 11, 1985, an extraordinary decree announced the expropriation of properties damaged by the earthquake in an effort to generate resources to solve the housing crisis (Gilbert 1994, 139). The government gave three reasons for taking such a drastic measure: (1) to rehouse the low-income families from the affected neighborhoods, (2) to restructure the central area of the city which contained poor housing and infrastructure conditions, and (3) to attempt to stop the social unrest caused by the earthquakes. However, not every affected building was included in the expropriations, nor were all the expropriated buildings severely affected

(Connolly 1990, 27–28). This lack of clarity and consistency in expropriation may be explained by a number of factors: unduly, hasty implementation due to a sense of urgency; political pressures from landlords on one hand and organized groups on the other to target specific properties; and the preservation of certain property values at the cost of others. The government's decision to expropriate property was a very radical step, but not one wholly unpopular with the owners, many of whom had been trying to rid themselves of the property and their tenants for many years (Gilbert 1994, 139).

Following the earthquake, the federal government established the RHP agency and program to oversee the reconstruction of the most badly affected low-income neighborhoods. Because most of the affected areas had been under rent control since the 1940s and the landlords were receiving negligible rents, there was little resistance to the government expropriation of damaged properties. From the beginning, area residents actively participated in the planning process. The RHP began constructing three-story multiple family condominiums, with the aiming to allow families to remain in their neighborhoods. In the interim, RHP supplied temporary housing on nearby public property, including streets and sidewalks. In the end, 48,749 relatively high-standard housing units were newly built, rehabilitated, or repaired.

The overall level of public housing production in Mexico for 1986–1987 was greatly increased by this earthquake recovery program. This demonstrates the importance of the RHP program.[3] The RHP program was focused largely upon rehousing low-income residents most affected by the earthquake in the central area of Mexico City. The RHP consumed over half of the entire post-earthquake city construction budget. About 87 percent of the housing units in the RHP program were newly built, 12 percent were rehabilitated, and 1 percent had minor repairs (RHP 1988, 110). This program succeeded for a number of reasons, including rapid action, massive funding, community outreach, improved conditions, and institutional coordination. These five successful outputs emerged from repeated analyses of the program documentation (e.g., studies, reports, and interviews). These successful outputs were largely based on institutional routines, and are described further in the next sections.

RAPID ACTION

After an initial period of hesitation and vacillation, the Mexican government responded to the growing crisis with the agility of an experienced political machine in need of quickly restoring its legitimacy and authority: "The major success was the rapidity with which it [the RHP program] was organized" (Eibenschutz 1995). Responding to increasing protests, the government began constructing around 22,000 provisional dwellings near the sites of the devastated *vecindades* in the week following the earthquake. The government also offered a rent subsidy to those choosing to live with relatives. Also, barely a week after the earthquake, President de la Madrid ordered the examination of Mexico City's building code to ascertain why so many structures failed. Another plan of action was unveiled on September 27, just eight days after the earthquake, by government officials meeting with residents of the damaged Benito Juarez neighborhood. Officials told displaced residents they could buy homes on the periphery of the city, but were met with tremendous resistance from irate residents who demanded that the government rebuild their housing on the current sites, even if that meant living several months in temporary shelters. This ultimately became the basis for the RHP program. RHP's swift implementation was a rarity for housing programs in Mexico.

The initial and most critical step taken to make the RHP housing recovery not only possible, but also successful, was the expropriation of properties with severe residential damage. The original expropriation decree was issued on October 11, 1985—less than a month after the earthquake—and expropriated 5,448 lots. The RHP agency and its self titled program were created three days later, on October 14, with a specific purpose and limited duration: to replace the concentrations of housing units lost to the earthquake. The first decree was issued amid tremendous public and political pressure for the government to respond to the needs of the housing victims, thereby resulting in a hurriedly executed document containing several technical problems. Thus, a second and revised expropriation decree was issued just days later, on October 22, 1985, and finally covered a total of 3,121 properties.

The expropriation decree, though drastic, did succeed politically. First, it quickly identified the group of beneficiaries for the largest housing reconstruction program, the RHP. Second, it effectively made available one of the vital resources in any housing reconstruction program: land. Third, many of the property owners were glad to dispose quickly of buildings that did not generate much revenue due to rent control. Ninety-seven percent of the people surveyed by the RHP program rented their dwellings and paid an average of 4,500 pesos per month, or about $6.50 per month (in 1985, 700 pesos equaled one U.S. dollar). Thirty percent of the population, however, paid less than 500 pesos per month, or about 70 cents a month. Rents were so low for two reasons: the 1942 rent control law that enabled people to hand over their dwellings and rents to family members, and the recent chronic inflation of the 1980s. Many landowners thus saw no profit in adequately maintaining their rental properties, and their willingness to relinquish them contributed to the rapid housing recovery process.

In fact, "[e]xpropriation is done all the time in Mexico, but they are [sic] used to build luxury hotels, or building a road, or in the case of illegal settlements, it is used for regularizing purposes" (Connolly 1996). Expropriation is legitimized by Mexico's Constitution of 1917, which puts forward the concept of land as a social right. The expropriation decree after the 1985 earthquake would not have been possible without the existence of Article 27 of the Mexican Constitution, which accords the state the power to impose upon private property "those modes which serve the public interest" (RHP 1988, 166).

The first precedent in Mexican urban and regional planning was the Ley General de Asentamientos Humanos (General Law of Human Settlements), published in 1976. This legislation formalized state involvement in urban and regional development. The law, passed almost a decade before the earthquake, empowered the state to intervene in a consistent and integrated way in the planning of human settlements. It contained a large number of general objectives to regulate and order human settlements into urban systems, to plan for improved access to employment and public utilities, to conserve the environment, to encourage public participation in the resolution of urban problems, and—perhaps most relevant to the RHP program— to exercise control over the real estate market and its main ingredient, land.

Mexican law allows expropriation only after the government meets two criteria: first, it must justify a cause in the public interest; and second, it must "compensate" the property owners. The severe devastation of the earthquake, especially to large amounts of multi-family housing, fulfilled the criteria of serving the public interest. The indemnification was provided by government bonds payable immediately at a 60 percent discount. The broad and general nature of the law, and its ambiguous definition of the public interest, provided public sector planning institutions with a tool which proved to be crucial to the success of the RHP program.

MASSIVE FUNDING

Ready money contributed enormously to the RHP program's success. The program's financial resources had two sources: funding especially assigned for housing recovery by the Mexican government and a loan from the World Bank. In all, RHP's total financial resources amounted to roughly 275 billion pesos, or about $392 million in 1985 U.S. dollars, of which about 55 percent came from the Mexican government and about 45 percent from the World Bank (Perló 1991, 16). Although the government did not openly admit it, it did not expect to recover its own real capital investment; likewise the World Bank only expected a 50 percent return (Riding 1986, 5).

When the RHP program was in full operation, its weekly budget was $13 million. Unlike the Ghost Town program in Los Angeles, RHP was a housing recovery program as well as a housing institution specifically created for housing recovery and subsequently dismantled. Thus, the operating and administrative costs are added to the funding received by the program itself. The RHP program received a total of $172 million in 1986 and 1987 combined as part of the national budget (Ebrard and Gamboa 1991, 25).

The external funds, from the World Bank, paid for the direct building costs, while the resources from Mexico's national budget financed all other secondary costs such as architectural studies and designs, construction supervision, temporary housing, rental assistance for the *damnificados* (earthquake victims), and operating costs of the RHP program.

The first of the World Bank loans for Mexico, $164 million, had been negotiated in 1981 for urban development in the Isthmus area. As this had not been used at the time of the earthquake, half of the funds were transferred to the housing reconstruction program. Additional financing was then negotiated for this program and its follow-ups, and now World Bank loans have become integrated into the funds channeled through the National Bank for the Public Works (BANOBRAS) to the National Fund for Popular Housing (FONHAPO).[5]

While such a massive funding from the World Bank for a Mexico City housing program was unprecedented at the time, it was in fact based on a number of existing institutional routines. For example, some of the money was channeled through pre-approved infrastructure projects established by the well-reputed BANOBRAS, the funding source for many Mexican infrastructure and urban development projects. Furthermore, at the time of the earthquake, FONHAPO was negotiating for housing finance with the World Bank, and the criteria and mechanisms for financing the RHP units were based on those discussed during the negotiations (Gamboa 1995). Thus, while the RHP was touted as a new and independent agency and program, the fact that it received its funding through the mechanisms of the BANOBRAS and FONHAPO—both largely successful housing and urban development institutions in their own right—suggests otherwise. This was confirmed in my interview with Roberto Eibenschutz, a former Director of FONHAPO: "This [RHP] organization was managed by people from FONHAPO. They profited from the knowledge, experience, and funding mechanisms of FONHAPO" (Eibenschutz 1995).

FONHAPO assists around 70 percent of Mexico's population with a demand for housing (Zepeda and Mohar 1993, 146). Its clientele comprises low-income families making two and a half times the minimum wage or less (around $172 per month in 1996). FONHAPO was established in 1981, under the authority of BANOBRAS. At the time of the earthquake, FONHAPO had a repertoire of routines for financing low-income housing, including mechanisms for appropriating sites and services, creating progressive or core housing, upgrading existing housing, and completed housing (Connolly 1993). These institutional routines directly benefited the RHP program: "The RHP program was not really all that different—the housing constituency was pretty much the same, the type of housing was also more or less the same, the types of credits were also more or less the same" (Eibenschutz 1995).

New and rehabilitated housing had to be affordable; for particular hardship cases, extra subsidies from donated funds were made available. According to information gathered by an RHP study of 7,000 heads of households involved in the recovery program, most of the earthquake victims were employed at very low wages (RHP 1988). Of this group of inhabitants, almost half of the male population earned below the minimum wage, and over half of the female population earned an income of three quarters or less of the minimum wage. Overall, about 57 percent of those interviewed were permanently employed, about 31 percent were temporarily employed, and 12 percent had other types of employment. The poverty of the affected community had to be addressed through a massive influx of funding, from international and national sources.

Furthermore, political pressure persuaded the government to offer large subsidies to the population in need of rehousing. While some middle-class families also benefited, larger numbers of poor households received subsidies (Gilbert 1993, 33). The affected inhabitants paid mortgages, with the payments pegged to the minimum wage earned in households with only one breadwinner. Most of the families had more than one wage earner, so the housing is considered affordable (Stockton 1986, 13). The result, of such generous financial conditions, was a high standard dwelling, with average costs around $1,350 for a newly built unit, $1,000 for a rehabilitated unit, and $500 for a repaired unit (Ebrard and Gamboa 1991, 26).

Because of the expropriation decree and subsequent institutional actions, the government was legally obliged to rehouse all of the affected population on site. This led to terms of funding which had to be accessible to all within the range of lower-income groups. The result was a fairly high level of subsidy, concentrated in the part of the RHP financed by the Mexican government: land and indirect (e.g., administrative) costs. Three-quarters of the program costs, which covered the costs of construction, was financed by a World Bank loan, via FONHAPO, with the routine World Bank loan terms (Connolly 1993). The loan terms varied according to the type of intervention—highest loan rates were set for new housing while the lowest were for minor repairs (RHP 1988, 59).

In the early 1980s, planning institutions had utilized similar strategies of highly subsidized housing in Mexico. During that period, the servicing of large external debt was drying up public funds for urban services, and driving up inflation and unemployment. To reduce high unemployment rates, the government provided generous mortgages through the newly nationalized banks for housing construction activities. FONHAPO—a leading institutional actor in the RHP program—was a major beneficiary of these funds, and through its sites-and-services program was able to provide more than 13,000 units by 1987 in Mexico City alone.

FONHAPO was the first housing institution in Mexico to connect its amortization scheme to the evolution of the minimum wage, so that its beneficiaries would be able to make suitable loan repayments. Such financial policies reflected the agency's understanding that the wage pattern is the closest indicator of their constituents' repayment capacity. Therefore, the loan, the subsidy, the repayment installments, and the terms of credit were all connected to the minimum wage, in order to offer the borrower a feasible loan scheme (Zepeda and Mohar 1993, 148).

At about the same time, Mexico adopted a new system of financing that requires the national banking system to underwrite the production of "social interest" housing at affordable interest rates. There was a sliding scale in which higher interest rates and more expensive housing units were intended for those with higher wages.[6]

Other institutional routines drawn from FONHAPO were also incorporated into the RHP housing recovery program. For example, the negotiations for the *convenio* (a democratic agreement) were with groups of beneficiaries rather than with individuals (Connolly 1993). FONHAPO does not traditionally provide funds to individuals but to public, private, or non-profit organizations. About 75 percent of its credits have gone to public housing developers, with the remaining 25 percent going to non-profit and non-governmental organizations, including those affiliated with urban social movements. Thus, FONHAPO is not directly involved in developing the housing projects it finances—which was the case in the RHP program as well.

IMPROVED CONDITIONS

Even before the earthquake, the minimal rents paid by families in dilapidated buildings meant that residential properties were worth very little (Comerio 1998, 136–137). Architects and planners had recognized the conditions of blight, but migration to the city, low wages for workers, and high construction costs had prevented the development of an adequate housing supply. However, the inhabitants of the historic central area found that the inexpensive rents, strong community ties, and relatively convenient access to jobs and transportation made the conditions tolerable and the area desirable.

Thus, the RHP's strategy to rehouse the affected community in the existing neighborhood greatly contributed to the successful output of improved conditions. Despite its strong public commitment to a decentralization policy, the government opted for the politically more acceptable (and thus more feasible) solution of rehousing the population affected by the earthquake on site, rather than undertaking reconstruction outside of Mexico City and relocating those who had lost their homes. This strategy also ensured, perhaps inadvertently, that many low-income families who lived close to their jobs in Mexico City and could not afford to commute would not be inconvenienced.

In order to house the same people in the original number of plots, building norms such as densities and plot ratios were very flexible. In particular, previous density-restricting regulations, such as the requisite one parking space per dwelling, were modified. By applying these modified regulations, the program was able, in most cases, to house the families on their original plots, i.e., with the same neighbors, and the program was administered on a plot-by-plot basis. This went a long way to preserving the community spirit of the population, most of whom had lived and worked in the area for more than one generation. In fact, the majority of the families had lived in the area for over thirty years, and, consequently, were deeply integrated into the community. Almost 40 percent of the earthquake victims also worked in the devastated area (RHP 1988). Resistance to being evicted from their homes and neighborhoods was in fact one of the main organizing principles of the post-earthquake popular movement (Connolly 1990, 28).

At first glance, infill development in such circumstances might seem unusual because the default strategy would be to disperse the earthquake victims to cheaper land and larger lots on the city fringe. However, planning institutions had already embarked on a policy of densification as a means of controlling the physical expansion of the Federal District of Mexico City. According to a 1981 master plan for Mexico City, the urban area—which includes all built-up areas—would be restructured, following a scheme of nine urban centers and several high-density corridors linking them with mixtures of public and private uses. According to the master plan, population density was to be raised to 520 inhabitants per acre by focusing redevelopment in underutilized areas. In the mid-1980s, prior to the earthquake, land was available for densification since nearly 18 percent of city lots in the DF were classified as vacant (Campbell and Wilk 1986, 302).

One of the most important contributions to urban planning in Mexico City was the Programa de Desarrollo de la Zona Metropolitana de la Ciudad de México y de la Region Centro (Development Program for the Metropolitan Area of Mexico City and the Central Region), developed by the Presidency in conjunction with the DF and the neighboring states of Mexico, Hidalgo, Morelos, Puebla, Queretaro, and Tlaxcala, published in 1983. The key element of interest here is an important precedent the plan contained: the utilization of infill strategies to optimize use of existing infrastructure (Campbell and Wilk 1986, 308).

Conditions also improved as residents made the welcome transition from the uncertain and tenuous tenure of renting to the more secure and long-term investment of ownership. Before the crisis, a full 97 percent of the community rented their units while 2 percent borrowed them, and only 1 percent owned them (RHP 1988). The shift from rental to ownership was inspired by the government's successful response to the proliferation of squatter settlements in the 1960s. At that time, planning institutions regularized squatter settlements by guaranteeing tenure rights and providing basic services to residents. In this way, the government attempted to consolidate settlements and increase neighborhood's tax base by collecting property taxes and user fees on services. Scholars have suggested that enabling home ownership for lower-income groups has also allowed the ruling PRI party to decentralize groups that are hostile to its rule and to consolidate (i.e., through rewards such as ownership) groups that are supportive (Pezzoli 1987). Such institutional actions (i.e., changing tenure of housing) are very much in the tradition of legalizing land holding, which has long been used to maintain and win political support. The regularization of land titles became increasingly important in the late 1960s, when social protest mounted, and several agencies were created in the early 1970s to handle the issue. Between 1969 and 1981, around 350,000 titles were distributed by the State of Mexico's planning institutions, and a further 330,000 were awarded in the DF. By 1982, around 80 percent of irregular settlement on agricultural and communal land had been regularized (Gilbert 1993, 35).

RHP beneficiaries not only gained home ownership, they also benefited from the greatly improved size, amenities, and design of the new housing units. The physical conditions in which most of the *damnificados* lived were among the worst in Mexico City (Perló 1991). Before the crisis, the average tenement dwelling size was a little over 200 square feet (RHP 1988). Around 25 percent of the units were in bad condition, displaying high levels of deterioration; around 62 percent were considered substandard; and only around 9 percent were in good condition. After the earthquakes, 18 percent were uninhabitable. Around 63 percent of the inhabitants shared bathrooms with other units, and 29 percent shared kitchens.

In contrast, each new RHP apartment had 430 square feet of living space and included a toilet, shower, laundry area, and kitchenette. In most cases, families of five or more lived in an apartment. Most families had more space than before the earthquake. "This is much nicer," said Pedra Hernandez de Monjaras, sixty-eight years old, who had lived in the old tenement for forty years. "Before, we had one room and toilet. Now we have two bedrooms and a toilet and shower" (cited in Stockton 1986, 13).

Although the RHP program quickly and dramatically improved living conditions for thousands of residents after the earthquake, it was not the first such effort. Vecindad improvement programs were in fact introduced by the National Institute for Community Development (INDECO) and the National Institute for the Housing Fund for Workers (INFONAVIT) in the 1970s, and slum improvement was a major goal of the Federal District's Directorate for Popular Housing (Gilbert 1993, 30). These institutional routines were confirmed by interviews in Mexico City:

> There had been other urban renewal from earlier on, actually . . . In the late '70s, INDECO, which was a housing institution which financed one-off projects. BANOBRAS had also set up an improvement program for *vecindades* . . . These are, kind of, previous institutional experiences of housing improvement in the central city area, turning tenants into proprietors. There wasn't completely a blank [before the RHP program].[7]

Furthermore, traditional components of Mexican architecture—such as vivid colors, central patios, large common entrance archways, and window surrounds—were incorporated into the designs. The result was a high-standard dwelling (usually better than the existing one) with a market value of around twice what the residents had to pay. This was largely due to the involvement of private architects and contractors, who had been exploring and implementing such housing (usually for the middle-income groups) long before the RHP program.

The revival of traditional elements of Mexican architecture in housing projects can be traced back several decades before the 1985 earthquake. In the 1920s, the upsurge of a new middle class and the large flow of provincial population coincided with a reaction against the imitation of European styles of architecture (Ward 1990a, 197). Designs that sought a national basis for inspiration incorporating colonial and vernacular styles grew in importance. As part of this larger movement, murals on public buildings, popular sculpture, and monuments all sought to cement this nationalistic ideology in the built environment of Mexico City. Later, house designs also incorporated the intensely Mexican ideas of texture, movement and, above all, deep color epitomized in Luis Barragan's buildings and gardens in the

1940s and 1950s, which inspired many contemporary Mexican architects. Architects such as Ricardo Legoretta adopted the international style of functionalist designs and pure geometry, but in ways that made the outcome a distinctively Mexican adaptation. Following Mexican traditions of strong bright colors such as purples, mauves, blues, and ochre browns used on exterior walls in provincial towns, together with the use of large archways, Legoretta developed an architectural style epitomized by large rough concrete textures, elaborate colors, and the interplay of bright light and dark shadow—all elements to be found in the designs of the RHP housing projects (see Figure 3.4, below). Rich colors, a range of entrance porches and arches, and emboldened surrounds for exterior windows were all traditional features embodied in the RHP and other central-city housing programs for low-income groups. This not only reinforced local residents' links with the past, it shaped the future demand for housing by public sector planning institutions, as groups increasingly demand similar designs for their projects (Ward 1990a, 221). As this brief history demonstrates, vernacular architecture and traditional styles are not really new in Mexico City; rather they have long been institutionalized through a series of public sector, monumental, and housing projects.

Figure 3.4 Pink stucco walls, red window border, and entrance archway in the façade of a RHP housing project at 54 Calle Herreros in the Colonia Morelos of Mexico City.
Source: Aseem Inam, August 1996.

COMMUNITY OUTREACH

Key to the implementation of the RHP program was the Convenio de Concertación Democratica para la Reconstrución de Vivienda del RHP, or the Agreement of Democratic Consultation for the Reconstruction of Housing of RHP. This *convenio* agreement resulted from long and difficult political negotiations. The *convenio* served as a social and political pact. In this pact, the leading role of the public sector planning institutions, and the legitimacy and apparent fairness of their actions, were acknowledged by the most important social and political organizations. Furthermore, the *convenio* incorporated the demands, participation, and organizations of the *damnificados* into the RHP housing recovery program.

The lead negotiator for the Mexican Government, the newly appointed Minister of Urban Development Manuel Camacho Solis, began negotiating with over one hundred groups involved in the earthquake housing issue, securing agreement on the details of the RHP program. The agreement was signed on May 13, 1986 by 106 different groups, including public sector and international institutions, non-governmental organizations, universities, technical support groups, and professional associations. The agreement defined a number of important issues. Housing units would be rebuilt on the same sites as the damaged dwellings, and would house the same people who had previously lived there. Provisional housing was provided nearby. The new homes would be around 450 square feet, with two bedrooms, living room, kitchenette, and space for laundry. Within these parameters, nonprofit and community-based institutions could present alternative housing projects and apply for funding as part of the program.

Far from novel, the "democratic agreement," carries on a long tradition of agreements the Mexican government has utilized to incorporate antagonistic groups into its economic and social programs. As a result, the only demonstration during the World Cup, soon after the earthquake, was a footrace organized by the earthquake victims in support of the agreement (Stockton 1986, 13). These strategies for dealing with lower-income housing constituencies and community groups were based on tried and true mechanisms of FONHAPO and INDECO in central Mexico City (Stolarski 1996). Many of the policy-makers of the RHP program actually came from FONHAPO, and brought with them the same institutional strategies. One such strategy was to negotiate with groups of beneficiaries—as was done in the "democratic agreement"—rather than with individuals. So, in order

to understand this [RHP] program, you have to understand FONHAPO, which is a very particular kind of housing institution in Mexico, and which had its golden age between 1982 and 1990. And FONHAPO's way of

operation is very much based on NGO [non-governmental organiza-
tion] experience, the kind of NGO like CENVI [Center for Housing and
Urban Studies] or COPEVI [Operational Center for Housing and Popula-
tion] that have been working in Mexico City. They work with the idea of
fortifying local institutions. They don't give individual loans, they give
collective loans.[8]

Urban sectors, particularly those most affected by the fiscal crisis in
Mexico City in the 1970s and 1980s, developed new organizations and urban
movements during those periods. The urban poor and popular sectors,
concerned with the decrease in living standards and the restricted opportunities for political participation, started to form independent groups outside
existing government channels. These neighborhood councils challenged
the existing institutional framework. Among the most independent urban
movements were the Frente Popular Independiente de Valle de Mexico in
1972, which later transformed into the Frente Popular Nezahualcoyotl; the
Unión de Vecinos de Colonia Guerreo in 1978; and the Coordinadora Nacional
Provisional del Movimiento Popular in 1980, which was later transformed
into Consejo Nacional de Movimientos Urbanos Populares (CONAMUP)
(Campbell and Wilk 1986). Thus, local groups already had an instituted
channel over which to make demands and be heard, to build consensus, or
to change priorities—as in the RHP program.

The Unión de Vecinos de la Colonia Guerrero (Guerrero Residents'
Union) was founded in 1976 to defend tenants' rights. It provided legal aid
to its members and, when necessary, mobilized the community against
evictions and rent increases. After the 1985 earthquake and following the
urban social movements' general trend, the Guerrero Residents' Union also
played a positive role in housing development. The Guerrero neighborhood was severely affected by the earthquake, and it was the Union that
mobilized and organized the victims. Joining forces with other community
organizations, the Coordinadora Unica de Damnificados was established,
representing around 30,000 *damnificados*. The combined political pressure
that this and other nonprofit institutions achieved produced the "Democratic Agreement for Reconstruction," which essentially guaranteed the favorable conditions of housing recovery for the affected community. For its
part, the Guerrero Residents' Union handled the rebuilding and rehabilitation
of about 1,000 dwellings on seventy properties in the neighborhood
(Connolly 1993, 81).

INSTITUTIONAL COORDINATION

The massive and complex—yet surprisingly rapid task of building, rehabilitating, or repairing 48,749 housing units was completed in about two years

with the participation of 1,244 private-sector institutions—738 building firms (sixty-four in charge of supervision), 184 suppliers, and 258 medium and small firms providing services such as architectural and engineering designs (Ebrard and Gamboa 1991, 22; RHP 1988, 110). However,

> there was a lot of support from a lot of institutions. For example, in the camps of temporary shelters, support was received in the form of supplies, from the Ministry of Public Education with programs for children, in the form of milk . . . There were many instances of coordinated support for the [RHP] program.[9]

This achievement is all the more remarkable given that governing and planning Mexico City is an extremely complex task, particularly in light of the constraints posed by its jurisdictional fragmentation, and by division of authority among the national ministries, the Department of the Federal District (DDF), the state governments, the municipalities, and the numerous planning and implementing institutions.

In order to coordinate the various recovery programs, including RHP, an inter-institutional technical coordinating group was established in December 1985. The group operated under the Secretary of Finance and included experts in economics, law, urban planning, housing, health, communications, decentralization, programming, and finance. The actual execution of the recovery programs was the responsibility of each sector's Ministry, including those of Housing and Urban Development, Transportation and Communication, Commerce and Industry, Health and Education, the Mexican Social Security Institute, and the DDF. Such institutional coordination, which was largely effective, owed its success not so much to newly created bodies or innovative strategies, but to three existing institutional routines: one technical, one administrative, and one political.

Institutional coordination mechanisms, such as a technical advisory committee, were created to oversee and inspect construction standards in non-governmental projects funded by RHP. The committee focused on the inhabitants' use of space, architecture, and planning considerations, historical context, the neighborhoods' social features, the *vecindades'* character, plus financial and legal concerns. The committee reviewed 160 plans, approved 120, and provided recommendations for the remaining forty.

Planning for the metropolitan area as a whole was addressed by the conurbation commission, one of the technical mechanisms established under the Law of Human Settlements of 1976. This commission was designed to facilitate integrated urban development in areas where formerly separate urban areas had coalesced. Headed by the Minister of SEDUE and comprised of the Mayor of the Federal District, the Governors of the neighboring states of Hidalgo, Mexico, Morelos, Puebla and Tlaxcala, and municipal presidents and delegates, the Conurbation Commission met only once—in October 1977. Although its Technical Secretariat worked up until February 1988 when it was disbanded, the Conurbation Commission is widely acknowledged to have had little impact on policy decisions apart from producing numerous planning papers (UN 1991, 30). However, it did manage to establish a precedent as well as a routine for subsequent institutional coordination in the RHP program.

The initial expropriation decree for RHP was carried out by the local government (DDF) of Mexico City, while the actual housing recovery program was established by the federal Mexican government. Furthermore, the agreement and coordination between more than a hundred institutions in the public, private, and non-profit sectors represented a major challenge. These apparently remarkable feats of institutional coordination were in fact facilitated by existing institutional relationships that depended largely on the highly centralized and top-down institutional arrangements of the public sector in Mexico, often emanating from the office of the Presidency. Also, while the World Bank's extensive involvement in housing recovery seemed to be without precedent, this was actually a modification of ongoing projects, loans, and negotiations for further housing support (Gamboa de Buen 1995; Stolarski 1996).

The discussion of massive funding above, has already demonstrated the significance of institutional routines from FONHAPO for the success of the RHP housing recovery program. Although institutional coordination was probably the least successful of the five outputs it was successful nonetheless. This success can be attributed to FONHAPO's tradition of dealing with and coordinating with a variety of institutions including non-profit institutions such as community groups and housing cooperatives, public sector housing institutions (especially at the federal level), and state and local governments. Public sector planning institutions served as intermediaries with community groups, or as a base for individual projects—the combination of such institutional coordination depended upon the nature of the institutional framework and the key institutional actors in housing in each locality. Thus, FONHAPO's institutional experience in coordinating with a variety of institutions, especially in the public and non-profit sectors, greatly benefited the RHP program.

Administrative mechanisms of institutional coordination contributed as well. The Comisión del Centro Conurbado del País (Commission for the Conurbated Center of the Country), established in 1978, formalized institutional relations and responsibilities among jurisdictions in the Mexico City region. To encourage cooperation among jurisdictions, it created and instituted a planning framework that had existed before only on paper (Campbell and Wilk 1986, 301). In addition, formalized planning activities began in

1978, with the formation of the Dirección General de Planíficación (General Planning Agency) within the Department of the Federal District and the elaboration of a master plan for the city. The DDF is subordinate to the Presidency, and from 1978, the planning agency had presidential authority to elaborate and implement a master plan (Campbell and Wilk 1986, 301).

The Presidential hand, above all gives these urban planning initiatives their importance, not the technical and administrative tools. In general, municipal governments within Mexico City fail to resist the corrosive influences of bought favors that largely demolish urban plans, land use controls, and locational regulations. Presidential intervention in metropolitan affairs signaled an important step in urban planning in Mexico City in the 1970s and 1980s (Campbell and Wilk 1986, 309). The national President was, in effect, also elected as Governor of the DF. The Mayor of the Federal District was appointed by the President of Mexico, as were the sixteen *delegados* or borough representatives. The National Congress is charged with legislative functions both for the nation and for the DF.

Mexico had long been dominated by a hegemonic and authoritarian party, the Partido Revolucionario Institucional (PRI), which held power for nearly seventy years. PRI's power at the local, state, and national levels has largely determined the established political routine. The party has often used internal political mechanisms to formulate and implement government policies. It has been authoritarian in both its internal structure and its firm control of electoral politics and the popular mobilization of the population (Pugh 1994, 171). This facilitates institutional coordination, especially in terms of vertical integration—i.e., among the national, regional, and local levels of government.

LIMITATIONS OF INSTITUTIONAL ACTION: SHORTCOMINGS OF PROGRAM

The RHP program has been critiqued for its extremely high costs, especially in terms of non-recoverable subsidies. The Mexican government opted to provide new and completed housing for earthquake victims on the sites of their respective demolished tenements. The RHP program meticulously solved the problems of the low-income tenement dwellers left homeless by the earthquake, but it relied heavily on subsidies. Government absorbed the costs of land expropriations as well as 60 percent of construction costs and administrative costs. As a crash program in response to a dramatic need, it could be considered an "artificial scheme based on a natural model," since it relied on standard architectural plans and direct administration of construction with no self-help components. Its high costs, however, limit the possibilities of replicating the Mexican model as a general housing solution—

especially for cash-poor institutions during periods of recession (Solo 1991, 300–301). In effect, this meant that the housing was very heavily subsidized, thus eroding the opportunity for developing a capital basis for an ongoing rolling housing program (Gilbert 1990a, 194–195).

This "Mexican model" is better understood, however, within the Mexican context, where publicly funded housing programs have long been a used to pursue social and political goals (rather than economic ones). One such goal is the co-optation into the state of those who are antagonistic to it, such as the urban lower-income classes. Seen in this context, the highly subsidized and high-standard RHP program was an extremely effective tool for not only pacifying but also strengthening the support of the affected communities for the state's political and administrative institutions, especially those dominated by the ruling PRI party.

A large portion of the beneficiaries could afford to pay higher loan repayments for units with high standards and prime locations in the center of the Distrito Federal—the heart of Mexico City. The RHP program ended up subsidizing its housing units at a higher level than was necessary. Furthermore, the high levels of subsidy and low levels of cost recovery were bound to have two negative effects: (1) to discourage non-crisis loans sought by SEDUE in the future from international funding agencies, and (2) to reduce the replicability of housing programs by eroding the rolling capital for ongoing urban planning and development.

However, some of the program's costs are not encountered under normal circumstances—costs such as demolition of buildings, temporary rental assistance, provisional shelters, and the rebuilding of infrastructure. Perhaps these costs reflect extraordinary expenditures during extraordinary times rather than simply being subsidies. The RHP was also a social and economic response program, (as a point argued further in chapter 9), so it is rather difficult to evaluate it using a standard cost-benefit approach.

A second major critique of the RHP program was that physical design was used to reproducel inequality and to create social divisions that did not exist before. According to this argument, the RHP program replicated and intensified social inequality through the arbitrary way in which the benefits of housing recovery fell among people with identical class and cultural backgrounds. Fate determined where the earthquake did most damage, but it was an inadequate government instrument—the expropriation decree— that determined exactly which families would benefit. Thus, families living cheek by jowl in adjacent *vecindades* found themselves in one of two camps: either included in the group to become owner occupiers and windfall beneficiaries of under-priced, high-quality housing; or excluded from the RHP program and at best likely to be included in the less well-financed Fase II program designed in part to cover those who were previously excluded. What was previously a broadly homogenous social class was split irrevocably between neighbors of the same class and between the downtown districts and the *colonias populares* of the periphery (Ward 1990a, 194–195).

However, this argument fails to consider the catalytic role the crisis situation played in strengthening existing community organizations and even creating new community organizations that were more inclusive and broadbased than before. For example, during the arduous negotiation processes for the *convenio* that nurtured institutional interaction and community leaders that had earlier been in only the nascent stages.

Furthermore, the RHP program was a rapid response to a crisis situation by planning institutions with particular roles and constraints. It was based on contingency and had to respond to unforeseen and non-preventable events. Most of the *damnificados* lost family members, suffered serious injuries, and were either left homeless or living in dangerous structures. Through the RHP recovery program, planning institutions attempted to target those who had suffered the most. The RHP program did not solve all or even many of the housing problems in the affected neighborhoods, but it did address most of the housing demands of the *damnificados*.

Figure 3.5 Failure of RHP program, or lack of responsibility of residents? Poorly maintained and vandalized main entrance to RHP project at 62 Pintores in the Colonia Morelos of Mexico City.
Source: Aseem Inam, August 1996.

The RHP program has also been accused of corruption in the form of kickbacks received by the public officials of the program from the many private-sector participants such as architects and builders (Greene 1995). The housing recovery money flowing from both external and governmental sources could have provided a motor for the faltering economy, but it instead spurred new rounds of inflation, setting back the country's longer-term economic program even further. Any large infusion of funds also raised the possibility of new corruption. While corruption and kickbacks plague most Mexican construction projects, including housing, there appears to be no documented evidence of such widespread occurrences in the RHP program. The legal terms of the expropriation decree determined, quite clearly, who were to be RHP's primary beneficiaries: those families occupying the expropriated lots at the time of, or immediately preceding, the earthquake. This targeted approach and the relatively clear policy substantially reduced the opportunities for traditionally corrupt mechanisms for allocating funds (Connolly 1993).

RHP PROGRAM IN PERSPECTIVE

One of the long-term implications of the largely successful RHP program is its potential replicability. Since tenements do not generally belong to their inhabitants, a first step in upgrading them involves purchasing them from the owner and converting them to condominiums or a cooperative. The Mexican government subsequently undertook a similar program, Casa Propia, which focused on tenements that were endangered, but not destroyed, by the 1985 earthquake. Under Casa Propia, the public housing credit agency FONHAPO provided tenants with financing to purchase apartments and to make minimum but necessary repairs to improve the buildings' resistance to tremors. Essentially, this program aimed at converting the tenants of the remaining old tenements into owners of their dwellings. Residents received credit for the purchase of the properties plus the cost of essential repairs. Casa Propia tended to reach families with higher income levels than RHP, and it provided up to 60 percent subsidy on the amount loaned (Solo 1991).

Also potentially replicable are the mechanisms adopted by the RHP program to address the many different properties, different landlords, and different inhabitants spread out in various parts of the central district. How does one deal with such diversity and dispersion during a housing crisis, such as the one in Mexico City? One approach tested was to "routinize" this diversity and dispersion by developing seven design prototypes. The prototypes shared the following common principles: the living room functioned as the center for family activities; the kitchenette and front door faced the common courtyard to facilitate communication among inhabitants and the supervision of children. Just as the funding and implementation strategies of the overall program were adapted to the specific situation so too were the design prototypes, which were modified according to plot locations, sizes, and shapes, and family size. Many of these adaptations were quite simple, such as using different colors to paint the projects in different neighborhoods.

The RHP program is also significant to planning as a unique example of successful urban renewal in Mexico City. The recession of the 1980s would no doubt have slowed the process of urban renewal. Commercial land prices plummeted in real terms between 1980 and 1984, making redevelopment schemes much less attractive. However, the process of urban renewal was reinvigorated by a wholly different and unwelcome source: the earthquake that hit the central area in September 1985. Ironically, the earthquake achieved something that many landlords had tried to do for years: remove the tenants so that they could redevelop their properties. However, while the earthquake severely damaged much of the housing stock, the owners were prevented from rebuilding for higher-income groups by the considerable tenant protests that developed after the disaster (Gilbert 1993, 28). The combination of the natural destruction of dilapidated residential properties and a low-income housing constituency that was vocal and articulate led to a fairly successful urban renewal and revitalization program. A different kind of success was accomplished in the Ghost Town Program in Los Angeles, as we will see in the next chapter.

Chapter 4

Successful Planning in Los Angeles

Tens of thousands of people huddled in parking lots and driveways, wearing whatever they were sleeping in or could grab. The ground was still alive with aftershocks, and the precariously balanced wreckage of their homes creaked and groaned and threatened further collapse with each tremor. The night was illuminated only by occasional fires, fed by broken gas mains, and the searchlights of circling helicopters; power was out over the entire city, in a cascade of outages that reached Alberta [Canada].[1]

AFTER THE 1994 LOS ANGELES EARTHQUAKE, also known as the Northridge earthquake, public-sector planning institutions played a crucial role in crisis response and recovery. Moreover, their efforts won enthusiastic praise from residents, public officials, evaluation reports, and the media. Mary Kapich, one of thousands of community members assisted by public institutions, said, "I was impressed with the speed [of recovery efforts], and the man [from the government] that came was very nice and very thorough, and gave us a lot hints on what to do" (cited in Simon and Levin 1995, A24). Within days after the government's inspection, she received a check to help repair the damage to her home. Los Angeles County Supervisor Zev Yaroslavsky said that "despite $5 billion spent so far by federal agencies on residential and commercial relief, the area's long-term rebuilding effort is a financial problem, not a governmental one. The insurance companies have made government look entrepreneurial" (cited in *Los Angeles Times* 1995, U2). A report of the highly independent and well-reputed U.S. General Accounting Office (GAO) issued six months after the earthquake stated, "Many state and local officials said that the emergency response immediately following the earthquake went very well . . ." (GAO 1994, 3).

The media also praised the recovery efforts, as in this passage from the *Los Angeles Times*:

> Local and national government led the way, responding with the most
> splendid emergency assistance program in U.S. history—far surpass-
> ing their reaction to the Loma Prieta earthquake or the Los Angeles riots.
> Firefighters and police risked their lives to save hundreds of imperiled
> apartment dwellers. Elected officials efficiently mobilized municipal work-
> ers and the National Guard to deliver food and water to hastily assembled
> tent cities. Cabinet officers jetted in from Washington to grant millions of
> dollars in aid on the spot, direct the rebuilding of freeways, protect ruined
> neighborhoods from looters and commiserate with the dying, the
> wounded, the homeless, the bereaved.[2]

The government's rapid, targeted, and efficient recovery efforts operated
in a number of different realms. The Federal Highway Administration and
the California Department of Transportation agreed to an expedited contracting process permitting State highway officials to advertise and award construction contracts in just three to five days, in contrast to the usual twenty-five
to forty weeks. Furthermore, only two days after the earthquake, $30 million
was approved for a transportation recovery plan to get Los Angeles moving
again (Wachs and Kamel 1996). Although the earthquake caused significant
damage, the utility industry ensured that the electrical, water, and gas systems
recovered exceptionally well. Within ten days of the quake, fewer than a
hundred scattered customers remained without water service. Most customers
had electricity again within a few hours.

Housing recovery efforts were singled out for special praise. The Urban
Institute's evaluation was quite positive, indeed, glowing: "The magnitude
of the devastation generated a similarly impressive relief response from
local, California, and federal agencies . . . But perhaps no response was
more aggressive, flexible, and unprecedented as that generated by the U.S.
Department of Housing and Urban Development (HUD) . . ." (Galster et al.
1995, i). Particularly effective was the Ghost Town program, targeted at the
neighborhoods of concentrated residential damage: "I think it [the Ghost
Town program] has been a huge success. We have funded now 98% of the
units that were in those Ghost Towns . . . Ninety-eight percent is an incredible
recovery . . . in two years" (Smith 1996).

Alvin Martin, a resident of the lower-income West Adams Ghost Town,
expressed gratitude for the rapid action of public institutions: "We were
able to get the foundation retrofitted right away and paid for by FEMA
[Federal Emergency Management Agency]. We were thankful for what we
got" (cited in Hong 1995b, U4). Peter Elias was president of the condomin-
ium association at Villa Saticoy, part of a Canoga Park Ghost Town where
half of the thirty-six units' owners abandoned their residences. Elias praised
the efforts of public institutions to provide safety and security in the Ghost

Towns: "In the beginning, I went by constantly to check on things. But as much as we boarded, the vandals got more creative, to the point they ripped the wrought-iron bars off the garage. Now the city has done a nice job with boarding and fencing, and I go there very rarely" (cited in Gordon 1995, U5). Fred Tehrani, who was awarded a $1 million loan seven months after the earthquake, owned a fifty-nine-unit apartment building in the Chatsworth neighborhood and said of the massive funding efforts of public institutions such as the Los Angeles City Council and the Los Angeles Housing Department: "If this [the funding] wasn't available, believe me, not only the building would have been destroyed but all our work and effort would have been destroyed" (cited in Martin 1994, B8).

The *Los Angeles Times* explained that the Ghost Towns, "pockets of destruction that became overrun by vermin, criminals and homeless after the Northridge [or Los Angeles] earthquake—were billed as the toughest challenge for the city's recovery program. But after a nearly two-year struggle by housing and public works officials and more than $300 million in public and private funding, authorities proclaimed a significant milestone in the battle to revive the areas" (Martin 1995, 1). "They did a super job," said Los Angeles City Council member Hal Bernson, who heads the city's Ad Hoc Committee on Earthquake Recovery, and who issued a commendation in November 1995 for the city's Ghost Town Task Force (cited in Martin 1995, 1). Los Angeles Mayor Richard Riordan praised President Bill Clinton and his administration for responding quickly to his request for extra housing funds required by the Ghost Town program. In turn, Clinton's Secretary for Housing and Urban Development Henry Cisneros said that the Riordan Administration's deft handling of earthquake relief gave him great confidence in entrusting the city with the money (Smith 1994, B5). This chapter examines the success of these post-earthquake recovery efforts more closely, focusing especially on the Ghost Town housing recovery program.

CRISIS: 1994 EARTHQUAKE

The earthquake occurred at 4:31 a.m. on January 17, 1994, with its epicenter in Northridge, about twenty miles west-northwest of downtown Los Angeles. The earthquake's magnitude was estimated to be 6.7 on the Richter scale, and it lasted approximately twenty seconds (Comerio 1995, 4). It left sixty-one people dead, over 18,000 injured, and 25,000 homeless. More than 55,000 structures were damaged, 1,600 of which were left uninhabitable (GAO 1994, 1). The State of California estimated total damage to be around $25.7 billion (Comerio 1998, 12). The magnitude of the earthquake, the number of human casualties, and the scale of destruction were significantly less than those of the Mexico City earthquake of 1985.

Los Angeles was spared much worse damage and loss of life through a combination of chance and preparedness. By chance, the shock occurred at a time when schools, businesses, and roads were largely deserted on a national holiday (i.e., Martin Luther King's birthday). The area also benefited from California's experience with earthquakes. A combination of laws, public programs, and private preparedness limited damage and enabled critical systems and services to function effectively in the emergency. Although the earthquake caused significant loss of life, damage, and disruption, it also created an unprecedented opportunity to learn about the actions of planning institutions during urban crisis situations.

The crisis was particularly relevant for planning institutions because it had such a devastating impact on the built environment. Striking directly under a heavily urbanized area, it has been called the most destructive earthquake in the United States since 1906, causing significant damage in almost every part of the city and county of Los Angeles. Several large commercial buildings collapsed. Hundreds of shops and offices were closed because of nonstructural damage such as fallen ceiling tiles and broken glass. Several hospitals were forced to evacuate their patients. The Los Angeles County school system shut down to allow for clean-up and repairs. Eight large public parking garages suffered partial or complete collapse. Seven major highway bridges were severely damaged or destroyed. Water mains broke and flooded streets; gas lines broke and in some instances started significant fires. The entire Los Angeles area lost electric power.

The region's housing stock suffered especially severe damage. Housing is critical because it makes up a vast majority—60 to 70 percent—of the building stock in most communities; because investment in housing constitutes a major portion of a household's budget as well as the U.S. economy; because it represents social infrastructures and neighborhood identity; and because it provides a basic necessity—shelter—to human beings (Comerio 1998, 15–17). The statistics clearly demonstrate that housing, and particularly apartment buildings in the City of Los Angeles, suffered the greatest impact in the earthquake: 92 percent of all building inspections were residential, and 90 percent of the vacated or seriously damaged units were in multifamily buildings (Comerio 1995, 1). The cost of the residential damage alone has been estimated at over $1.3 billion (HUD 1995, vi).

Assessments of initial damage showed that approximately 65,252 residential units sustained damage of $5,000 or more; 19,439 housing units were ordered vacated (LAHD 1995, 1). In broad comparison, the Loma Prieta earthquake (near San Francisco in 1989) was also largely a multifamily housing disaster, damaging 43,200 units, 11,600 of which were either completely destroyed or rendered uninhabitable. The 1992 Hurricane Andrew disaster in Florida affected 107,900 housing units, mostly single-family, 49,000

Table 4.1 Inspections of Residential Damage in Los Angeles County

Units	Red Tagged (significant structural damage)	Yellow Tagged (unsafe to enter)	Green Tagged (non-structural damage)	Total Inspected
Single family	1.078	6,040	56,239	64,405
Multifamily	15,191	33,810	324,759	376,234
All types	16,269	39,850	380,998	440,639

Source: Mary Comerio, "Los Angeles Housing Losses" (Berkeley, CA: Center for Environmental Design Research, 1995), 13.
Note: The red, yellow, and green tagged columns do not add up to the Total Inspected due to a number of units of unknown tag color.

of which were completely destroyed (LAHD 1995, 4). Furthermore, the residential damage was concentrated (92 percent) within the city limits of Los Angeles, much like as was within the boundaries of the central DF in Mexico City.

Multi-family units suffered the most damage. In Los Angeles County, seven times as many apartments as homes were damaged by the earthquake. Table 4.1 summarizes the large scale of the residential damage, and highlights the large extent to which the housing crisis involved multi-family housing units in the Los Angeles County region.

SUCCESSFUL INSTITUTIONAL ACTION: GHOST TOWN PROGRAM

The city council, the mayor, and the most significantly, the LAHD realized that neighborhoods which had suffered massive and concentrated housing damage would permanently blight the city unless immediate steps were taken to stabilize and rebuild them. One of the first such initiatives documented was a motion presented by Richard Alarcon, a member of the City's Council's Ad Hoc Committee on Earthquake Recovery, on May 20, 1994. Alarcon moved that "the Los Angeles Housing Department, the Department of Building and Safety, the Los Angeles Police Department, and the city Attorney create a task force to address the issue of vandalism for earthquake damaged buildings and report to the Ad Hoc Committee on Earthquake Recovery within two weeks" (Alarcon 1994).

A Ghost Town was later officially defined as "a concentrated area with 100 or more dwelling units that have incurred at least $5,000 worth of property damage per unit" (LAHD 1994, 2). The LAHD took the lead in identifying Ghost Towns and in developing recovery strategies for each area. Officials identified Ghost Towns by following up on city council office referrals, conducting field surveys, and analyzing data collected by the city's Department of Building and Safety. The data, mapped visually on

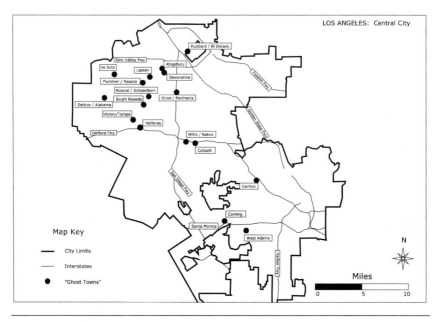

Figure 4.1 Map showing locations and dispersion of Ghost Towns
(i.e., concentrations of severe residential damage) in the City of Los Angeles.
Source: Los Angeles Housing Department, "Report on the earthquake recovery program and prioritization plan"
(Los Angeles: Los Angeles Housing Department, 1995), 7.

GIS, displayed concentrations of severe damage in the San Fernando, Hollywood, and Central Los Angeles areas.

In June of 1994, the City designated the Ghost Towns from the forty-seven most devastated census tract areas, as seen in Figure 4.1. The residential damage was obviously concentrated; around 63 percent of all the vacated units were in thirty-eight census tracts in the City of Los Angeles, and in the seventeen neighborhoods dubbed Ghost Towns, 60 percent of the housing stock was lost. Table 4.2 summarizes the spatial distribution of housing damage, and highlights the concentration of damage in the Ghost Towns in particular, and in the city of Los Angeles in general.

In the Ghost Towns, whole blocks were damaged and vacant. Spoiled food and garbage attracted rodents and posed a public health hazard. Empty buildings drew looters, vandals, squatters, drug dealers, prostitution rings, and gangs whose trespassing caused additional damage, often worse than that caused by the quake itself. The threat of fire increased, as did burglaries: "Scavengers have picked through the rooms so thoroughly that there is almost no sign left of the lives that were lived here [in the Sylmar neighborhood of Los Angeles] before the January 17 earthquake. Only a few mattresses

Table 4.2 Comparative Residential Damage Concentrations in Los Angeles

Geographic Area	Number of Census Tracts	Total Units Inspected	Total Vacated Units	Percent of Units Vacated
Ghost Towns	18	11,126	6,601	59%
Tracts with 1 to 99 vacated units	407	758,211	5,929	0.8%
Tracts with 100 or more vacated units	38	97,044	11,994	12%
San Fernando Valley	250	457,360	14,647	3.2%
City of Los Angeles	756	1,299,953	18,801	1.5%
County of Los Angeles	1,652	3,163,343	19,046	0.06%

Source: Mary Comerio, "Los Angeles Housing Losses" (Berkeley, CA: Center for Environmental Design Research, 1995), 21.

and broken couches remain. Air conditioners, refrigerators, even door handles and wall thermostats, have been stripped away" (Mydans 1994, 12).

The residents remaining in these neighborhoods were overwhelmed as they continued their lives next to derelict structures and closed businesses (see Figures 4.2 and 4.3). "Things are getting worse rather than better," said Richard Close, president of a homeowner's association in the Sherman Oaks section (cited in Mydans 1994, 12). "In areas where 70 percent of residences are vacated we are finding that the remaining 30 percent of people are now moving out because they don't want to live in a ghost town . . . The cleaners, the shoemaker and the little retail establishments just don't have the population they need to survive. So even if they physically survived the earthquake, now they are finding major economic problems." As masses of residents began abandoning their rented and owned properties and local businesses lost the customer base of entire neighborhoods in the weeks following the crisis, the housing institutions in Los Angeles (especially the LAHD) realized that a few property owners could not possibly revive the neighborhoods by moving back.

The City of Los Angeles and its housing institutions moved quickly to clean up, control crime, and restore these Ghost Towns and their surrounding neighborhoods. The LAHD, in response to city council member Alarcon's motion (1994), chaired the Ghost Town Task Force. Before the Los Angeles earthquake, the principal federal disaster assistance programs in the country were the Small Business Administration (SBA) and FEMA. These programs, however, were designed primarily to assist single family homeowners. As such, they left significant gaps in the recovery from the earthquake, where 92 percent of the damage was to multi-family housing units. In order to fill the gap, the LAHD reorganized itself into a crisis-recovery mode by reassigning *regular* staff, refocusing *existing* programs, and designing and

Figure 4.2 Severely damaged and abandoned single-family housing unit in the low-income West Adams Ghost Town in south central Los Angeles.
Source: Aseem Inam, March 1996.

obtaining funds for programs through *established* sources (LAHD 1996). The Ghost Town housing recovery program produced several successful outputs such as rapid action, massive funding, improved conditions, community outreach, and institutional coordination. Many of these outputs emerged from institutional routines—established and tested arrangements, policies, programs, and practices that characterize particular institutions. The following sections describe the successful outputs of the Ghost Town program and the institutional routines on which they were based.

RAPID ACTION

Rapid action, the most significant output of the housing institutions' recovery efforts, was embodied in a series of quick decisions, events, and accomplishments. HUD and the local housing institutions received high marks for their speedy response. "They have moved incredibly quickly. HUD has moved in a way that the department has not moved in many years . . ." said Jan Breidenbach, the executive director of the Southern California Association of Non-Profit Housing, a Los Angeles-based organization of subsidized-housing developers (cited in Stanfield 1994, 392).

On July 18, 1994, the City Council approved the first construction loans through LAHD's Earthquake Emergency Loan Program for a total of $7.5 million (LAHD 1994, 2–4). Just few days later, on July 23, the LAHD and its institutional partners implemented the complete multi-phased plan to recover and restore the thirteen Ghost Towns then identified in the San Fernando Valley, Hollywood, and Mid-City areas. The city hired private security guards to keep vandals out of damaged buildings (Martin 1994, B3). On July 27, Riordan asked Clinton to redirect unspent FEMA funds to housing assistance for Ghost Town condominium and apartment owners. In August, Clinton agreed to seek the transfer of $225 million in emergency aid redistributed from highway and school retrofitting projects, which subsequently won passage from Congress (Smith 1994, B3-B5). With these funds, the cities of Los Angeles and Santa Monica were eventually able to make thirty-year, no-interest loans to owners of damaged buildings (HUD 1995, 8).

The rapid pace of institutional action continued. In December 1994, 1,030 residential buildings occupied the Ghost Towns, and of this total 29 were demolished and 301 were vacant. As of May 1996, only 83 vacant buildings remained. Of the 301 originally vacant buildings, 269 buildings

Figure 4.3 Earthquake-damaged apartment building in Colbath Ghost Town
in the San Fernando Valley area of Los Angeles.
Source: Aseem Inam, March 1996.

representing 6,473 units were undergoing or had completed reconstruction. A total of 7,503 housing units, 99 percent of total units damaged, had funds committed for rehabilitation. Construction had been completed on 5,065 units, which was 67 percent of the damaged units (Earthquake Ghost Town Task Force 1996, 2). The success of the LAHD's strategy is highlighted by the simple fact that despite the severe devastation and abandonment in the Ghost Towns, less than 500 units were demolished in the first year after the event due to the rapid recovery efforts (Comerio 1995, 44).

This rapid action can be credited largely to *existing* institutional arrangements, including ongoing relationships between the LAHD, HUD, and financial institutions. The existing database and the Geographic Information Systems (GIS) mapping of local housing conditions also facilitated rapid action. The Housing Department provided loans to owners of Ghost Town properties partially through the federal Community Development Block Grant (CDBG) program. Most often, CDBG projects allow input from the city council, the planning commission or planning department, and citizens before they are proposed or funded. However, after the earthquake, these lengthy negotiations and provisions were waived due to the urgency of the situation. HUD and LAHD were able to respond so quickly partly because they drew from discretionary funds and advanced CDBG and HOME allocations. In a telephone interview, Jan Opper, Senior Program Officer in the Office of Block Grants at HUD, confirmed that the rapid institutional actions followed existing routines (Opper 1996). The legislation required for appropriations under the authority of the well-established CDBG and HOME programs was based on previous legislation utilized for the Hurricane Andrew crisis in Florida and the Midwest floods. Several Congressional appropriations helped replenish these funds and provide additional monies. This massive funding, the second successful output, is further described in the next section.

MASSIVE FUNDING

The physical devastation of the Ghost Towns was exacerbated by the accompanying financial devastation. For example, Barry Wegman, a lawyer, owned a $159,000 condominium in a thirty-unit building in Studio City that was severely damaged in the earthquake. The building did not have insurance, and his owners' association voted to abandon it. "We're giving up everything," he said (cited in Mydans 1994, 12). "It now goes to the banks. I'm financially wiped out. My cash flow is next to nothing." The poor financial conditions of the residents were especially severe in the low- and lower-middle income communities. One of the residents of the lower-income West Adams Ghost Town, Michael LaChapelle, had lived all of his thirty-six years in his house. His earthquake insurance had expired in November

1993, two months before the crisis. The house shifted eight inches off its foundation during the earthquake and was immediately red tagged, designating it uninhabitable. Two weeks after the quake, LaChapelle was laid off from his job as an auto mechanic (Renwick 1994, 17). The LAHD was already familiar with the difficult financial conditions in the Ghost Towns, as described by Barbara Zeidman, former Assistant General Manager of the LAHD, in an interview with the author:

> Interestingly enough, they [Ghost Towns] . . . tended to be neighborhoods, in at least half the instances, where we already had a concern about their condition before the earthquake. We knew that there was a financial problem in the buildings. Many of them were upside down: that is, their debt exceeded their income, and so their ability to service mortgages was questionable. If you couldn't service your mortgage before or if you were not making your expenses before, and we were going to ask you to add more debt to the building, nobody is going to do that.[3]

Given such dire circumstances, applications for federal assistance set records, and the government pledged $11.2 billion in aid, more than for any previous disaster in the United States. After consulting with local institutions, HUD provided $30 million on April 1, 1994 out of its contingency fund for local governments, enabling housing institutions to launch wholesale efforts to rebuild the Ghost Town neighborhoods. HUD subsequently provided, on August 2, 1994, an additional $225 million for neighborhood recovery efforts after Congress passed a supplemental appropriation (Galster et al. 1995). The money, which came from leftover federal money for repairing freeways and schools, provided interest-free (and thus subsidized) loans. The funding pressures of the Ghost Town problem can be partly traced to the defeat in June 1994 of a $2 billion statewide bond issue for earthquake recovery, which would have included $576 million to provide loans for building repairs. Even though the federal government was paying 90 percent for these repairs, California could not pay its 10 percent of the disaster-repair costs. Without state help, earthquake victims further besieged federal institutions (Mydans 1994, 12).

FEMA and California's Office of Emergency Services spent $6.5 million in emergency grants to Ghost Town property owners. About $200 million in additional funding poured into the Ghost Towns through private insurance, loans from the SBA or loans from private banks (Martin 1995, 20). In addition, soon after the city had identified the Ghost Towns as a serious problem, the SBA agreed to review 28,000 disaster loan applications that had been denied or withdrawn and give top priority to loan requests from property owners within Ghost Towns. The review covered business and home loan applicants who suffered more than $10,000 in damage and were denied loans because they could not prove they could repay. By late September 1994, nine months after the crisis, the SBA had already approved 179 loans totaling nearly $55.5 million to Ghost Town property owners.

The City of Los Angeles's Ghost Town Task Force recommended initial board-up costs of abandoned housing be paid from the Building and Safety Department's Contract Nuisance Abatement funds, part of their existing general budget. The Chief Administrative Officer of the City of Los Angeles used the Disaster Assistance Fund, which had been intended for other purposes but which could be used to pay initial board-up and private security costs. Approximately $1 million in FEMA funds was already available in June 1994 for the Public Works Department to utilize for fencing Ghost Town properties.

Most of the funding was obtained through the tried-and-tested routines of the CDBG and HOME Investment Partnership programs. The major changes in CDBG and HOME in the housing recovery efforts involved extended income targeting and a wider range of permissible activities.

For more than two decades, the CDBG program has provided a flexible source of funding for community development and revitalization. CDBG funds may be spent on housing, economic development, public facilities, social services, land acquisition, or other related activities. The nature of CDBG-funded projects meshed well with the operations of the Ghost Town program. For example, under normal circumstances, 62 percent of local owner-occupied housing rehabilitation (a critical component of the Ghost Town program as well) carried out by CDBG-funded local institutions in the United States (such as the LAHD) was initiated through the use of CDBG funds (HUD 1995, 1). Furthermore, under normal circumstances, CDBG has been primarily a neighborhood-based program—like the Ghost Town program—with cities allocating an average of 54 percent of their 1992 funds to neighborhood-based strategies.

One of the stated objectives of the CDBG program administered by HUD is to meet an urgent need, defined as an activity

> that is designed to alleviate existing conditions which pose a serious and immediate threat to the health or welfare of the community which are of recent origin . . . [and] that the recipient is unable to finance the [alleviation] activity on its own. A condition will generally be considered of recent origin if it developed or became critical within 18 months preceding the certification by the recipient.[4]

Housing and related infrastructure recovery after the earthquake clearly fell within this objective of the well-established program. Other requirements of the CDBG program, however, had to be modified or simply waived. For example, existing program regulations limit the CDBG subsidy to 50 percent of a down payment for home purchase by a low- or moderate-income household. HUD waived this regulation after determining that the subsidy would have to exceed 50 percent of a down payment in order to assist many of the low- and moderate-income households in the Ghost Towns. Similarly, under existing regulations of the HOME program, participating local institutions must provide 25 percent complementary funding from local revenues as a condition for receiving federal funds. HUD, however, waived these requirements in order to facilitate flexible and rapid crisis recovery.

The federal HOME Investment Partnership program was the second major source of funds for the Ghost Town program. This block grant program was first funded in 1992 at $1.5 billion (HUD 1996, 4). In 1992, two years before the earthquake, the LAHD had already obtained $35 million from the federal HOME investment partnership (Squier 1993, 2). Under normal circumstances, participating jurisdictions can utilize HOME funds to support four types of housing assistance: acquiring and developing rental housing, rehabilitating owner-occupied housing (as was the case with the Ghost Towns), facilitating home ownership, and providing tenant-based rental assistance. In the first year of the program, participating jurisdictions emphasized rental housing, with about 60 percent of program funds allocated to support rental housing (also a major concern of the Ghost Town program). The program targets to lower-income families: all program funds must benefit families with incomes below 80 percent of their area's median income—which was one of the indirect goals of the Ghost Town program and is described more fully in the concluding sections of this chapter.

A senior HUD official explains how existing institutional routines, such as the CDBG and HOME programs, are used and adapted in crisis situations:

Using the vehicle of CDBG and HOME and some others because the departments knew them—both CDD and Housing [LAHD] —knew how to use them, knew the rules and regulations . . . That was a really good vehicle rather than a new program. I think that would be something you would learn from experiences: to use some of the existing vehicles to get the money out and tweak them a bit . . . When an earthquake hits or some disaster happens, people call Jan [Opper (Senior Program Officer, Office of Block Grants, HUD) to find out] what can be offered from HUD, particularly on the side of HOME and CDBG. He is ready. He has got a letter within a 24-hour period of time or less saying: we have waived the following things that you can use your CDBG dollars for.[5]

The City of Los Angeles provided zero- and low-interest loans up to $50,000 to single-family homeowners from a pool of federal disaster aid and local housing funds. The new money helped rebuild approximately 17,000 units, or about half the number that Riordan had said were at risk for lack of necessary funds. Loans were targeted especially for the recovery of Ghost Town housing units (HUD 1995, 8).

In addition, LAHD developed a Ghost Town Finance Unit by re-organizing its existing staff to expedite loan processing in these hard hit neighborhoods, utilizing $22.5 million in HOME supplemental funds awarded by HUD in addition to other available funds (LAHD 1995, 10–11). The new loan process grew out of the pre-crisis process, and was common to most local housing institutions. Institutional personnel were already quite familiar with the procedures.

The Loan to Lenders program, a funding effort initiated by the City of Los Angeles, provided banks the money to issue low-interest loans to building owners. For example, Home Savings of America, one of the banks participating in the program, had issued $500,000 in loans by November 1995 (Martin 1995, 20). The banks and other lending institutions had to be extremely flexible with landlords to keep the properties from falling into foreclosure, but it was in the bank's interest to help landlords make repairs and reoccupy the units with paying tenants.

For Ghost Towns, the SBA received a total of 1,707 residential applications through August, 1995; the majority (73 percent) were from individual condo-minium owners. The SBA approved 1,108 of these applications for a 60 percent approval rate and total funding of over $97 million. The majority of the funding, about $63 million, was provided for apartment buildings (LAHD 1995, 14).

With $284 million in available funding for earthquake recovery loans, the LAHD worked closely with property owners, lenders, developers, and the SBA to design and implement a recovery-assistance program addressing the unique needs of the affected housing stock, including multi-family and single-family rental units, single-family owner-occupied units, and condo-miniums (as was the case in Mexico City) in the Ghost Towns. These efforts produced the Earthquake Emergency Loan Program (EELP), a fast-delivery mechanism with the following objectives: (1) to fill the gap when funds available through federal and state institutions (e.g., FEMA and SBA) and private institutions (e.g., banks and insurance companies) were insufficient or when these sources rejected an applicant's request for funding, (2) to create incentives to rebuild for property owners and lending institutions, and (3) to establish loan terms that responded to the economic effects of the recession (LAHD 1995, 15–16).

In order to address the problems associated with various categories of damaged housing, the LAHD developed several components of the EELP. The major problem facing owners of single-family housing was the lack of earthquake insurance or the inability to pay high insurance deductibles. Alternative assistance was available through SBA's Home Disaster Loan Program and California's Individual Family Grant Program. However, applicants had to demonstrate the ability to repay all loans. The LAHD's Single Family Home Program was designed to assist homeowners who were rejected for funding by other sources, or whose funding from other sources was insufficient (LAHD 1995, 16).

As described previously, public sector housing institutions drew upon past experiences to help initiate financing, to coordinate between private sector financial institutions and homeowners, and to ensure collective efforts rather than simply individual ones for neighborhood recovery:

> We have been very proactive in Los Angeles for . . . maybe 20 years in providing low-cost housing and residential units of various types that were government-subsidized. So, we had a built system already of moving money through the loan process—zero-interest loans, low-cost loans. We had already been through that . . . with the riots for one . . . But we have a very proactive Housing Department here that had been building residential units for a long time. So, we were familiar with the concept of getting loans to people.[6]

For example, LAHD had considerable experience in the types of housing loans used in the Ghost Town program. In 1991 the LAHD, then known as the Housing Preservation and Production Department, provided loans to 447 homeowners and apartment building owners to rehabilitate 2,256 units of housing. This represented a total public and private investment of $24 million (Squier 1992, 1).

IMPROVED CONDITIONS

The devastated neighborhoods experienced the third successful output, improved conditions, in the form of safety, stability, and physical improvement. Conditions in the seventeen abandoned Ghost Towns were dismal: in the deserted neighborhoods, rats and cockroaches proliferated. Stagnant swimming pools bred mosquitoes, and city officials either ordered them drained or stocked them with insect-eating fish. On Hubbard Street in the Sylmar Ghost Town, vandals shattered windows and sliding glass doors and threw a toilet out a window (Mydans 1994, 12). For social and economic reasons, it was imperative to restore physical conditions to their previous level. However, the Ghost Town program accomplished even more: it helped improve neighborhood conditions so much that they eventually surpassed their pre-earthquake state.

The immediate task for those aiming to improve conditions in the Ghost Towns was to ensure the safety of any remaining inhabitants and of the housing units abandoned by the community. The Los Angeles Police Department (LAPD) conducted sweeps in Ghost Town neighborhoods to clear vacated properties of squatters and vandals. In July 1994, the LAHD initiated a one-year security plan for Ghost Town neighborhoods with over $6 million in FEMA funding. The City of Los Angeles provided an additional $200,000 to finance private security through October 15, 1995 for six Ghost Towns where significant construction activity began later than in the others (LAHD 1995, 12). The Housing Department surveyed private security companies and determined the cost of and need for such security at each Ghost Town location. The Housing Department was then authorized to expend funds for this security service for a maximum of 120 days at each location (Earthquake Ghost Town Task Force 1994, 1).

Concurrent with boarding-up, the Public Works Department fenced those Ghost Town properties that had not yet been fenced by their owners. In consultation with the LAPD, Public Works posted "no trespassing" signs, and property owners were asked to authorize the LAPD to arrest trespassers. The Housing Department consulted with the appropriate LAPD Bureaus and Senior Lead Officer contacts in the Neighborhood Watch program regarding LAPD sweeps to clear the properties of existing squatters and vandals (Earthquake Ghost Town Task Force 1994, 2).

The second task for improving conditions was to facilitate the physical, and thus the psychological, stability of the devastated neighborhoods. The LAHD and several other institutions and community groups worked together to stabilize the Ghost Towns and surrounding neighborhoods against the deterioration and escalated crime levels observed after the earthquake (LAHD 1995). To improve deteriorating conditions in these neighborhoods, the Public Works and the General Services departments boarded, fenced, and cleaned over 400 earthquake-damaged buildings between June 28, 1994 and July 17, 1995 (LAHD 1995, 12). If a property owner took no positive steps toward repair or rehabilitation of a structure within 120 days of July 1, 1994, the Building and Safety Department was asked to commence abatement proceedings leading to the demolition of the building as a danger and hazard to the community.

Like the RHP program in Mexico City, the Ghost Town program aimed to revitalize each affected neighborhood on site rather than relocating earthquake victims to cheaper land or larger lots in other parts of the metropolitan region. Generally, disaster victims have so many new things to manage that they strongly desire to return to pre-disaster social patterns (Bolin and Stanford 1991). For example, one of the Ghost Town neighborhoods, West Adams, was an area with low- to moderate-income households. Many residents were senior citizens living on fixed incomes who had been in this neighborhood for twenty years or more. "This is not a transient group of people. They've had considerable structural loss, which has led to lots of emotional and psychological pain for them," said Cheryl Grills, an associate professor of psychology at Loyola Marymount University who conducted a survey of earthquake damage in South Los Angeles for the Community Coalition (cited in Renwick 1994, 16).

The third task was to improve physical housing conditions. In many areas, the quality of housing was even better than pre-earthquake conditions due to stricter standards and regulations accompanying low-interest loans (for example, see Figure 4.4). Institutional routines such as HUD regulations promoted the safety and soundness of all public and HUD-insured housing by requiring these structures to meet the Minimum Property Standards established by the Department, which are more stringent than many local code standards. Under newly revised Minimum Property Standards for single-family and multi-family housing, seismic safety was mandatory. In some instances, property owners were able

> to redesign some of the apartments that they remodeled or rehabbed to have larger units because the demand for 3-, 4- and 5-bedroom . . . apartment buildings is far greater than the actual numbers of units out there. And so, in some instances, they were able to enlarge that and to serve a need that's out there.[7]

Furthermore, Greig Smith, Chief Deputy to Councilman Hal Bernson of the 12th District in Los Angeles (where most of the residential damage occurred), suggested in an interview with the author that

> five years after this [1994] earthquake, this [Ghost Town] community will be better than it was. These were 1960s apartments, most of them, that were degenerating. They were getting run down; some of them were beginning to be very strong crime problems; there were gang elements moving in before the earthquake. Now, if you look at them, they are beautiful. They are subsidized housing, but they are bringing in elements that are productive to the community. This is terrible public policy as far as reconstructing a community, but you take a lemon and make lemonade out of it, and that's what we did. We used this to rehabilitate tremendous blocks of areas that were degenerating very quickly.[8]

Figure 4.4 Apartment building undergoing repair and improvement work
on Carlton in the Carlton Ghost Town of Los Angeles.
Source: Aseem Inam, March 1996.

Ensuring the safety and stability of deteriorating housing and neighborhoods was a well-established institutional routine long before the earthquake:

> The City [of Los Angeles], for 20 years, has had a very successful, largely single-family, rehab program . . . in the single-family oriented neighborhoods, like the ones in Crenshaw and West Adams . . . All you did was move over and say, "Now we're doing earthquake stuff." So, you didn't have to do a whole lot of new program design.[9]

In early 1992, the LAHD targeted severely deteriorated blocks where community revitalization required the concentration of multiple local government resources. In the Distressed Property Program for example, the LAHD and other planning institutions in Los Angeles worked with nonprofit and community-based institutions to return crack houses and abandoned buildings to use as affordable housing (Squier 1992, 1). Also in 1992, the LAHD initiated the Impact Rehabilitation program, designed to bring the weight of public and private sector resources to bear on deteriorating neighborhoods whose residents and business owners suffered the extremes of crime, violence, and disinvestments. Beginning with a joint venture with the Police Department on Blythe Street in the Van Nuys area of Los Angeles,

Impact Rehabilitation built partnerships with residents, landlords, business owners, community organizers, social service providers, and other local institutions to make the streets safer and the housing livable. Though still dominated by a gang of drug dealers, the Blythe Street partnership resulted in police patrols on foot, ninety units of rehabilitated housing, funding for fifty new affordable housing units, child care, and most critically, a program and an institutional routine for improved conditions in distressed neighborhoods. Impact Rehabilitation has been just one part of LAHD's larger rehabilitation efforts in Los Angeles. The program invested $12 million to rehabilitate 1,400 homes and apartments in low-income neighborhoods (Squier 1993, 1). The routines of the Distressed Property and Impact Rehabilitation programs served as precedents for the promotion for the post-earthquake safety and stability.

COMMUNITY OUTREACH

The Los Angeles Housing Department reached out to the community through many programs and partnership initiatives, some of which were targeted specifically to Ghost Town neighborhoods. The Department contacted individual property owners to offer substantial assistance, participated in community meetings, and collaborated with the nonprofit, community-based institution, Habitat for Humanity, to rebuild a low-income Ghost Town. This effort grew out of the Department's routines in dealing with its housing constituencies.

The LAHD also created the city's only all-purpose hotline for all housing needs and earthquake information by expanding the role of its existing Rent Stabilization Ordinance Information Line. Within the first year of the earthquake, a total of 162,000 calls had poured into the Public Information Section (LAHD 1995, 8). Other community outreach activities of the LAHD included leadership and participation in the neighborhood-based Disaster Assistance Centers (DACs), Reassurance Teams, and an "Earthquake Recovery Forum" at the Los Angeles Convention Center. This forum helped multi-family housing property owners overcome financing obstacles, fill vacancies, and obtain individual assistance from the SBA, private financial institutions, and the financing programs of local public institutions such as the LAHD. The event was co-sponsored by the LAHD, the Apartment Owners Association of Greater Los Angeles, and HUD. LAHD also participated in other events sponsored by various charitable and public institutions during the three months immediately following the earthquake.

For those property owners who applied to LAHD for assistance, the Department's construction specialists conducted individual building inspections and developed cost estimates in order to expedite loan underwriting.

Loan underwriting included an analysis to determine if properties required loan modifications from senior trust deed holders. LAHD finance officers worked with each of the lenders and owners to reach agreement on loan modifications that ensured the financial feasibility as well as physical recovery of properties. Together, these efforts have enabled nearly all owners in Ghost Towns to secure financial solutions for their buildings. A designated staff person continued to monitor construction progress and liaison with owners and lenders throughout the seventeen Ghost Town neighborhoods (LAHD 1995, 11–12).

Dan Falcon, who headed the Ghost Town Task Force's financing unit, said a key challenge in the recovery was convincing landowners to take out repair loans. Some landlords were already over-leveraged, and taking on even more debt was risky. A financial specialist working for the city met with groups of landlords from Ghost Town neighborhoods to assure them that it made financial sense to rebuild. Often housing officials drafted financial projections to demonstrate that a landlord could pay off a repair loan and still make a profit. "We had to convince everybody psychologically that it was a good idea," Falcon said. "That was no easy task either" (cited in Martin 1995, 20).

In addition, community meetings provided loan information, LAHD staff participated in neighborhood clean-ups, and city officials collaborated with Habitat for Humanity, to restore part of the West Adams Ghost Town. Earthquake recovery staff at LAHD attended Neighborhood Watch and other community meetings in the Ghost Towns and surrounding neighborhoods to inform residents and to solicit feedback on LAHD programs.

These community outreach efforts have their roots in a number of institutional routines. In 1991, the LAHD took part in a variety of community outreach projects that involved partnerships with the nonprofit, community-based sector. For example, it provided funding for an institution called Concerned Citizens of South Central Los Angeles for a building with eighteen housing units and a print shop offering job training for local residents. It also offered loans to another institution, A Community of Friends, to acquire and rehabilitate a dilapidated building to house twenty-four mentally disabled individuals who received on-site support services (Squier 1992, 2).

The well-established, and indeed institutionalized, approach of Habitat for Humanity is essentially one of partnerships: with planning institutions who donate land, with corporations who donate funds, and with individuals who contribute labor—especially the future homeowners, whose labor is considered to be sweat equity. Habitat for Humanity has been working, since 1991, in the largely lower-income neighborhoods of Los Angeles, such as East Los Angeles, Pico Union, and South Central Los Angeles, where the West Adams Ghost Town was located. In addition to its house-building activity, Habitat for Humanity has been involved in community outreach in Los Angeles through activities such as cleaning up empty plots of land, painting over graffiti, planting trees, and completing house repair projects. Thus, Habitat for Humanity was a well-established choice for an institutional partner in the community outreach efforts of the Ghost Town program.

INSTITUTIONAL COORDINATION

The Ghost Town program also succeeded through institutional coordination, using effective coordinating mechanisms such as the Ghost Town Task Force within the City of Los Angeles; collaborative efforts between different types of institutions such as the SBA and LAHD database; and of course pooled funding from institutions at the federal (e.g., FEMA, SBA, and HUD), state (e.g., the Calforina Office of Emergency Services (OES)), and local (e.g., Los Angeles City Council and LAHD) levels, and from institutions in the public as well as private sectors.

Six months after the quake, the City of Los Angeles established a task force specifically to broker deals between lenders and Ghost Town landlords, hoping to provide financially strapped owners a break on mortgage payments while they were rebuilding. A memorandum from the Earthquake Ghost Town Task Force (1994) six months after the earthquake listed no less than eleven different institutions to be involved in the Ghost Town effort, including the City Council, the Mayor's Office, the City Attorney's Office, the City Administrative Officer's Office, LAHD, Los Angeles Department of Building and Safety, Los Angeles Public Works Department, LAPD, Los Angeles General Services Department, OES, FEMA, HUD, and SBA. The coordination and interaction among these institutions is described in an interview with a senior housing policy maker in Los Angeles:

> I think the cooperation he [the General Manager of the LAHD] had with Building and Safety and the Planning Department; and the Mayor, and Councilman Hal Bernson—they really made it a priority with the [City Council's] Ad Hoc Committee . . . I think those would be the key players locally. Again, with the kind of information they provided to us in HUD, we were then able to take the next step and advocate for the financial resources to address the Ghost Town issue.[10]

In times of crises, Los Angeles can turn to *established* precedents of institutional coordination. This is especially true of horizontal integration; that is, coordination at the same level (e.g., local). For example, following the Los Angeles riots of 1992, Council member Mark Ridley-Thomas set up an Ad Hoc Los Angeles Recovery and Revitalization Committee, consisting of the Departments of Housing, Community Development, City Planning, the Community Redevelopment Agency, and the County Transportation Commission (Leavitt 1996, 114). They agreed that targeted areas in South Central Los Angeles needed a strategy and development plan that could be implemented within three to five years.

Vertical integration played a role in the form of cooperation at most governmental levels. The governor declared a state of emergency; the President declared a national state of emergency; and the head of the FEMA, the U.S. Secretary of Transportation, and the U.S. Secretary of Housing and Urban Development flew to Los Angeles. In Los Angeles, officials quickly decided to let local institutions lead the effort, with other institutions playing facilitative and supporting roles (Wachs and Kamel 1996). For example, the city successfully worked with federal institutions such as FEMA to pay 90 percent of the estimated $1 million to provide a security plan and to police the ghost towns for 120 days. The city's leading housing institution, the LAHD, and the SBA worked together to reach all affected property owners in the Ghost Town areas. The two agencies shared a single database for tracking the status of all properties in the Ghost Towns, and both agencies had access to the same automatic referral system.

Vertical integration is usually ensured by the routine of federal crisis management. Federal participation in disaster response and recovery is managed by FEMA. Established in 1974, FEMA has become the primary source of federal funds for disaster recovery. FEMA itself administers just a handful of programs. The agency's more important role is as the primary intake and coordinating institution for a wide variety of federal, state, and local government recovery programs. FEMA accomplishes this function by establishing local Disaster Assistance Centers, or DACs. DACs are staffed by FEMA personnel as well as those from state and county social service agencies, whose salaries are temporarily paid by FEMA (Comerio, Landis, and Rofe 1994, 26).

Several routines helped facilitate horizontal integration, especially partnerships between the public sector and the private or nonprofit sector. For example, in order to assist the City of Los Angeles's response to the 1992 riots, the LAHD joined with the Planning Department in inviting the Urban Land Institute, a private sector institution, to develop strategies for revitalizing and reusing distressed commercial corridors. In addition, LAHD joined the Community Development Department, the Planning Department, and the Community Redevelopment Agency to develop a physical and economic framework to establish long-term solutions to urban blight and loss of employment opportunities (Squier 1993, 2).

Such routines, or established institutional practices, appear in the housing sector as well. The Los Angeles Housing Partnership was formed as one of the first Blue Ribbon Committee recommendations implemented by the City. The committee based the partnership on existing models in Chicago and Boston, whereby a public-private entity would provide financing and technical assistance to non-profit developers in the city. Gary Squier, general manager of the LAHD (then known as the Housing Preservation and Production Department), described it as "the hub of a wheel . . . being the coordinator, pulling together public capital, lender debt, equity investment, predevelopment funds, at a one-stop shop through which non-profit developers could get all the support they needed to put together affordable housing. . . ." (Squier cited in Goetz 1993, 160). The Housing Partnership continued to play a minor role as a developer of affordable housing, but the more grandiose vision of the Partnership did not emerge. However, the Partnership did establish a precedent for institutional coordination by coordinating public funds; this model would later be effectively utilized in the Ghost Town program.

In 1991, the mayor's office increased its efforts to assist non-profit developers. In coordination with the local office of the Local Initiatives Support Corporation and several private foundations, the city contributed $1.5 million and leveraged over $4.5 million from private sector partners for a Community Development Collaborative to provide technical assistance and development support to the region's non-profit housing sector. In practice, the Collaborative was even closer to the "hub of the wheel" described above by Gary Squier than the Los Angeles Housing Partnership ever was, in terms of gathering financing from an array of public and private sources and then passing on the financing and assistance to community-based groups (Goetz 1993, 160).

LIMITATIONS OF INSTITUTIONAL ACTION: SHORTCOMINGS OF THE PROGRAM

Critics have pointed out several limitations of the Ghost Town program, including the perception that institutional action was not rapid enough, and the program's alleged neglect of low-income neighborhoods. For example, "[n]early seven months after the quake, Los Angeles [was] still plagued by single blocks or entire neighborhoods of these vacant, damaged buildings, populated by squatters, drug addicts and gangs, as they await[ed] demolition or repair . . . Though emergency repairs were rapid, and the city's freeways were reopened ahead of schedule, government regulations and bureaucratic procedures, insurance conflicts and a lack of money [had] slowed housing reconstruction, especially in apartment buildings" (Mydans 1994, 12). Massive funding was provided through loans from a variety of public sector sources, which did help the program succeed, but also slowed it down somewhat due to the variety of institutional actors involved and the complexity of the loan application process. Moreover, the Ghost Town problem was initially difficult to understand and analyze due to the dispersed pockets of damage, the problem of coordinating with landlords and tenants in multi-family housing, and—unlike in Mexico City—a genuine lack of community initiative in housing recovery.

Critics also charge that the program neglected low-income neighborhoods: "the financing and the repairs have come slowly to low-income neighborhoods, where crime and depressed property values have made it difficult for landlords contemplating making repairs" (Martin 1995, 3–20). Rachel Tucker, a resident of a low-income neighborhood, was not surprised at the slow progress in fixing earthquake damage in her neighborhood. "It's because we're minorities . . . that's the bottom line," said Tucker, who is black. "Most people here can't take off their jobs and go downtown and fight City Hall" (cited in Martin 1995, 20). Housing recovery in lower-income Ghost Towns such as in the West Adams area was slow not only because of the lengthy loan application process, but also because many of the homeowners were retired, living on fixed incomes, and reluctant to take on a large debt. However, the charge that minority communities were ignored is difficult to substantiate because the evidence suggests housing recovery efforts were targeted specifically to areas of greatest devastation, regardless of their racial composition. Figure 4.5, clearly indicates that the

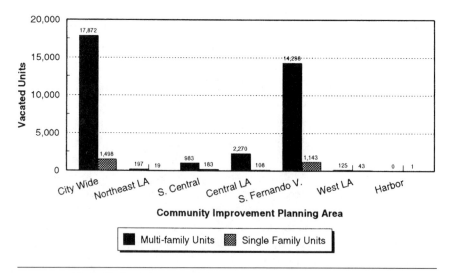

Figure 4.5 Graph showing distribution of post-earthquake vacated housing units in various parts of Los Angeles, as of March 1994.
Source: Hamilton, Rabinovitz and Alschuler, Inc., The 1994 Los Angeles rental housing study: Summary. (Los Angeles: City of Los Angeles Housing Department, Rent Stabilization Division, 1994) 21.

greatest housing damage, and thus the greatest demand for housing recovery, was not in South Central Los Angeles (where many minorities live), but in the San Fernando Valley, close to the epicenter of the earthquake.

GHOST TOWN PROGRAM IN PERSPECTIVE

The Los Angeles earthquake housing losses compelled local and state attention and special federal assistance because of the concentration of damage in multi-family structures, and the associated potential for blight, abandonment, and long-term decline in the property values of entire neighborhoods. In contrast, the Mexico City housing losses caught the attention of public sector planning institutions for largely political reasons, including the concentration of voter groups such as labor unions in the affected neighborhoods and the mass mobilization of affected communities. Moreover, in the months following the earthquake in Los Angeles, pre-earthquake economic conditions such as high rental vacancies, declining property values, declining rental income, high mortgage debt, and severe reduction of owner equity made it clear that recovery would not happen without significant public intervention.

The Ghost Town housing recovery program must also be placed in the broader context of the crisis situations' massive scale. For example, seven months after the earthquake, FEMA had received 606,643 applications for assistance; that surpassed the previous record of 304,000 applications filed after Hurricane Hugo in 1989. The agency expected to pay out a total of $5.5 billion for the Los Angeles earthquake. Similarly, the SBA processed more applications for low-interest loans than it had in all disasters over the past five years combined, including Hurricane Hugo, the Loma Prieta earthquake in San Francisco, the 1992 Los Angeles riots, Florida's Hurricane Andrew, Hurricane Iniki in Hawaii, Typhoon Omar in Guam, and the 1993 Midwest floods (Mydans 1994, 12).

Given the huge scale of the devastation of the Los Angeles earthquake, institutional actors not normally designed to deal with crisis situations, such as housing institutions, could very well have been overwhelmed and helpless. Instead, housing institutions such as HUD and LAHD became driving forces of effective action and policy. In addressing issues of crisis recovery, these institutions turned to some of their long-standing policies and practices. Traditionally, owners receiving rehabilitation loans from LAHD under normal circumstances for properties with five or more units are required to set aside several units for low-income or very low-income households; these restrictions applied to projects receiving earthquake funding as well. Loan terms were adjusted depending upon the number of units a property owner was willing to reserve for low- and very low-income households; more set-aside units resulted in better loan terms: "A link between the Section 8 [Certificate subsidized rent program] and this is, when the Ghost Towns are rebuilt, one of the requirements was . . . [that] there would be some priority for some of those who were in the Section 8 program to go into the apartment buildings that were then improved by the Ghost Town money" (Gruel 1996). The affordability restrictions had two objectives: first, they offset the inflationary effects subsidized loans have on property sales prices, and second, they created affordable housing. LAHD estimated that as many as 2,000 affordable units were created throughout the city as a result of these requirements (LAHD 1995, 16).

The concern regarding the loss of lower-income and affordable rental housing stock during crisis situations has been a *long-standing* one for the City of Los Angeles. In 1988, Los Angeles City Council member Ernani Bernadi (1988, 188) expressed concern that "low income tenants will suffer . . . if their buildings are brought to seismic code requirements under *private, high-cost financing* [emphasis mine] because the resulting higher rents will be beyond their ability to pay. Where are these tenants to go?" This suggests a *public, low-cost financing* mechanism, as was utilized in the Ghost Town program, to maintain and indeed increase the stock of affordable rental housing. The mechanism applied in the Ghost Town program, then, is quite similar to the City of Los Angeles's *existing* 15 percent Ordinance, which requires developers of housing projects of five or more units to make a reasonable effort to make available 15 percent of the units for sale or rental to low- or moderate-income households (Bernadi 1988, 189).

The Los Angeles case study reveals two insights: (1) the role of institutions as relatively autonomous actors with impacts on urban planning and development, and (2) the role of institutional routines in effective institutional actions during crisis recovery. The next chapter presents a brief counter-point by discussing two examples of failed institutional action, the Hoy No Circula program in Mexico City and the Rebuild Los Angeles program in that city. In contrast to the successful programs analyzed above, these programs lack many of the five outputs and the guidance of institutional routines.

Chapter 5

When Planning Institutions Fail

Beyond the legal limits of Mexico City's self-destructive sprawl, the view from the mountainside neighborhood of El Zacaton was breath-taking—literally. A photochemical soup spread across the urban valley 1,500 feet below. Skyscrapers, factories, highways, and homes loomed grayish-brown through translucent smog as more than twenty million people and three million cars coughed, choked, and gasped their way through ozone levels more than double those considered safe for humans. The cloud spread across the horizon, burning eyes and lungs even up in fast-growing El Zacaton (the Pasture), where construction workers, oblivious, continued carving the city deeper into one of its few remaining forests, illegally building makeshift homes to accommodate a population boom that brings 1,000 new residents to Mexico City each day.[1]

The world was shocked by the video tape showing a black motorist being beaten by white police officers. No one had expected that a jury viewing this tape would find the four police officers to be not guilty of using excessive force against Rodney King. The Los Angeles Police Department was unprepared when the personal shock over the trial outcome turned into angry and violent crowd behavior. Koreans did not seem to anticipate that the black rage against the white establishment would be diverted into looting their grocery stores and burning their small businesses. City officials, the police and local merchants did not expect Hispanic immigrants, who were becoming known as the new "silent majority" on the Los Angeles scene, to be found in large numbers among the participants in the rioting and looting that took place after the verdict.[2]

AIR POLLUTION, though very much an unstable condition and a major disturbance to the existing urban system, is unlike earthquakes and riots in that it is an ongoing crisis: "It's deceptive when they declare an emergency. The reality is that we are in a pollution emergency practically every day of the year."[3] Although such a crisis has a less dramatic onset, it can still command the attention and effort necessary to prompt response and recovery programs.

The Hoy No Circula (HNC, or No Driving Today) program is an unprecedented effort to limit 20 percent of vehicular circulation in Mexico City each day of the week in a large-scale effort to reduce air pollution. However, according to Raúl Tornel, representative of the Comisión de Ecología de Concamin (Confederation of Industrial Chambers of the United Mexican States), the HNC program constitutes a scandal and corruption (Urrutia 1996). A World Bank study has shown the HNC program to be ineffective in curbing automobile use, with some indicators even pointing to increased automobile usage as a result of the program (Eskeland and Feyzioglu 1995, 1). Despite some initial success based on reduced traffic congestion and curtailed air pollution, the HNC program did not achieve the desired results—households circumvented the ban by buying a second car (Onursal and Gautam 1997, 156).

The actual source of the meager air quality improvement is debatable. The Secretary for Urban Development for Mexico City suggested that the reduction in pollution is not really attributable to HNC; in fact, the verification of emissions from engines has had the most impact (Eibenshutz 1999). Government regulation of the auto industry has caused the development of engines with a significant reduction in pollutant production. However, many of the potential air quality benefits were offset by a 14 percent increase in the number of Mexico City's registered personal automobiles in 1990, immediately after the HNC program was introduced, as wealthy residents sought to evade the inconvenience of the program.

As a result of the apparent failure of the HNC program, a double ban has been in place since December 1995 (Onursal and Gautam 1997, 103). Under this program, 40 percent of the vehicles (except buses) in the metropolitan area are prohibited from use when air pollution exceeds a certain level, IMECA 250. For example, in October 1997, about half of the cars in Mexico City were banned from the streets as part of the City's efforts to control smog (Los Angeles Times 1997, 12). Cars with license plates ending in an odd number were prohibited from driving, and drivers who broke the rules were fined about $100.

Instead of analyzing and addressing the multi-faceted nature of the air pollution crisis, the government continues to implement the program—rather than stopping it all together or modifying it substantially—based on purely technical justifications. The failed HNC program has been inherited by each successive administration. It has proven difficult to discontinue due to the fact that the cancellation would cause a heavy increase in the amount of traffic circulation and hence an increase in contaminant emissions (Lezama 1999). According to Ernesto Rico, Director General of the Secretary of the Environment in the Government of Mexico City and the person most directly responsible for the management of the HNC program,

> if we now discontinue the HNC program and all the automobiles circulate on all days, we would be releasing around 800 tons of daily contaminants into the air, which would then constitute daily environmental emergencies; that is, we would arrive at emergency levels in ozone as in PM-10 and smaller suspended particles. Also, it would complicate the situation regarding cruising speed; that is, we would tend towards congestion in almost all the streets of Mexico City. The average speed is 33.4 kilometers per hour. If the HNC program was lifted, speed would lower to 22 kilometers. Then, in that case, we would have an increase in the consumption of combustible fuels in the metropolitan area, which is a very large amount of consumption for the geographical conditions that we have in the area.[4]

The program thus continues, still shadowed by large questions regarding its effectiveness. Its lack of effectiveness has been attributed by more than one observer to institutional factors (e.g., Garza 1996). These factors will be discussed further—in parallel with the failed Rebuild Los Angeles (RLA) program in response to the 1992 riots—in the rest of this chapter.

In Los Angeles, three days after the riots sparked by the Rodney King verdict began and while fires were still smoldering, Mayor Tom Bradley called Peter Ueberroth, the successful organizer of the 1984 Olympic Games, to discuss the development of a private-sector initiative that would spark a Los Angeles renaissance (Grigsby 1993). RLA was launched one day after Bradley's initial phone call. The premise of the effort was that previous federal efforts to stimulate urban revitalization had failed, and that if reinvestment were to occur, then people with proven track records—private sector business leaders—would have to assume the lead, as "a showcase of how private industry could lead the city to recovery" (Gordon 1996, A1).

After taking a helicopter tour of the devastation, Ueberroth vowed to make the city's reconstruction effort "a blueprint for revitalizing inner cities' across the nation (*Los Angeles Times* 1992, 123–126). Ueberroth soon launched a public relations campaign proclaiming an infusion of dollars by major corporations to inner-city business development, job training programs, and charities. RLA established six objectives to be accomplished within five years (Grigsby 1993): to create more jobs; to increase the number of business owners; to improve work force skills; to engage the public sector more actively—albeit as a secondary player to the private sector—in solving local problems; and to build community pride. RLA's strategies included helping to interest Vons, a large grocery store chain, in building twelve new stores in the riot-affected neighborhoods.

RLA was supposed to be a conduit between the poor, riot-affected neighborhoods and business investors (Fulton 1997, 22). In 1993, a year after its creation, RLA's fifty staff members—including lawyers, business executives, and community development specialists—were essentially deal facilitators who spent their time identifying worthy needs in the South Central and other neglected areas, and then linking those neighborhoods with likely investors. Only about a third of the staff was paid from the RLA budget; the rest were either on loan from private companies or working as volunteers. The organization was intended to disband after five years, and it did.

RLA was under nearly constant attack from one sector of the community or the other—an indication of just how hard it was to forge a consensus among the city's four major racial groups (Fulton 1997, 22–23). RLA was formed in May 1992, but months passed before a board of directors could be selected, as major interest groups argued over representation. The African American political leadership, which had been in place in South Central Los Angeles for over a generation and regarded the area as their territory, wanted to control the incoming resources. Korean merchants wanted to recoup their investments and rebuild their shops. The Latino leaders simply wanted to be included in the process so they could work toward political enfranchisement, especially for the poorly organized Central American immigrants. As for the whites, the downtown power structure wanted control over the private funds flowing into South Central Los Angeles, while the middle class on the west side of the city and in the San Fernando Valley wanted to feel shielded from the violence elsewhere in the city. RLA did not appear to understand the complexity of racial dynamics in Los Angeles.

Once the initial Board was appointed, angry groups held daily press conferences complaining that they had been left out (Fulton 1997, 23). In response, Ueberroth simply expanded the Board. In 1993, there were eighty members, ranging from the State of California Treasurer Kathleen Brown to Danny Bakewell, an African American activist. RLA was also attacked in the local press as too fragmented and slow moving to serve any useful purpose. The RLA claims of business support were questioned when the *Los Angeles Times* reported that nineteen of the sixty-nine businesses on an RLA list of businesses interested in investing in the area denied any involvement with the organization. Furthermore, many community leaders argued that it was not enough for companies to provide jobs in the inner city. To have true economic clout, they contended, the poor neighborhoods must also become stakeholders in the new businesses. In the final analysis, community leaders felt that RLA did not accomplish their goals, and community members agreed (e.g., Battle-Bey 1999).

By early 1994, Ueberroth's initial objectives had failed to materialize and RLA underwent a drastic downsizing. Some questioned what the region had to show for the $8.5 million in federal and private funds that RLA received and used mainly for salaries and support services (Gordon 1996, A1). By then, RLA had had a "rocky history amid ethnic tensions, unwieldy leadership and inflated expectations" (Gordon 1996, A1). Los Angeles Councilman Mark Ridley-Thomas, who resigned from the RLA Board after two years, said RLA "will be recorded as a missed opportunity . . . [and] . . . it's hard to really point to the impact that RLA has had" (cited in Gordon 1996, A1).

One year after the institution and the program were launched, RLA claimed that it had attracted $585 million in new corporate investments. However, an analysis of the total showed that it was clearly exaggerated (Feldman 1994). For example, one program included in the $585 million amount as a four-year, $40 million, post-riot investment from the Southern California Gas Company's home weatherization program. The program, designed to make older houses across all of Los Angeles—and not just those in the riot-affected areas—more energy-efficient, had in fact been operating since 1983, long before the riots occurred. By many measures the

Figure 5.1 An aerial view of the air pollution covering the valley which constitutes the Mexico City metropolitan area.
Source: Aseem Inam, August 1999.

program proved to be a failure, as will be discussed in greater detail in the following sections.

CRISIS: POLLUTION AND RIOTS

A number of observers have pinpointed the mid- to late-1980s as the period when the extreme air pollution crisis was created, and perhaps more significantly, was perceived at an institutional level. During the 1980s, the number of cars in Mexico City increased more than 5 percent annually. From 1983 to 1986, the acidity of rainwater in Mexico City increased significantly because of increasing concentrations of sulfur and nitrogen oxides in the air (Ezcurra and Mazari-Hiriart 1996, 26). Population growth and economic concentration in the 1980s accelerated air degradation in the Mexico City metropolitan area (Garza 1996, 315).

The crisis was recognized and came to head for a number of reasons. In 1985, birds in midflight began to fall from the sky over the city and one-third of the city's trees died from pollution. In the same year, an automated network for monitoring the atmosphere (Red Automática de Monitoreo Ambiental, or RAMA) was established with assistance from the United States Environmental Protection Agency. The system uses an automatic air-monitoring network with thirty-two stations and a manual network with nineteen stations. RAMA reports the level of several atmospheric pollutants such as ozone (O_3), suspended particle matter (PM), sulfur bioxide, nitrogen bioxide, and carbon monoxide (CO). These reports are based on a metropolitan index of air quality (Indice Metropolitana de Calidad del Aire, or IMECA), which scales each pollutant from 0 (best) to 500 (worst). The pollution index is expressed as a percentage of the acceptable norm. When the IMECA for ozone exceeds 240, when PM-10 exceeds 175 or when ozone exceeds 225 and PM-10 exceeds 125, a Phase I pollution contingency is declared and emergency measures implemented (Connolly 1999, 68). The first reliable set of data from these systems was available in 1987, two years before the initiation of the HNC program.[5]

In Mexico City in 1989 an estimated 4.4 million tons of air pollutants were emitted by vehicles (mobile sources) and economic activities (stationary sources) (Garza 1996, 320–322). The 1989 inventory of emissions stressed that mobile sources in the transport sector were responsible for 76.7 percent of total pollution, environmental degradation for 14.9 percent, and industry, services and energy for the remaining 8.4 percent. Internal combustion vehicles were consequently the main source of air pollution in Mexico City, although their importance varied significantly with regard to the type of pollutant, since they accounted for 96.7 percent of the carbon monoxide but only 2.1 percent of total suspended particulates. Pollutant emissions from mobile sources were calculated on the basis of gasoline consumption, the vehicle fleet in the city, and the annual kilometers driven.

Mexico City's atmospheric pollution is aggravated by its geographic conditions, paradoxically the same conditions that make it such a good place to live (Connolly 1999, 67). Due to its location at the heart of a great land mass and to the protected nature of the valley, with mountain barriers on all sides except from the direction of the prevailing wind, atmospheric stability prevents natural dispersion of pollutants. The combination of high altitude (i.e., more than 7,000 feet or 2,000 meters above sea level) and tropical latitude makes for temperate sunny daytime weather and cool nights: perfect for ozone creation and thermal inversions. A thermal inversion occurs when a layer of cold, dense, thermally stable air prevents pollutants emitted at ground level from dispersing upward and produces high pollutant concentrations, frequently reaching critical levels (Onursal and Gautam 1997, 127). The lower oxygen content of the air, due to the altitude, also means that internal combustion engines are 23 percent less efficient that at sea level, with a corresponding effect on emissions. Thus, among all major cities of the world, Mexico City has the most serious air pollution (Wirth 1997).

Like the smog of Mexico City, the 1992 Los Angeles riots also grew out of humanly created conditions—though their onset was much more sudden and violent. On April 29, in Simi Valley, north of Los Angeles, an almost entirely white jury (with one Asian man) acquitted four white policemen who, on the night of March 3, 1991, had brutally beaten African American Rodney King (Keil 1998, 205). The beating had been caught on tape by an amateur videographer and was later broadcast to millions.

The verdict came as a shock to most people, because the beating was so clearly sadistic and unfair (Jencks 1993, 79–84). At 4:17 p.m. on the day of the verdict, violence erupted at the intersection of Florence and Normandie Avenues in South Central Los Angeles—where a white truck driver was filmed being pulled from his truck and beaten almost to death. The verdict sparked five days of rioting. The riots left 60 people dead, another 2,383 injured, and 623 documented fires (Keil 1998, 205).

The nature of the post-riot crisis appeared, on the surface, to be primarily economic. Over 10,000 small businesses were economically impacted by the riots, and 1,100 building structures were damaged or destroyed at a cost of nearly $1 billion (RLA 1997, 45). Ninety-five percent of the damaged buildings were concentrated along commercially zoned corridors of historically African American South Central Los Angeles and Koreatown, although adjacent residential areas remained untouched. Nearly 70 percent of the damaged or destroyed properties were retail stores, including 225 liquor and convenience stores. An estimated 20,000 people were put out of work immediately after the riots (*Los Angeles Times* 1992, 130).

The 1992 riots rank as the most deadly U.S. civil disturbance in the twentieth century. At an estimated $1 billion in insured losses, the unrest was also the costliest in U.S. history. It was also the first disaster of its sort in which the government's primary response was to hand over the responsibility of rebuilding efforts to the private sector (Feldman 1994, A1). In the face of the crisis, the goal of RLA was to jump-start rejuvenation of the economy of the poorest, most long-neglected communities of greater Los Angles—a challenge of unprecedented scope.

FAILED INSTITUTIONAL ACTIONS: HNC PROGRAM IN MEXICO CITY, AND RLA PROGRAM IN LOS ANGELES

As a precursor to the HNC program, in 1987, Mexico City promoted a voluntary non-driving program, but it failed because drivers refused to co-operate (Garza 1996, 324). The origins of the HNC program itself have been variously attributed to a civil servant in Mexico City's Department of Ecology (Lezama 1999), to former Secretary of Urban Development and Ecology Guillermo Carrillo, who proposed using colored stickers to restrict vehicular circulation during certain days of the week (Eibenschutz 1999), and to the DDF in general (Rico 1999). According to Luisa and Mario Molina, professors from Mexico who teach at the Massachusetts Institute of Technology, an environmental group named Mejora tu Ciudad (Improve your City) led by Cecilia Kramer persuaded drivers in Mexico City to participate in a voluntary initiative to avoid the use of cars once a week (Molina and Molina 2002, 333). The initial response to this voluntary program was favorable, but declined due to a lack of wider public awareness and greater resources to publicize and manage the program. Whatever the exact origins of the program, it was conceived as a temporary one—much like the other case studies in this book—but became the only long-term recovery program among the four case studies.

The program became mandatory on November 20, 1989 as part of the short-term emergency program developed by the government during the winter months in response to the crisis of extremely high ozone concentrations caused by severe thermal inversions (Molina and Molina 2002, 333). Based on the last digit of license plate, 20 percent of all private vehicles were banned on each weekday; restrictions did not apply on weekends. The aim of the program was to reduce congestion, pollution and fuel consumption by reducing vehicle kilometers traveled. Studies that winter indicated that fuel consumption decreased while subway ridership and average speeds on the road increased. Due to this initial success, HNC became a permanent measure, and a major component of the first major air quality management program (the 5-year PICCA) in 1990.

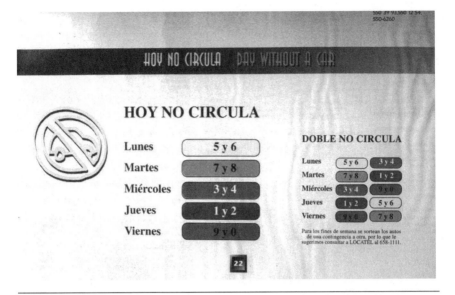

Figure 5.2 Announcement explaining the Hoy No Circula program in the Mexico City telephone directory, including the restrictions imposed on different colors and numbers of automobile license plates by day of the week.
Source: Mexico City Telephone Directory, August 1999.

Initially, all vehicles except high-use vehicles, fire trucks, ambulances, and police cars were prohibited from circulation one workday per week. In late 1991 the program was extended to include vans, taxis, and microbuses. Circulation of taxis was also prohibited on alternate Sundays.

During the first few months of the program's implementation, the results appeared to be satisfactory; however, when the program became permanent, residents of the metropolitan area were confronted with a scheme of constraints, which radically modified their transportation decisions. Automobile owners were reluctant to give up driving. They perceived public transit as a poor substitute to the convenience of automobiles. Thus, households made decisions which were costlier, both socially and environmentally: They bought older and more polluting vehicles as second or third cars and simply moved their trips from the banned days to other days of the week, thus increasing kilometers traveled, gasoline consumed, and volume of emissions into the atmosphere.

In contrast to the more effective Ghost Town and Renovación Habitacional Popular programs, the HNC and RLA programs demonstrate a lack of the five successful outputs: rapid action, massive funding, community outreach, improved conditions, and institutional coordination. The lack of each successful element in both programs is discussed in the following sections.

LACK OF RAPID ACTION

The first formal proposals for the HNC program in Mexico City emerged as early as 1986. They were much discussed and strongly resisted (Eibenshutz 1999). Even though the urgency of the crisis was clear, officials delayed implementing the first recovery actions for three years. Finally, the lack of rapid action is reflected in the somewhat resigned attitude of the government, with the Director General of the Secretariat of the Environment for Mexico City admitting that "efforts for lower emission levels of contaminants are very slow; we have barely obtained a reduction of 4 percent in emissions" (Rico 1999).

In Los Angeles, an internal report undertaken by RLA board member Dan Garcia in 1993 highlighted several symptoms of slow and ineffective action by that organization (see Figure 5.3) that included the unclear nature of its objectives and a lack of information about the conditions of damaged properties. Furthermore, Garcia was concerned that without a comprehensive local-state-federal strategy (i.e., institutional coordination), existing ethnic tensions would be heightened and ultimate recovery of the city would be frustrated (River 1993). According to Los Angeles's Planning Director, Con Howe (1999), RLA lacked grounding in the area, its issues, and its leaders, and thus attempted to "create something out of thin air" and began "fumbling about what [was its] role."

LACK OF MASSIVE FUNDING

The government of Mexico City failed to dedicate the magnitude of resources commensurate with the scale and urgency of its air pollution crisis. The Mexico City government had forty-five technicians divided into six groups with one ecological police officer for each group, while the municipal governments in the State of Mexico each had fifteen ecological patrols and an equal number of technicians (Rico 1999). This small band of technicians and police officers was expected to serve a metropolitan area of around eighteen million inhabitants.

Moreover, it is important to realize that HNC works by constraining transportation choices for those who can least afford it. The anti-pollution program does not affect the portion of the population that can afford new automobiles. However, for the lower-income user, both the need for the vehicle to pass the emissions standards twice a year (to be able to drive at all) and the once a week ban (twice a week when pollution exceeds the

Figure 5.3 An example of slow and ineffective action by RLA is this vacant parcel of land between 85th and Manchester—one of several—along Vermont Avenue in south central Los Angeles, seven years after the riots in 1999.
Source: Aseem Inam, July 1999.

specified limit) reduce the advantages of car ownership. A whole array of public and private investment patterns enforces car dependency. New and wider roads pave the way for more cars. Traffic congestion continues to be addressed with road-widening schemes and new over-passes. Officials even justify this approach on environmental grounds by arguing that vehicles pollute more when moving slowly; thus, congestion is scapegoated as the main problem.

In Los Angeles, the RLA program also suffered from underfunding. An early RLA report estimated that an investment of $6 billion and 75,000 to 94,000 new jobs would be needed to revitalize the city's impoverished neighborhoods (Feldman 1995). However, the City of Los Angeles spent a mere $4.1 million from its own budget on specific post-riot revitalization programs. State funds for post-riot revitalization amounted to $68 million and federal funds $700 million, although much of the latter amount was directed toward policing costs, emergency assistance, and loans for riot victims (Feldman 1994).

An analysis of RLA's funding by the *Los Angeles Times* newspaper suggested that $87.7 million had either been overvalued, or had actually been made by private foundations and non-profit entities, and therefore should not have been counted as corporate commitments. Furthermore, of the $207 million committed by various companies to open thirty-one chain supermarkets in the area, $104 million remained unexpended in 1997, five years after the riots. In the end, after five years of operation, RLA actually raised only $10.2 million, which included $4 million in federal government grants, a $2 million foundation grant, and private sector support of $4.2 million (RLA 1997, 13). Of the $10.2 million, $3.4 million was directed to other non-profit organizations, with RLA retaining only $6.8 million for its five-year operation.

LACK OF IMPROVED CONDITIONS

One of the HNC program's biggest failures is that it does nothing to improve conditions in the long run. Rather, it is at best a permanent stop-gap measure. In this sense it exemplifies one major drawback of planning approaches to environmental problems such as serious air pollution: they are based on notions of sustainability in a rather narrow and conventional sense. Sustainability does not connote constancy, but rather continuity and resilience in the face of change—that is, the successful management of change in ways amenable to human well being, including the maintenance and reasonable access to open spaces and the preservation of ecosystems. The problem with such a notion of sustainability is that it suffers from a crucial missing element, that of improvement. Ideally, planning would promote an enhanced environment, which is not only healed from past abuse but is also more vibrant. Such improvement has failed to materialize in Mexico City. In fact, some studies show that HNC has even worsened conditions there. Eskeland and Feyzioglu modeled gasoline consumption as a function of gasoline prices and income, using data from January 1987 through December 1992 (Eskeland and Feyzioglu 1995, 6–7). When data from the post-program period were compared to data from the pre-program period, the results showed that actual demand for gasoline increased after the program was implemented. Other studies show that in the first few months, fuel consumption dropped by 6 percent (Garza 1996, 324). However, it subsequently rose by an average annual rate of 4.5 percent between 1989 and 1993, equal to previous years. For example, in 1990, a year after the introduction of HNC, more than 100,000 new automobiles were sold in Mexico City, an increase of 20 percent over the previous year. By 1994, five years after the program began, it had theoretically prevented the operation of 600,000 vehicles a day, but it has not prevented increases in gasoline consumption and pollution levels.

Similarly, four years after the riots, Los Angeles still suffered the after effects of its crisis. While 900 buildings and properties had been utilized or revitalized, 200 remained vacant or unrepaired (Gordon 1996). Major supermarkets failed to rebuild in South Central Los Angeles as expected because high land costs left their stores unable to compete with smaller markets, which could target individual neighborhoods because their non-union wages were $5 less an hour than those of the major chains.

According to Dr. Clyde Oden, the Chief Executive Officer of WATTS Health System, (one of the largest non-profit employers in South Central Los Angeles), the idea of a "silver bullet" was doomed to failure because RLA embodied the simplistic image of the area perceived by the business community outside the riot-affected neighborhoods (Oden 1999). Furthermore, the process of engagement is as important as the solution itself; and RLA failed to acknowledge the issues of local residents and incorporate their participation in the solution. In Oden's experienced perspective., the lack of improved conditions in the riot-affected areas can be blamed primarily on the approach of RLA, which was superficial and high-level (i.e., top-down), rather than grass roots.

LACK OF COMMUNITY OUTREACH

Just as RLA was limited by its superficial understanding, HNC failed in part because of its lack of understanding of automobile ownership and travel patterns of various communities in the Mexico City metropolitan area. Both federal and local government failed to research patterns of automobile usage by the community and therefore did not anticipate that people would circumvent the ban. For example, one problem with attempting to control automobile usage by prohibiting driving them during specific time periods is that restricting trips—especially non-work trips—that were to be taken during a certain day could conceivably be taken on another day. Eskeland and Reyziglu estimate that since the HNC went onto effect, Mexico City has turned from an exporter of used vehicles (average 74,000 per year) to a net importer (average 85,000 per year), and that since the advent of the program subway ridership has actually declined over the years (Eskeland and Reyzioglu 1995).

Twenty-two percent of vehicle owners in the metropolitan area purchased a second vehicle just to bypass the requirements of the HNC program (Onursal and Gautam 1997, 156). These included 170,000 inexpensive old vehicles brought in from surrounding regions, mostly by households having more drivers' licenses than cars. The second car was not only used as a one-day replacement for the principal vehicle but was also driven during the other (permitted) days of the week by other members of the household. As a result, the total kilometers traveled by many households increased. Accelerated gasoline consumption and increased air pollution after this driving ban suggest that the intended results were not achieved. However, the Mexican government has not given up on the HNC, because it is estimated that eliminating the program would result in an increase of daily gasoline consumption by 132,000 liters, an increase in daily vehicle circulation by 385,000, and a consequent increase of 756 tons in daily pollutant emissions.

A second clear indication of the lack of community outreach is the government's ignorance of—and even indifference to—the community's reaction to the HNC program. Government officials claim that the program is either unpopular or corrupt in the eyes of the populace (Rico 1999; Urrutia 1996). Yet credible surveys from 1993 show that 56 percent of ordinary citizens and 70 percent of city council members indicated that the HNC program aids the air pollution problem, and that 45 percent of ordinary citizens and 63 percent of city council members agreed that the solution to the air pollution problem is to decrease the circulation of private automobiles (Wirth 1997). Thus, a sizable portion of the public and elected officials viewed private automobiles as a major source of air pollution.[6]

The RLA program in Los Angeles also suffered from a lack of community outreach. Jesse Peterson, a resident of a riot-affected area, complained, "The people that are in charge of rebuilding L.A. are not the people that the community chose to be in charge. How can we get more real people involved in this committee? We did not get any notice of this task force."[7] City Council member Mark Ridley Thomas responded that the "task force process is the way in which that can happen . . . if Rebuild LA is not where you want to make your investment, then . . . attach yourself to some other organization [such as Community Build or Operation Hope] that makes sense in your mind . . . Rebuild LA just simply isn't the only game in town and we should stop acting like it is."[8] Council member Thomas thus encouraged community members to reach out to other institutions, and in effect not really make an effort to interact with RLA.

In 1993, Bernard Kinsey, one of the co-Chairmen of RLA, claimed that his job was to sell the inner city to business (Walters 1993). However, Kinsey spent most of his time trying to sell RLA to the community, especially in the face of criticism of RLA and the frustration over the lack of progress the city of Los Angeles had made in filling the needs exposed by the riots. This was compounded by the fact that very few community organizations were included in RLA decision-making (Battle-Bey 1999). RLA failed to make into what community organizations were already doing in South Central Los Angeles. Similarly, according to Louise Manuel inquiries into the non-profit organization, the Local Initiatives Service Corporation, the community perceived RLA as "useless" to them and believed that "nobody came to ask [them] what [they] needed" (Manuel 1999).

One attempt at community outreach was the creation of a Volunteerism Task Force, which established a network of volunteers who received newsletters and announcements of various RLA work projects. It also set up an information and referral hotline to match volunteers with various non-profit organizations involved in the riot-recovery activities. The Task Force, however, soon realized that the stop-gap nature of these measures did not address the larger need for a regional volunteer network. As a result, the Task Force restructured itself into a Working Committee to develop a regional volunteer system, and hired a full-time staff person (RLA 1997).

With official revitalization efforts such as RLA moving slowly, grassroots community groups turned elsewhere for help (see Figure 5.4). The Coalition of Neighborhood Developers, which began in 1989 and was composed of fifty-six non-profit civic, church, and economic development agencies in South Central Los Angeles, received a $32 million commitment from the Local Initiatives Support Corporation (LISC) to build affordable rental housing and develop a retail shopping plaza that would include a new supermarket. LISC is a national organization founded by the Ford Foundation that channels private-sector resources to nonprofit developers (Feldman 1994; Fulton 1993).

Figure 5.4 The facilities of the Watts Labor Council Action Committee at 10950 South Central Avenue in Los Angeles were burnt down in the riots, and rebuilt by the organization itself.
Source: Aseem Inam, July 1999.

"We didn't burn our community, just their stores" (cited in Jencks 1993, 89) asserted one gang member. For better or for worse, gangs are a major constituency of the community in South Central Los Angeles. As this comment suggests, lack of economic self-determination was an underlying cause of the riots and therefore a key issue that had to be addressed in any strategy. The Los Angeles branch of the California Green Party proposed a community banking system, support for local ownership and control, the recycling of profits back into the community, cooperative zone funding, and cooperative food markets as well as health care facilities. At issue here are two different views of how the economy should work, the dominant corporate model of RLA and the Green model of C (for Cooperative) LA.

LACK OF INSTITUTIONAL COORDINATION

Air pollution control measures in general, have been hampered not only by lack of public support and participation, but also by unclear or overlapping institutional responsibilities (i.e., lack of institutional coordination) (Onursal and Gautam 1997, 281). The HNC program fell into this trap as well. Instead of harnessing and modifying existing resources (i.e., institutionalized routines), HNC has relied on creating even more institutions, which, though sometimes justified in the face of new challenges, leads in most cases to ever increasing and larger bureaucracies, a phenomenon I call "institutionalitis": creating a new institution as an automatic and superficial response to planning problems.

In 1972, a Subsecretariat of Environmental Protection was created within the federal government's Secretariat of Health. In 1982, the Secretariat of Urban Development and Ecology was created to deal with matters linked to urban environmental quality. In the aftermath of a deadly sewer system explosion in the city of Guadalajara in 1992, the federal environmental administration was divided into two new offices: a National Institute of Ecology, authorized to draft environmental regulations, administer environmental protection efforts, and coordinate natural resource management; and an Environmental Attorney General, created to oversee enforcement of environmental legislation.

Furthermore, in response to citizen protests about the area's deteriorating air quality, the Department of the Federal District, which used to administer a large part of Mexico City, created a Metropolitan Commission for the Protection of Air Quality in 1992. In December 1994, a new secretariat was created to encompass all federal environmental functions, including those dealing with "brown ecology" (environmental pollution) and "green ecology" (natural resource management). Functions that had previously been dispersed among various federal agencies were centralized under the Secretariat of Environment, Natural Resources and Fisheries. The complexity and size of environmental institutions increased, but this did not necessarily lead to a corresponding increase in the effectiveness of environmental programs such as HNC.

The program was supposedly coordinated by a steering committee and a technical secretariat, established by the federal government and consisting of representatives from the Federal District Department; State of Mexico; Secretariats of Ecology and Development, Finance, Programming and Planning, and Industry and Agriculture; Pemex; Mexican Petroleum Institute; and BANOBRAS.

At present, the most important institutional actor is the municipal Secretaría del Medio Ambiente, or Secretariat of the Environment, of Mexico City (Lezama 1999). The Secretariat of the Environment has a Dirección General de Prevención y Control de la Contaminación del Aire (DGPCCA), or Office of Air Pollution Prevention and Control, which is directly responsible for HNC. Within this office is a Dirección de Gestión de la Calidad del Aire (DGCA), or Office of Air Quality Management, which actually administers the program on a day to day basis. Furthermore, all the environmental programs are discussed in the Comisión Ambiental Metropolitana (CAM), or the Metropolitan Environmental Commission, which was constituted by the federal government through the Instituto Nacional de Ecología (INE), or National Institute of Ecology, and the municipal governments of the State of Mexico, which are suburbs of the DF. The local representatives of the environment, the federal representatives, the senators, the non-governmental organizations (NGOs), and the chambers of commerce and industry all participate in the CAM. All of these representatives are supposed to meet and dictate the environmental programs or projects that need development in the metropolitan environmental zone (Rico 1999).

This complex institutional structure is flawed in three ways. First, while the structure appears to be broad-based, it is in fact rather centralized within the DDF and lacks important institutional actors such as those responsible for transportation policy and planning. Second, as the lack of community outreach demonstrates, the structure does not really represent the sectors, such as community groups and public transit representatives, which are crucial to the effectiveness of the program. Finally, designing and implementing a program such as HNC to reduce transport air pollution in the Mexico City metropolitan area is complicated because national, regional, and local institutions are involved and coordinating them is difficult. The problem is local in the sense that issues like vehicle inspection, traffic management, and public transport are in the hands of the Ciudad de Mexico (formerly the Federal District). The problem is regional because the metropolitan area includes the city itself and seventeen municipalities in the neighboring State of Mexico. From an institutional and legal standpoint, the subject has been national, because until 1997 the city was the Federal District and continues to the capital of the country, but the city government was also—especially when HNC was initiated—a direct arm of the federal government.

The RLA program in Los Angeles also faced challenges of institutional coordination. During the first phase, from the inception of RLA in May 1992 until February 1994, RLA's approach was top-down. Its vision was that together business, government, and the community—though it never actually specified its "community," or constituency—would bring prosperity to neglected areas. This would be accomplished by securing substantial outside private sector investments by major corporations, by cutting red tape and through volunteerism. However, for several months after its founding, it seemed that tensions within the organization, and between RLA, minority groups and political leaders, would rub away the veneer of spirited cooperation that enveloped the city's initial response to the devastation of the riots and the creation of RLA.

RLA changed its leadership and direction in response to criticism, especially from minority communities, leading to the 1993 appointment of four co-chairmen, Peter Ueberroth (white), Barry Sanders (white), Tony Salazar (Latino), and Bernard Kinsey (African American). In 1994, RLA's diverse Board, by then encompassing over ninety members, replaced the remaining four co-chairs (Ueberroth had resigned earlier) with a single chair, ARCO's Chairman Lod Cook, and a full-time president and chief executive officer, former Deputy Mayor for Economic Development, Linda Griego, who reported directly to the board (RLA 1997, 11–12).

RLA's new leadership narrowed its focus to economic development, and adopted, according to RLA, a bottom-up strategy in order to determine what residents needed in the riot-affected neighborhoods (RLA 1997, 12). To form a revitalization strategy, RLA conducted local industry surveys and community needs assessments. Based on these assessments, RLA launched two principal programs, the formation of manufacturing networks, and retail revitalization of vacant lots. The first program encouraged small to medium-size manufacturing companies already located in the target neighborhoods to join together in cooperative endeavors that enabled them to expand and thereby increase jobs in neglected communities. The second program helped transform post-riot vacant lots into new commercial facilities and involved such new business establishments as an AutoZone automobile parts store at the corner of Normandie and Florence, the flash point of the riots (see Figure 5.5), Smart and Final Supermarkets, McDonald's, Taco Bell, and Chief Auto Parts (RLA 1997, 12).

By looking strictly at the roster of RLA's board of directors, one might have concluded that all of the city's cultures, if not classes, were repre-

Figure 5.5 A new automobile parts store, AutoZone, built—at least in part due to the efforts of RLA—at the intersection of Normandie and Florence avenues in south central Los Angeles. *Source:* Aseem Inam, July 1999.

sented. However, RLA had a ninety-six-member board consisting of elites representing a number of constituencies and sectors which were ideologically conservative to moderate, and which regularly followed policy leads and activity guidelines from its directors (Regalado 1994, 207). The organization changed its grandiose focus from being the city's economic, race-relations, and school-district savior under Ueberroth to a more streamlined entity directing its energies to small-business assistance and start-ups in inner-city communities, ultimately, for the better.

Still, critics charged that RLA was disorganized, that its board was unwieldy, that its non-governmental status was a crippling flaw, and that the gargantuan, 1,200-member task-force structure diluted resources, energy, and purpose (Walters 1993). The collaborative philosophy of the rebuilding effort was questioned when John Ferraro, then president of the Los Angeles City Council, criticized RLA because it moved forward on policies without consulting the council (Grigsby 1993, 350). Over time, RLA itself recognized that it was ill prepared to handle the challenges and work presented by its own task forces (RLA 1997, 20). RLA staff members were not experts at volunteer management, nor were they hired with this particular skill in mind. In some cases, the task forces themselves further diffused the organization's focus. Thus, there was a lack of institutional coordination within RLA itself, among its vast leadership of co-chairs, directors, and task force members, and between itself and other critical institutions such as the Los Angeles City Council.

LACK OF INSTITUTIONAL SUCCESS AND LACK OF INSTITUTIONAL ROUTINES

All of the flaws of the HNC program described above can be traced to one crucial missing piece: institutional routines, or workable precedents from the Mexican context that might have been modified and applied as appropriate. Interviews with representatives of key institutional actors revealed the following: "In Sao Paulo, Brazil, there is a program called Rodisio which prevents circulation of automobiles during certain hours of the day" (Lezama 1999). "I believe there is a program in Chile, and they tried something in Athens, Greece and in Bangkok, Thailand. There were not precedents in Mexico" (Eibenshutz 1999). "I was quite impressed by a recent example in Singapore controlling traffic in the central city. They have an electronic system in which each vehicle has an apparatus and when entering the restricted zone, it is registered electronically and a card, such as a bank card, is charged," but as far as precedents in Mexico are concerned, "No, not that I know of" (Rico 1999). Thus, much of the inspiration for the HNC appears to be from cities in other parts of the world, but little thought was given to using precedents that could work in the specific political-economic context of Mexico and the local planning practices of Mexico City.

In Los Angeles, from the moment the announcement was made that RLA had been formed, the switchboard was swamped with telephone calls (Grigsby 1993, 352). People offering to volunteer their services came from throughout Los Angeles. Unfortunately, no apparatus—that is, no routine— was in place to respond effectively. In most cases, calls went unanswered and people with very good intentions became either disillusioned or angered by what they felt was RLA's lack of interest. Another insight from the RLA effort is that success requires the involvement of existing (versus brand new) business and community organizations (Grigsby 1993, 352). In the days immediately following the riots, RLA's management focused its attention on large corporations, attempting to persuade them not only to remain in South Central Los Angeles, but also to increase their levels of investment and encourage others to do likewise. While securing major commitments from big business initially had great symbolic importance, RLA staff largely neglected key community stakeholders—small business owners and community-based organizations—in their partnership development activities.

LIMITATIONS OF DEFINING FAILURE: SUCCESSFUL ASPECTS OF THE PROGRAMS

The HNC program in Mexico City, though clearly ineffective, is nonetheless not a complete failure, especially if viewed as part of a larger set of programs to combat air pollution. Vehicle emissions controls, circulation restrictions, and emergency contingency measures have brought carbon monoxide to acceptable levels and have also virtually eliminated the occasional high peaks of extreme pollution from ozone and particulates (Connolly 1999, 67). An alternative explanation for increase in the consumption of gasoline is that it is not due so much to the HNC as to the increased sale of automobiles. "At present we have an average of between 225,000 and 250,000 automobiles sold each year, and then we have an increase in the use of gasoline" (Rico 1999). Still, according to the criteria of successful outputs developed for this study, the program falls far short of overall effectiveness.

In Los Angeles, the RLA organization clearly failed to achieve its initial goal of attracting over $500 million in post-riot development contributions and tens of thousands of new jobs. Still, it made some important contributions in its more limited mission of conducting urban economic research for small- and medium-sized businesses, starting self-help networks in the local toy, food, furniture, garment, and biomedical industries, and attracting new retail stores to the riot-affected areas. Through its data collection and research, RLA dispelled long-held myths about the lack of economic potential and significance of the riot-affected neighborhoods to the Los Angeles metropolitan region (RLA 1997, 11). The neighborhoods are a source of great industrial strength because they are home to over 15,000 manufacturing companies that employ 360,000 companies and generate in excess of $54 billion a year.

With the cooperation of the electricity provider Southern California Edison and the financial services company Dun and Bradstreet, RLA began collecting data about businesses in South Central Los Angeles. RLA identified small companies involved in a wide range of economic activities, from manufacturing computers to processing sausages, and accounting for more than a fifth of Los Angeles County's total output of goods and services. Many of these were small, family-owned companies, often employing fewer than fifty people. RLA staff and graduate student interns interviewed over 250 company, trade association, and industry experts (RLA 1997, 24). The staff analyzed the results to identify common themes and priorities, such as job training, which was identified as one of the top three priorities for all industry sectors. In furniture, food, and textile production, for example, access to capital and environmental issues were identified as important concerns.

When RLA ceased its operations in 1997 after five years of existence, the databases on local companies and industries were transferred to the Community College District of Los Angeles. While RLA clearly failed in its original mandate of economic development through investment and job creation, the organization has left a legacy of detailed, unexpected, and exciting information on small businesses in what is usually considered to be depressed area of Los Angeles. As a means of discovering local assets rather than simply focusing on liabilities, the databases also provide hope for other central cities in the United States.

IMPLICATIONS AND ALTERNATIVES

Roberto Eibenschutz, the Secretary of Urban Development and Housing in the Government of Mexico City, suggests a more comprehensive approach to the air pollution crisis:

> The poor people have or should have access to public transit and public transit should be privileged and should have competitive elements with private transportation. What needs to be done is to develop a better system of public transit. Substitute the fixed-rate collective taxis with normal and decent public buses, improve the surface public transit. We are now thinking of an elevated train system from the State of Mexico to the Federal District. Extend the metro lines, transportation by bus—these are the important things in terms of transportation. But we have to do it from both sides, at the same time as the public transit is being improved, we have to make more difficult, control and restrict the use of private transportation because this is what is really generating problems. Other policies being considered include the re-use of already developed areas of the city. We are trying to avoid expansion of the periphery, avoid the dispersion that implies multiplying transportation services and generating more trips of longer distances between peripheral and central zones.[9]

However, there has in reality been no such comprehensive approach, and furthermore, such an approach must include more than transportation and land use planning. Mexico City has no overall public transit policy (Connolly 1999, 76). Policies for promoting public transit only envisage investment in improving bus services or extending the metro. The fundamental issue of travel behavior is not addressed. Thus, planning and building legislation, including the provision of parking, are in no way related to transport, even less to the environmental problem. And although automobiles' overwhelming contribution to pollution is recognized, there have been virtually no attempts to curb car ownership and use, except as emergency measures when pollution levels become intolerable. The number of cars

Figure 5.6 A common sight in the Mexico City metropolitan area is traffic congestion caused by numerous automobiles occupied by only one or two people per car.
Source: Aseem Inam, August 1999.

registered in the DF and metropolitan municipalities in Mexico City has grown much faster than population, almost doubling from 1.3 million in 1986 to 2.4 million a decade later. The private automobile is a convenient way to move around Mexico City with average journey times of only thirty-five minutes compared to fifty minutes total average on all modes of public transportation.

Car parking is widely and cheaply available at a maximum cost of about $1 per hour, usually much less (Connolly 1999, 77). Parking near supermarkets and other commercial centers is often free. New buildings, including most housing, (which is clearly a planning issue), require parking spaces throughout the city. Recent policies have actively promoted the construction of new downtown underground car parks, for which the government has provided land and other indirect subsidies. Shopping malls combined with restaurants and multiplex cinema halls, first introduced for the upper echelons of the market, are now multiplying all over the city and cater essentially to automobile users. Pedestrian access to these establishments is often complicated and unpleasant.

In the Mexico City metropolitan area, the fleet of automobiles grew from 48,000 in 1940 to 3,000,000 in 1995 (see Figure 5.6). In absolute passenger numbers, high-capacity public transport (e.g. metro, buses, trolley-buses, and trams) has also increased since the 1960s, but this increase has not kept pace with the more rapid demographic and economic growth in Mexico City (Wirth 1997). More significantly, low-capacity privately owned transport (e.g., automobiles, taxies, minibuses) expanded rapidly after the 1960s, as measured by the absolute number of units in operation, the number of passengers transported, and relative percentages.

About three million vehicles are estimated to circulate and contribute to air pollution in Mexico City (Onursal and Gautam 1997, 132). Of the vehicles registered in the DF 71.2 percent are private cars, 17.8 percent are freight vehicles, 5.4 percent are taxis, 1.9 percent are buses, 1.1 percent are government vehicles, and 2.6 are other vehicles. About 42 percent of the vehicle fleet in metropolitan area is more than ten years old, and 68 percent of the vehicle fleet was manufactured before 1991 and thus is not equipped with catalytic converters. The deep recession Mexico experienced during the 1980s partly explains the large proportion of older vehicles in the metropolitan area. Tax exemptions for vehicles older than ten years and low repair costs also have encouraged prolonged vehicle ownership. Although private cars are used by only 15 percent of the population, they make up more than 71 percent of the total vehicular fleet (Onursal and Gautam 1997, 134).

In Mexico City, private automobiles generate 35 percent of all air pollution and 65 percent of the pollution from passenger transport, yet they provide only 20 percent of the passenger transport (Wirth 1997). Private automobiles generate high levels of air pollutants that harm the public health and impact a much larger population. They cost the economy an estimated $1 billion annually and cause 4,000 to 5,000 deaths annually. Relative to other forms of transportation, including minibuses, taxis, buses, trolleys, and light rail, private automobiles generate substantially more air pollution per passenger trip. The use of public transit vehicles can reduce emissions per passenger traveled (Onursal and Gautam 1997, 101). For example, in Mexico City the use of a bus in lieu of a catalytic converter-equipped automobile is estimated to result in a reduction of 40 percent of NO_x emissions, 95 percent of HC emissions, and 98 percent of CO emissions per passenger-kilometer traveled (*The Economist* 1997, 26).

In Los Angeles, RLA calculated that the private sector had spent $389 million on urban revitalization in the five years since the riots, and the government a further $900 million, far less than RLA's consultants, McKinsey, estimated would be need to do the job. In 1997, half of the 500 buildings that were seriously damaged or destroyed in the riots were still in ruins. The riot area was still pockmarked with vacant sites, some of them occupied by squatters and street vendors. Many of the companies that sounded most eager in 1992 have broken or trimmed their promises. Vons, a supermarket chain that had promised to invest up to $100 million in the area, had not opened a single new grocery store, due partly to a change in management. There was still only one grocery store for every 16,571 people in the riot-affected neighborhoods, compared with one store for every 7,795 people in the larger Los Angeles metropolitan region.

However, all was not necessarily devoid of hope in South Central Los Angeles in 1997. Home ownership was notably higher than in most other inner cities. Since 1992, South Central Los Angeles had seen $1 billion a year issued in mortgages (*The Economist* 1997, 26). Property prices in many parts of the area rose throughout the 1990s, at a time when prices in chic areas like Bel Air were falling. The main reason for the rising prices was that the riot-affected neighborhoods were economically more vibrant than inner city neighborhoods elsewhere in the country.

The strongest proof that South Central Los Angeles's riot-affected neighborhoods have a future is that their populations continue to grow. The exodus of African American professionals and Korean shopkeepers is more than compensated for by the influx of Latinos. Latinos make up more than 60 percent of the population of South Central Los Angeles, the capital of African American rap music, and more than 70 percent of the population of Watts, known as a hotbed of African American radicalism (*The Economist* 1997, 26). This phenomenon is driving up housing prices, creating new businesses and filling once-empty streets with people. Immigrants and entrepreneurs are doing incrementally and in piece-meal fashion what corporations and governments thought could be done in one program: rebuilding South Central Los Angeles.

The secondary case studies discussed in this chapter demonstrate the extent to which failed planning actions, such as the HNC program in Mexico City and the Rebuild Los Angeles program in Los Angeles, were measured by lack of outputs such as rapid action, massive funding, improved conditions, community outreach, and institutional coordination. The lack of some outputs in these programs, such as lack of community outreach, was clearly more significant than others. However, these programs also failed due to an absence of institutional routines, which are effective embodiments of institutional legitimacy, specification, and fit.

Chapter 6

Routines, Comparisons, and Future Directions

THE BOOK HAS FOCUSED ON THE ACTIONS of planning institutions to examine and articulate a plot dominated by public sector institutions acting more or less autonomously. This type of plot, derived from an institutional framework of analysis, allows one to acknowledge patterns of policy formulation and implementation (i.e. institutional action) that are often ignored. The case studies of successful housing recovery following the Mexico City and Los Angeles earthquakes, and of unsuccessful recovery from the crises of air pollution and riots, point to the significance of routines in planning institutions. A repertoire of routines—well-established and tried-and-tested institutional arrangements, policies, programs, and practices—is not only utilized for repetitive and uncomplicated situations. Routines are also the basis for an institutional approach to novel situations, including crises. For in the end, novelty is not a property of a situation so much as it is of our reaction to it; and the most standard institutional response to novelty is to find a set of routines that can be used. Problems do not have an intrinsic structure; they have a structure by reference to solutions that individuals and institutions can imagine, which is all the more reason to break problems up in ways congenial to our human understandings. Furthermore, by shaping a change to make it more consistent with existing procedures and practices, institutions maintain stability in the face of pressure to change. In this part of the conclusion, I discuss the role of routines more generally in institutional action, and also more specifically, in relation to the case studies, as sources of institutional legitimacy, specialization, and fit (or lack thereof).

The ubiquity of routines makes public institutions appear to be bureaucratic, rigid, and insensitive—often, justifiably so. The simplification provided by routines is clearly far from perfect. However, some of the major capabilities of planning institutions come from their effectiveness in substituting routine-bound behavior for individually autonomous behavior. Routines make it possible to coordinate many simultaneous activities in a way that makes them mutually consistent. Routines help avoid conflicts; they provide codes of meaning that facilitate interpretation of ambiguous worlds; they constrain bargaining within comprehensible terms and enforce agreements; and they help mitigate unpredictability by regulating the access of participants, problems, and solutions to choice opportunities (March and Olsen 1989).

Routines embody collective and individual identities, interests, values, and worldviews, thus constraining the allocation of attention, standards of evaluation, priorities, perceptions, and resources. Most significantly, routines embody collective and individual identities, interests, values, and worldviews (i.e., informal institutions) which enable public sector agencies (i.e., formal institutions) to implement policies and strategies that are legitimate to their constituencies, adaptive to the circumstances, and wide-ranging in their choices. Without routines policy formulation and implementation would be lost in a jungle of detail and uncertainty. With them, subsidiary questions can be handled summarily, and inexperienced participants will avoid major errors. Legally and psychologically, it is comforting to have an established way of separating the desirable from the undesirable. Routines are a necessity.

The importance of routines during crises is derived from the fact that continuity, or what people did before a crisis, is the best predictor of what they will do when a crisis occurs. Disaster literature stresses such factors as previous experience, pre-disaster community characteristics, and pre-disaster social networks' influence on collective behavior (Neal and Phillips 1995). In essence, studies show that pre-existing social and institutional relationships facilitate emergence and provide potentially innovative, successful solutions to assisting disaster victims.

Interviews in Mexico City and Los Angeles revealed that most of the public officials involved in the housing reconstruction programs were from existing housing institutions, had considerable expertise in housing finance and development programs, and drew upon their years of experience in the field to come up with ideas, rather than thinking of new ones (Dunne 1996; Gruel 1996; Gamboa 1995; Stolarski 1995). The use of old or existing strategies in dealing with novelty (like crises) can be effective for a variety of reasons. Institutional routines can be appropriate for the task at hand, and for a specific context for various reasons, including institutional legitimacy, institutional specialization, and institutional fit, which I will further describe in this chapter.

INSTITUTIONAL LEGITIMACY

Studies of public sector planning institutions often explain policies through motives of political expediency, social equity, or economic efficiency

(Johnson 1989: Self 1982). Empirical evidence, however, points to another critical factor: the need for legitimacy. Public institutions come into being if they are able to establish their legitimacy, and persist if they are able to sustain their legitimacy by serving collectively valued purposes over time. At a simple instrumental level, planning institutions need to communicate to their observers that the actions they take are legitimate. Legitimacy is established by showing that actions accomplish appropriate objectives or by showing that actions are taken in appropriate ways.

Institutions establish that they are good policy formulators and implementers by following an institutionalized process in a way that symbolizes the qualities that are valued in each society. They consult relevant people, consider alternatives, gather information, and act decisively but prudently. Plans, information gathering, analysis, consultation, and other observable features of normatively approved policy formulation are often explicable less in terms of their contribution to decision outcomes than as symbols and signals of propriety in policy formulation and implementation, that is, institutional action (March and Olsen 1989).

In Mexico City, the RHP housing recovery program was as much an economic measure (in response to the severe recession) and a social measure (to pacify massive protests by earthquake victims) to strengthen the institutional legitimacy of the government, as an end in itself to fulfill immediate housing needs. One manner in which institutions established legitimacy for these actions in Mexico City was through the *convenio*. This "democratic agreement" was signed eight months after the earthquake by 106 public institutions, universities, technical support groups, professional associations, and international organizations. The agreement defined and standardized the housing reconstruction process. Upon deeper analysis, however, the agreement also turned out to be a mechanism for non-governmental organizations, such as community groups, to be co-opted into the government's strategies and actions. This is very much in the tradition of the corporatist tendencies of Mexican governments whereby pressure groups such as labor unions or chambers of commerce are consulted and granted concessions— which may range from political representation, to subsidies, or to special contracts for projects. Land and urban services have traditionally played an important role in the Mexican corporatist model of patronage.

Institutional leaders, through policy initiatives and symbolic action, also asserted institutional legitimacy. After a lethargic and ineffective beginning in which it seemed to ignore those affected, the housing recovery effort advanced rapidly. Partially, this was due to the fact that initially

> it was a bit like wartime Britain—everyone was pulling their weight, sort of like a disaster situation. So, that explains the first time-lapse because

that was the first real emergency situation, you know, people were dying. And after October [1985], it was about 10 days or something, then people started thinking about housing.[1]

The turning point came after an economist, Manuel Camacho Solis, was named Minister of Urban Development and was able to reach agreement on a housing reconstruction strategy with dozens of neighborhood committees, church groups and foreign relief agencies. "My orders from the President were to negotiate and that's what we did," Camacho Solis said (cited in Riding 1986, 5). "It took one month to reach an agreement, but we have been able to work well since then." Camacho Solis displayed tremendous determination and resolve: "We will meet this schedule [of completing the RHP program by February [1987], period," he said (cited in Stockton 1986, 13). In February of 1986—five months after the earthquake, Camacho Solis was picked out of the Ministry for Budget and Planning, where he was a deputy minister, and given the task of solving the housing problems of the earthquake victims. President Miguel de la Madrid had dismissed his predecessor the day before because the problem of housing the earthquake victims threatened to become a major political embarrassment to the Mexican government. Responsibility for earthquake construction largely fell to Camacho, and his competent and efficient disbursement of these large-scale resources, and his politically sensitive handling of what had threatened to become a major political problem in the center of Mexico City, won him much respect.

In the highly centralized and hierarchical nature of institutional arrangements of Mexico, the support of the office of the President was critical. President Miguel de la Madrid was in the streets at least a dozen times—similar to site visits by President Bill Clinton and senior members of his cabinet to Los Angeles in 1994—visiting with those hardest hit by the earthquakes, giving them encouragement and promising them aid. Public institutions emphasized the symbolic nature and political character of such gestures. For example, on a government television broadcast, an announcer intoned: "Isn't it impressive how our President goes to see the homeless? Aren't we fortunate to have such a leader? We can see how much it helps the people that he visits them" (cited in Meislin 1985, 3).

Similarly, site visits by U.S. Secretary of Housing and Urban Development Henry Cisneros to the Ghost Towns in Los Angeles were as much a symbol of the government's political legitimacy as a spur to rapid action. Secretary Cisneros was among the first federal officials on the scene of the earthquake, arriving in Los Angeles within hours of U.S. Transportation Secretary Frederico Peña in the afternoon on the day of the earthquake. Clinton visited Los Angeles just two days after the earthquake. In the eyes of some, Clinton played Santa Claus to stricken homeowners in the vote-rich precincts of the San Fernando Valley and northern Los Angeles County (Davis 1998, 47–48). The Clinton administration, including powerbrokers from southern California such as Warren Christopher and Mickey Kanter, broke records in speeding $13 billion in earthquake relief to Los Angeles. Setting aside an amendment to the 1974 Disaster Relief Act that required state and local governments to pay 25 percent of all recovery costs, the administration assumed 90 percent of the burden. It was a dramatic contrast to former President George Bush's relatively meager efforts after Hurricane Andrew in Florida in 1992 and benign neglect of South Central Los Angeles after the 1992 riots.

Observing the crisis from such close quarters helped institutional leaders quickly shape federal recovery policies in the days immediately following the earthquake:

> The first day the Secretary [of Housing and Urban Development] was here, he met with local housing authorities and housing departments and said, "OK, what's happening?" He kind of listened to them to see how we can tweak it [the housing program]. You had the decision-makers here: the Secretary could say, "Do it!" . . . and write the letter and get it done. So, there wasn't a long bureaucratic process. One of the pluses of the Secretary and also James LeWitt [head of FEMA, was that] they went out to each site and talked to people. And so the Secretary could say that, "I met this family and their building is here." . . . I mean he could really paint a picture as well for Congressional members who might not have come out here from other states.[2]

Gary Squier, General Manager of the LAHD, provided leadership and policy initiative at the local level. Squier's background in housing advocacy groups and short time in the local government enabled him to push for rapid institutional action.

Los Angeles housing institutions further expressed their legitimacy through due process: community outreach efforts such as contacting owners of Ghost Town properties personally, participation in public forums such as Neighborhood Watch meetings, and public-private partnerships such as those with private financial institutions and nonprofit, community-based institutions, including Habitat for Humanity. These institutional practices are as much processes of policy formulation and implementation as visible symbols of democratic decision making.

The institutional initiative provided by extraordinary leadership in both cities helped shape each recovery program on the basis of particular strengths of each institution. The Mexico City case study also demonstrates the importance of physical proximity of federal institutions and leaders in legitimizing processes in the same city—frequent site visits and direct negotiations with affected communities. Access to key federal government leaders in Los Angeles was also through site visits, but on a much more sporadic basis. The decision making process depended to a larger extent on existing institutional arrangements, particularly between housing institutions at the local and federal levels.

Institutional legitimacy is often spurred in reaction to demand for action by planning institutions based on a perceived need. Thus, the restoration of neighborhood confidence was critical since the Los Angeles earthquake had the potential to make a significant one-time reduction to market values in the most severely affected neighborhoods. This potential for value reduction came on top of the multi-year downward trend and impacted the climate required for housing recovery. The negative market psychology of declining rents, declining values and damaged property was likely to effect the neighborhoods with the highest level of damage, although some citywide effects were seen as well (Hamilton, Rabinovitz, and Alschuler. 1994, 56).

LACK OF INSTITUTIONAL LEGITIMACY

In the case of the HNC program in Mexico City, its own institutional leaders undermine the institutional legitimacy of the federal and local governments to some extent. Politicians, policy advisors, academic researchers, ecological activists, and even urban planners fit into an income bracket whose lifestyles revolve around cars and who buy cars for the younger generation out of concerns for their personal safety and convenience (Connolly 1999, 78). Thus, the population that is supposed to severely reduce or even abandon transportation by automobile in favor of a potentially improved public transit system is always someone else. Furthermore, these institutions have no specific programs nor campaigns for energy conservation in Mexico City and relatively little effort had gone into identifying areas for improved energy efficiency and alternative sources (Connolly 1999, 64–65). Public debate on the environmental significance of energy consumption is mostly limited to the impact of fuel consumption on Mexico City's atmospheric pollution.

In Los Angeles, Rebuild Los Angeles was perceived as a grandiose abdication of public sector responsibility for the riots and the rebuilding aftermath, since it was essentially a private sector entity created by the public sector (Regalado 1994, 206–207). Advertised and self-promoted as a three-part coalition of equals involving private, public and community sectors, RLA was perceived as never more than a private sector driven organization with minimal participation of public sector representatives and even more limited contact with community organizations and individuals. In fact, within hours of Ueberroth's appointment, some members of the very communities he would call on for help began questioning whether Ueberroth could effectively relate to the plight of the city's riot-torn neighborhoods. Undaunted, Ueberroth pushed forward, vowing repeatedly to solicit and heed input from African American, Asian, and Latino politicians, from business leaders and from others with a stake in the rebuilding effort (*Los Angeles Times* 1992, 123–126).

The minority communities were not pleased; whatever Ueberroth's accomplishments, he was, after all, a white businessman from Orange County who had little familiarity with the damaged parts of South Central Los Angeles. Partly because Los Angeles Mayor Tom Bradley and California's Republican Governor Pete Wilson presented Ueberroth as a messiah, RLA suffered from the perception that it was supposed to solve most, if not all, of the problems in south central Los Angeles. So difficult was the task of defining the organization, that one of Ueberroth's co-chairs, lawyer Barry Sanders, defined RLA mostly in terms of what it is not: not a fundraising organization, not a charity, not a redevelopment agency (Fulton 1997, 22). In addition to this lack of symbolic and perceived leadership at the local level, the weakness of the leadership at the federal level was symbolized by the fact that Bush disembarked from Air Force One an entire week later (*Los Angeles Times* 1992).

INSTITUTIONAL SPECIALIZATION

Routines also represent the specialization of institutions. Planning institutions usually build-up an array of programs and policies that cater to specific sets of issues, usually divided by sectors such as housing, economic development, environmental remediation, or transportation. Such a repertoire of specialized programs and policies constitute a set of core competencies, which can then be adapted to ambiguous situations that are not necessarily narrowly defined in terms of institutional purposes and capacities. In the private sector, core competencies turn a business into a successful learning organization because such routines, procedures, and skills allow them to produce a stream of distinctive products that cannot be easily imitated by a rival: for example, miniaturization for Sony, optics for Canon, or timely package delivery for Federal Express. These routines evolve into well-established program and policy packages that sit on shelves either literally, or figuratively speaking. These can subsequently be utilized and adapted according to particular situations, including crises.

Routines are particularly effective for clearly defined problems with lucid objectives to be attained, a specific time frame of operation, and a distinct geographical area, as was the case with the RHP program in Mexico City. During crises, the shock and sense of urgency of a crisis generates pressures for rigorous, time-bound performance. The RHP housing recovery program was clearly defined because

> there was a real need or necessity, [and] a limited and defined time period—2 years—after which the program and the institution were to cease to exist. The purpose of the program and institution was to produce 48,000 housing units. This was an advantage, because this did not place a larger demand on the program.[3]

Under normal circumstance, the processes of institutional specialization take on a variety of forms. The rhythmic accumulation and discharge of small obligations creates routines that in turn shape expectations of cooperation. The repetitive use of knowledgeable and experienced institutional personnel is yet another form of the specialization process. Specialization through an inventory of routines constitutes a reserve against contingencies, often leading to apparent redundancy within or between institutions. In developing countries especially, trade-offs must be made between the costs of apparent redundancy and duplication and the increased probabilities of succeeding in attaining planning and development goals. Some theorists argue that the creation of redundancy in specialized programs, resources, and skills, far from being inefficient and wasteful, is essential for increasing the reliability of service delivery. Caiden and Wildavsky point out that the ability of developed countries to obtain the resources needed for production and service delivery owes less to management efficiency than to complex redundancy (Wildavsky 1974). When a large number of institutions with resources and skills are performing the same or similar functions, the failure of one institution or one program is not critical. Others fill the gap, thereby increasing reliability and reducing uncertainty. Arrangements in developing countries often lack the benefits of redundancy—the surplus, the reserve, the overlapping or competing networks of skills and data—to cushion the reverberating effects of uncertainty (Rondinelli 1993, 170–171).

In Mexico City, planning institutions had built a repertoire of routines, including funding mechanisms (e.g., for targeted low-income groups), procedures (e.g., working with community groups), and policies (e.g., of social appeasement) that served as the basis for many of the actions undertaken in the RHP program. Interviews in Mexico City confirmed that many of the public officials entrusted with strategies for the "new" RHP housing reconstruction program were in fact from FONHAPO, a national trust fund for low-income housing (Gamboa 1995; Eibenschutz 1995; Stolarski 1995). This institutional specialization and memory, embodied in the FONHAPO personnel and routines, was critical to the success of the subsequent RHP program.

FONHAPO has been relatively successful in reaching its goals due to a number of early innovations within the Mexican context. Many of these innovations, tried and tested in the early 1980s, were either modified or applied directly to the RHP program following the 1985 earthquake. First, FONHAPO awarded housing credit to public and private institutions, including non-governmental organizations—key actors in the RHP program as well. Second, the targeted beneficiaries of FONHAPO were the low-income populations—who also happened to be among those most adversely affected by the earthquake. Third, FONHAPO financed various types of housing credit packages, including sites and services, core housing, improvements, and finished housing; this experience of dealing with various types of housing was adapted to the RHP as well. Fourth, FONHAPO's relative success and credibility in the Mexican housing sector made it an attractive candidate as an entry door for World Bank housing finance, and for eventual use in the RHP program.

The lead planning institutions in the Ghost Town program, LAHD and HUD, possessed a set of specialized institutional routines that matched the nature of the crisis. This helped them shape an effective targeted approach to the problems of housing finance in the Ghost Towns. The fact that 85 percent of the Ghost Town units received financing for repairs within the very first year is a testament to the effectiveness of the recovery program. The City of Los Angeles' extensive knowledge housing conditions within the city and use of damage data to understand the scope of the recovery problem allowed them to formulate a multi-family recovery program and to convince HUD of the need for specialized funding:

> I think that some of the targeting approach that both the Housing Department and the Community Development Agency . . . knew how to kind of look at an area and what was needed. [Also,] the kinds of housing programs that the City offered currently were a lot of rehab[ilitation], and had some direct relationship with developers and builders, and I think that that assisted them in being able to respond.[4]

This is in stark contrast to the aftermath of the Loma Prieta earthquake of 1989 where the only multi-family housing financed was a small number of apartments, and those owners had to rely almost entirely on private funds (Comerio 1995, 44).

Throughout both the emergency response and recovery efforts, HUD modified policies and issued waivers to allow HUD funding to be used by local governments and affected households as flexibly and quickly as possible. HUD also delegated significant authority to the Los Angeles field office, which allowed for immediate actions to occur to address urgent issues surrounding the earthquake. The CDBG, in existence for about twenty years, was utilized for the rapid funding of housing recovery through modifications such as the waiving of certain requirements. Even before the earthquake, HUD launched a review intended to assess and remove obstacles to the use of CDBG and HOME for activities related to crises.

At least part of the match between institutional specialization (e.g., housing routines) and the nature of the crisis (e.g., housing devastation) was fortuitous following the Mexico City and Los Angeles earthquakes. Moreover, there was a substantial effort by housing institutions to define the problem in terms that they could understand and consequently address with existing routines. For example, the Ghost Town problem was defined through data gathering and visual mapping of red-tagged (i.e., seriously damaged) residential structures using in-house GIS technology. The LAHD also mounted a considerable effort of communicating the extent of damage and abandonment in the Ghost Towns by arranging for site visits with local and federal institutional representatives.

Thus, specialized institutional routines were effective in Mexico City and in Los Angeles because there was a match between the crisis and the specialization (i.e., in terms of housing demands and housing programs); the objectives were clear (i.e., reconstruction of housing); the time frame of operation was specific (i.e., about two years); and the affected geographical areas were distinct (i.e., concentrated areas of residential damage within the administrative boundaries and jurisdiction of the local government).

LACK OF INSTITUTIONAL SPECIALIZATION

In contrast with the case studies of successful programs, the lack of institutional specialization is brought into relief by the sheer scale and multifaceted nature of the air pollution crisis in Mexico City versus the overly narrow approach of the HNC program. A study by the Mexican government determined that to bring ozone levels down to the international norm of 0.11 parts per million overnight the government would have to ban all private automobile, bus, and truck traffic every hour of every day; suspend all electricity generation in the metropolitan area; cut all factory production in the city by 50 percent; and install hundreds of millions of dollars worth of catalytic equipment at all city industries (Fineman 1996, A11). Institutional specialization was also needed given not only the sheer magnitude of the challenge—as seen in the hypothetical example above—but also in the multi-faceted nature of the crisis. In spite of its practical complexity, the measures to modify—by decree—the transportation needs of millions of Mexico City residents who must go to their jobs, schools, shopping centers, and places of entertainment have been overly simplistic (Mumme 1991).

In the year 2000, the program was at an impasse, because it had not produced the results expected; yet it would have been counterproductive to release 600,000 additional vehicles onto the streets each day. The policy approach has been to impose a set of simplistic and questionable constraints rather than to also provide multiple incentives (for example, to car pool, to increase use of public transit, or to induce land use patterns that promote a substantial reduction in trips).

In Los Angeles, contrary to conventional opinion, the 1992 riots were not simply those of an African American underclass; they were something more complex and dynamic, a multi-ethnic uprising: 51 percent of the defendants in court were Latino, only 36 percent were African American, and the rest divided among other Los Angeles minorities. Sixty-eight percent of the damaged buildings were retail stores and the next highest percentage, 6 percent, were restaurants, while residential areas were hardly affected (Jencks 1993, 79–84). Many residents and observers felt that unless formidable political reforms were adopted and economic assistance arrived to deliver both an increased tax base to fund services, and widespread job growth within and around inner-cities through the metropolitan region, relations among the city's communities and groups, long-divided along class and race/ethnic lines, will improve little (Regalado 1994). Mike Davis points out that looking for singular essentialist—for example, by focusing only on issues of economic development, as RLA did—modes of explanations for the riots of 1992 would prove unsuccessful (Keil 1998). For black youth, the uprising was a struggle for their civil rights; for the Korean merchants, whose stores were looted and burned, it was a pogrom; and for the city's poor, it was a protest against bad times. Official attempts by RLA to continue the project of a world-class city under a new program of market-oriented global capitalism was countered by voices from the same communities that had presented social alternatives even before the riots.

INSTITUTIONAL FIT

The fit of an institution refers to how well its structural and decision-making processes match the customary values and behavior of its societal context. The personal correlate of fit is the sense of competence—the ability to do something well, to be adequate or sufficient. These words shift in meaning as expectations shift. Organizational literature has begun to recognize this critical aspect of institutions (Corwin 1987; Harrison 1994). Perhaps Kevin Lynch, as part of his theory of good city form, has developed the most interesting and useful description (Lynch 1981). This section draws essentially on Lynch's arguments about good city form as a metaphor for good institutional form based on the definition of fit described above. Such an approach contains certain limitations, notably in taking the metaphor too literally; nonetheless it does provide a rich and suitable frame of discussion.

Two broad dimensions of institutional fit are: (1) manipulability, which is the extent to which an institution can presently be changed in its use or form, and (2) resilience, which is the ability of the institution to withstand shocks and crises. Manipulability and resilience are dimensions, not absolutes, and the devices of adaptability must deal with these tensions. Both measures express the conservation of two goods that remain valuable: the ability to respond, and the ability to recover. There are some general formal means for achieving these ends, such as excess capacity (i.e., redundancy), good access, the independence of parts, the use of modules (i.e., routines), and the reduction of recycling costs. There are complementary process means: better information at the point of decision, flexible planning procedures, and the loosening and renewing of the patterns of control.

A critical component of fit is the ability of institutions to adapt to their environment. However, the environment of institutions is not always stable and adaptation to it is not necessarily instantaneous. Institutions preserve themselves partly by being resistant to many forms of change and partly by developing their own criteria of appropriateness and success, resource distributions, and constitutional rules. Institutions are sustained by being embedded in a structure of routines, by socialization, and by the way they organize attention.

A related observation is that the long-term development of planning institutions is less a product of intentions, plans, and consistent decisions than of incremental adaptation to changing problems with available routines (or solutions) within gradually evolving structures of meaning. Although it is difficult to estimate when an opportunity to attach a favored routine or solution to some problem will arise, a solution that is persistently available is likely to find an occasion. The implication is that governance becomes less a matter of engineering than of gardening, less a matter of hunting than of gathering (March and Olsen 1989, 94). The flexibility of any particular institution depends on acquiring good information about external changes and upon its capacity to process this information and respond appropriately.

Institutions transform transactions into discussions, for discussion is precisely the process by which parties come to reinterpret themselves and their relation to each other by elaborating a common understanding of the world. This is one of the ideals behind community participation and outreach attempted by both the RHP and Ghost Town programs, but in different guises.

Institutional fit, most significantly, should be appropriate to the conditions and processes of specific crisis situations. Modifying and experimenting with tried-and-tested practices and programs can lead to better institutional fit to the environment. The application of alternative forms of institutional understanding and conduct also includes planners and administrators to view social-problem solving as an incremental process of social interaction, trial and error, successive approximation, and learning. Institutional action is often the application of established rules, standard operating procedures, and typical roles that evolve through a process of selection and adaptation to different situations over the long term. Institutional fit is based on adequate and appropriate knowledge of the institution's particular constituency.

Planning institutions in Mexico City and Los Angeles were able to refine their activities as better information became available or as initial damage conditions changed. The first expropriation decree in Mexico City was modified due to awareness, criticism, and pressure arising out of errors in rushed judgment. A general outcry arose when it was discovered that among the expropriated properties were undamaged single-family dwellings that should never have been included in the scheme (Russell 1985, 58). This process of adapting and learning from mistakes is very much a part of institutional fit.

In addition, interviews in Mexico City with senior officials in the RHP program revealed that they had an extraordinary personal knowledge of and contacts with low-income housing communities; that is, their institutional constituencies (Gamboa 1995, Stolarski 1995). As well-defined constituencies, these communities tended to be louder and more articulate in their demands about housing. If institutional knowledge and adaptation constitute the supply side of fit, then the articulated needs of the institutional constituencies make up the demand side. This was further enhanced by a survey undertaken by the program to profile the socio-economic conditions in the earthquake-effected neighborhoods. This process of institutional fit was ongoing during the program:

> The procedures were adapted [or fitted] during the functioning of the program. There were many things that we did not know what to do about, and when the problem presented itself, we took the decisions. For example, what to do with the people who had abandoned their housing units? There was a decision to establish a program of rental assistance . . . Another example [of fit], many of the existing housing units had housing and commerce. The original proposal was to have a housing program [only]. As we became more aware of the problem of the people, it was decided that it would require housing and commerce to adapt to the actual needs of the population.[5]

The program itself became part of the process of subsequent institutional fit. The RHP program was instrumental in converting former tenants into owners of their dwelling. The FONHAPO credit packages were modified and utilized to finance these dwellings. These strategies were tried, tested, and subsequently became the precedents for a subsequent housing program in central Mexico City called Casa Propia. This program also aimed at converting tenants into owners, and provides credit for purchase of the properties plus the cost of essential repairs.

In Los Angeles, the initial number of Ghost Towns, thirteen, was increased to seventeen as more information and knowledge entered into the housing institutions. The proficiency of data collection, particularly in terms of crisis definition and institutional fit, is well illustrated by the Ghost Town program. The 1994 earthquake was the first major disaster where extensive residential damage was systematically collected and used in the recovery process (Comerio 1995). The most extensive structural damage was within the city of Los Angeles and the institutional coordination between the Building and Safety Department and LAHD was particularly effective; this led to an overall data set that had better information than from any of the other affected jurisdictions. The availability of detailed information on the number and types of housing units lost, the location of these units, and the socio-economic conditions of the affected communities allowed planning and housing institutions in the City of Los Angeles to focus both the emergency housing and the long-term recovery programs to the needs of their constituencies. Southern California Representative of HUD, Wendy Gruel, confirmed in an interview that

> they [LAHD] were very quick to analyze and be able to back-up what they had. They used [the Los Angeles Department of] Building and Safety's data as well as staff going out and looking at some areas. I think at that time they started realizing that there were these Ghost Towns in these neighborhoods.[6]

Moreover, when the earthquake occurred in January 1994, the consulting firm of Hamilton, Rabinovitz, and Alschuler were in the midst of preparing a report on the conditions of rental housing in Los Angeles. Much of the data collected and analyzed in the report was quite relevant to the housing damage suffered during the earthquake:

> One of the things which was sort of interesting is that the City of Los Angeles has a very moderate program of rent regulation. But it has also been the source of primary information about the city's housing stock. That was its prime value as far as I was concerned. We had just completed or were 2/3 of the way through this every 5- or 6-year look at the rental housing system in an academic oriented analysis. So, we knew a

> lot about financial conditions of buildings, and we had used some GIS
> mapping there to begin to plot ages of buildings, buildings clearly iden-
> tified as being in financial trouble, buildings where we knew we had
> heavy citation history—often, that is an indicator of lack of fiscal health.[7]

The report stated that there was a basis for serious concern about the lack of housing stock in the region since "[r]esidential permits issued in 1993 were 82% below the number issued in 1990," especially in light of the more than 19,000 housing units vacated subsequent to the earthquake, an unknown number of which would be permanently removed from the stock through demolition (Hamilton, Rabinovitz, and Alschuler 1994, ii). In addition, the report predicted at the time that a "likely long-term effect of the earth-quake will probably be upward pressure on rents, somewhat exacerbating the affordability problems measured before January 1994" (Hamilton, Rabinovitz, and Alschuler 1994, iv). This was certainly a spur to rapid action for housing recovery.

In the aftermath of the Los Angeles earthquake, the LAHD utilized the GIS mapping system to analyze building inspection data and develop a clear understanding of the extent of the damage. Maps produced with this system depicted both the scope and concentration of the damage, which led to the quick identification of areas with massive destruction such as the Ghost Towns. GIS mapping was then used to track the rehabilitation of damaged properties through a variety of data sources, including the Depart-ment of Building and Safety's permit data and LAHD's loan data. This capa-bility was particularly useful in tracking the financial and construction status of individual Ghost Town properties, and was critical, given the complex and diverse nature of the Ghost Towns in terms of socio-economic and housing conditions.

The other aspect of institutional fit is the ability of an institution to adapt to a particular situation. In response to the extensive housing damage caused by the earthquake, the LAHD began assessing housing needs so that it could make a significant contribution by reorganizing itself to a disaster recovery mode. Staff was reassigned, existing programs were refocused, and funds obtained for new programs that would assist persons unaided by the federal recovery process. The Ghost Town program relied on the Housing Department's sophisticated knowledge of local housing conditions, gathered through the Department's staff experience, and a vast database.

There was an outpouring of federal assistance for housing, which was unprecedented in previous disasters. This was in part, because the damage was concentrated in the city of Los Angeles, a city with sophisticated planning institutions with adequate routines, embodied for example, in the housing database, an experienced staff, existing loan processes, and established relationships with federal and financial institutions. The Clinton Administration, sensitive to the recession plaguing southern California, offered relatively easy access to the staff and resources of HUD, an institution not traditionally involved in crisis-related activities, to assist in the recovery effort.

LACK OF INSTITUTIONAL FIT

The HNC program operates on a basis of poor institutional fit; that is, neither a supply-side strategy of trial-and-error processes based on previous institutional experiences nor a demand-side strategy based on extensive knowledge and stores of information on the precise and complex nature of the problem. Jose Luis Lezama, a professor at El Colegio de Mexico in Mexico City and a leading scholar of environmental policies in Mexico, claimed he did not know of a single conclusive study or analysis of the impacts of pollution in Mexico City (Lezama 1999). As late as 2001, a full twelve years after the HNC was initiated, Mexico City's Secretary of the Environment Claudia Sheinbaum, suggested that a "complete evaluation of anti-pollution policies has never been done" (cited in Weise 2001).

To compound the lack of institutional fit, instead of studying, revising, or scaling back, the program continued with no systematic learning and feedback mechanisms in place. Thus, in 1990, under the Comprehensive Program to Fight Air Pollution in the Mexico City metropolitan area, the Metropolitan Commission extended the HNC program to school and worker transportation (Garza 1996, 325). In December 1995 the government introduced a new program called Doble No Circula (DNC), or No Driving for Two Days), which is used when emergency air pollution levels (above IMECA 250) are reached (Onursal and Gautam 1997, 149). The program prohibits 40 percent of the vehicles from circulation.

Perhaps one of the most important insights from the failed RLA case study concerns the flawed institutional framework by which the entire effort initially was organized (Grigsby 1993, 352–353). In an example of poor institutional fit, RLA did not seem to recognize that conditions in much of Los Angeles, in contrast with the Ghost Town case study, were not the result of a downturn in the economy or a mere lack of jobs. Rather, conditions of concentrated poverty, poor public services, high incidence of crime, and overcrowded, substandard housing were due to multiple factors. One factor was the restructuring of southern California's economy. The restructuring had resulted in the closure or relocation of a number of manufacturing firms that heretofore were located in the impacted areas and had provided employment opportunities with high wages and worker benefits. It was naïve to think that one institution could possibly alter these trends. This is why the response of the private sector was largely symbolic. A more effective strategy for RLA was to have initiated partnerships with small businesses and community-based organizations (i.e., community outreach and institutional coordination). Furthermore, a specific set of strategies to redress the number of businesses that were actually destroyed or damaged was sorely needed (i.e., improved conditions).

If Los Angeles' demographics and its socioeconomic makeup had been changing in the 1990s, some of its institutional structures—and, especially, its approach to planning in the riot-affected areas—had lagged far behind for several reasons (Fulton 1993, 21). First, the city's diffuse political system encourages an equal distribution of public resources in the fifteen city council districts. Second, the extreme geographical separation of various racial and ethnic groups has discouraged the creation of forums where different interests could interact. Third—and maybe most important in planning terms— California's whole planning structure is set up to deal with new growth rather than challenges in existing developments. According to the Planning Director of Los Angeles, Con Howe, Los Angeles has had "a lot of people who know about hillside development and subdivisions in the mountains, and not enough who know about working with and revitalizing deteriorating neighborhoods" (cited in Fulton 1997, 22).

LEGITIMACY, SPECIALIZATION, FIT, AND POLITICAL IMPETUS

The discussion in this section has illustrated three factors responsible for the effectiveness of institutional routines: institutional legitimacy, specialization, and fit. The routines were utilized for the RHP program in Mexico City and the Ghost Town program in Los Angeles as tools for attaining short-term objectives of housing recovery, and long-term objectives of urban renewal in Mexico City and neighborhood stability in Los Angeles. The routines were adopted on the basis of a sense of expediency, and adapted on the basis of a logic of appropriateness.

Institutional legitimacy, specialization, and fit are interrelated. In the successful case studies, institutional legitimacy was demonstrated and strengthened through a highly assertive and visible leadership. One of the mechanisms of this assertiveness and visibility was for institutional leaders to personally visit the affected communities as a display of concern as well as first-hand information gathering. Much of the information gathering was done on the basis of institutional specialization (e.g., to find out the extent of *housing* damage). Such a process of institutional legitimacy and specialization also enabled institutional fit in two respects: understanding the situation in the field, and providing access to the leadership of the housing institutions for appropriate policy formulation. This process is illustrated by the following example.

In Los Angeles, Cisneros and Riordan toured the San Fernando Valley area's Ghost Towns in August 1994, drawing attention to the strategy to jump-start repair work in apartment neighborhoods with heavy earthquake damage. Sidestepping rubble and ducking under the roof of a partly collapsed garage, the two leaders met the owners of two apartment complexes. Riordan praised the Clinton Administration for its quick response to his request, made about a week earlier, for the extra housing funds. Rejecting criticism that the money will be taken from other urgent projects, Cisneros said it was needed to address a crisis that could leave the city with permanent blight. "You can see that this is uninhabitable, unacceptable for the long run," Cisneros said, standing before the eerie facade of a broken sixty-nine-unit building on Kingsbury Street that leaned in all directions (cited in Smith 1994, B5). "Just put yourself in the shoes of an apartment owner who had tenants who are gone after the damage. They can no longer make bank payments and have no choice without help but to walk away. The loser when an apartment owner walks away from an apartment like this is the community." Through such visible and powerful gestures during a crisis situation, Cisneros and Riordan asserted their respective administrations' legitimacy to initiate large-scale action, focused on their institutions' specializations, and enabled institutional fit through on-site information gathering and policy formulation:

> We went several times up there [to the Ghost Towns] with elected officials, with the Mayor, with the Secretary [of HUD], with the Assistant Secretary, with Senator Feinstein, you name it. We went out because it really did exemplify . . . and it was such a visual . . . And so a lot of money was put into the Ghost Towns because L.A. publicized it and could package it. Because everybody said we need more money for transportation or we need more money for whatever, and so how do you demonstrate that there is a greater need for housing?[8]

However, institutional routines, while responsible for much of the success of the RHP program in Mexico City and the Ghost Town program in Los Angeles, were by no means the only contributing factors. The policy impetus for the institutional initiatives was largely exogenous to the institutions: urban crises that created a sense of urgency, particularly through the visual impact of damage and abandonment. Mexico City attracted attention at the international level due to the thousands of deaths in the earthquake, the upcoming World Cup Soccer championship, and mass community mobilizations. Los Angeles was highly visible in the national eye due to the devastating 1992 urban riots, a series of subsequent natural disasters, including fires and floods, and the political significance of California in national elections.

There were a number of sources of external pressure for rapid institutional action in Mexico City. Following the earthquake, there was a veritable wave of protests from those who had lost their homes. On September 27, 1985, 3,000 people marched to the official home of the President, Los Pinos; five days later, 15,000 people demonstrated; on October 26, 30,000 earthquake victims marched to the President's home; and three days later, a further 6,000 people held a meeting in Mexico City's main square, the Zocalo (Gilbert 1994, 139). The demonstrations continued in November and December of 1985, when 15,000 people marched to the President's home.. In March of 1986, people were still demanding action with 50,000 earthquake victims threatening to camp out in the main football stadium two months before the World Cup was scheduled to begin. The protesters were insisting that the government re-house them in the same areas as they had been living.

There was also concern in the Mexican government that the earthquake victims could become the nucleus around which significant political opposition to the all-powerful ruling PRI party might coalesce (Stockton 1986, 13). In the days that followed the Mexico City earthquake, President de la Madrid was strongly criticized for failing to provide leadership and the authorities were blamed for delays in rescue operations. Anger increased when the Government seemed to minimize the number of dead, when victims who had apparently been tortured were found in the ruins of the city's judicial police headquarters and when the collapse of many government-owned buildings, including schools and hospitals, suggested they had been poorly constructed as a result of corruption. On the other hand, the earthquake was remarkable for the spontaneous response of ordinary Mexicans who dug with bare hands for survivors or brought food and blankets for rescue workers. It was no less unusual that religious, professional, and scholarly groups assumed important roles in the crisis, while committees of the homeless became centers of pressure on the government in the months that followed. The community's pressure continued, often through constant physical presence on the sites of the housing projects, and led to greater transparency in policy formulation and implementation in the RHP program.

The U.S. government's response to Hurricane Andrew a few years earlier in Florida and other natural disasters in the recent past had been criticized as being too slow and disorganized. In order to counter such criticism, Clinton's administration purposely took quick and decisive action to participate immediately and intensively in the Los Angeles earthquake recovery efforts. HUD's decision to participate in the earthquake recovery efforts so quickly and comprehensively was also politically motivated. If the earthquake were to have occurred in a less prominent city, the U.S. government and HUD might have been only minimally involved. Extraordinary resources had to be channeled into Los Angeles because the earthquake occurred when the city was still recovering from the destruction brought by another crisis, the riots sparked by the Rodney King beating and court verdict. Planning institutions were also concerned about the well-publicized criticism that low-income groups did not receive adequate housing assistance after the Loma Prieta earthquake:

> [A]fter the . . . 1989 San Francisco [Loma Prieta] earthquake, one of the big problems they had was that they got only 50% of their housing back up and running within 3 or 4 years. To this day I think they only have 60 or 70% total rebuilt. And we said, "We can't let that happen; what can we do?" The federal government had suffered a lot of criticism from their response to some recent disasters; Hurricane Andrew was the most recent. So, FEMA was feeling put upon by the federal government and by us to be much more proactive after this disaster . . . So, the money flowed very quickly for a change, and we have to credit the Clinton Administration, even though I am a Republican.[9]

Thus, while mass mobilization and international pressure played a role in the success of the RHP program in Mexico City, the Ghost Town program's success in Los Angeles was partially aided by the memory and mistakes of previous disasters and the political significance of California during nationwide elections. The institutional routines utilized in the two programs took different forms and evolved through different processes in Mexico City and Los Angeles, as discussed in the following sections.

COMPARATIVE INSIGHTS:
SIMILAR SUCCESSES, DIFFERENT CONTEXTS

In this section, the similarities, differences, and underlying factors for the two primary—and successful—case studies will be discussed on two levels: elements of the political-economy, which generally occur nationally, and elements of planning practices, which generally occur locally. As constraints, these factors provide institutional designers with valuable insights into what is possible within a given society and thus help set feasible goals for institutional development. Policy and institutional changes are regularly introduced that do not reflect the very real limits of administrative capacity, international market conditions, social tolerance for change, and other such factors. Systematic awareness of contextual constraints therefore plays a valuable role in shaping feasible proposals for increasing institutional effectiveness. As opportunities, these factors provide institutional leaders with resources to mobilize societal interests, to use the realities and myths of historical experiences for generating support or tolerance for change, to seize opportune moments (e.g., crises) for launching policy initiatives, and to utilize existing human resources for developing feasible options for improved effectiveness. The contextual factors that set limits on what is possible also provide grist for generating creative responses to public problems (Grindle and Thomas 1991). This type of creative problem solving is present in the successful Mexico City and Los Angeles cases.

While the political-economic and urban planning contexts of Mexico City and Los Angeles are quite different, there are substantial similarities between the two housing recovery programs. The success of both programs depended to a large extent on existing institutional routines, which were effective for similar reasons of institutional legitimacy, specialization, and fit. However, the institutional routines in the two programs are similar for different reasons. The factors of institutional legitimacy, specialization, and fit were expressed in different ways in Mexico City and Los Angeles due to their each city's political-economic and planning conditions. This is because even within the strict procedures for technical work, the discussion, refinement, and acceptance of such judgments are themselves structured by institutionalized norms and practices unique to each context. For example, the expropriation of land in the central part of Mexico City following the 1985 earthquake was a technical and legal decision on the part of the government. However, the fact that these decisions can be made and have effect at all is the result of the norm of considering land as belonging to the community and for the public interest. In the United States, where land is viewed much more as private property and a commodity, it would be extremely difficult to imagine a similar expropriation of land by the government. Technical and legal decisions make a difference, not so much because they are

Table 6.1 Comparative Framework for Successful Planning in Mexico City and Los Angeles

Elements of Comparison	Mexico City RHP Program	Los Angeles Ghost Town Program
Political-Economy		
Political structure	Centralized political structure	Federal crisis management
Economic conditions	Economic safety net	Economic development
Planning Practices		
Policy inputs	Mass community mobilization	Lack of community initiative
Policy outputs	Co-optation	Neighborhood revitalization

Source: Aseem Inam

technical, but because they are made within socially accepted practices (i.e., informal institutions) of tradition, authority, and expertise that are often context-specific. Table 6.1 outlines the comparative framework of the two housing recovery programs in the broader contexts of planning practices and the political economies of Mexico City and Los Angeles. The table also summarizes the key findings and differences discussed in this chapter.

POLITICAL ECONOMY

In examining the political economy of Mexico and the United States, I focus on two relevant components: the political structure, and the economic conditions of each country, as relevant to the routines and outputs of each housing recovery program. In treating the component parts of the political structure I distinguish, first, three broad classes of objects: (1) specific institutions, such as legislative bodies, executives, or bureaucracies; (2) individuals who occupy particular roles, such as particular presidents, legislators, and administrators; and (3) typical public policies, decisions, or enforcements of decisions; that is, routines. These institutions, individuals, and routines may in turn be classified broadly by whether they are involved either in the political (i.e., input) process or in the administrative (i.e., output) process. By political or input process I refer to the flow of demands from the society into the polity and the conversion of these demands into authoritative policies. Some structures predominantly involved in the input process are interest groups, political parties, and the media of communication. By the administrative or output process I refer to that process by which authoritative policies are applied or enforced. Institutions predominantly involved in this process would include federal agencies, planning and housing departments, and local authorities and courts.

Mexico: Centralized Political Structure

In most of the developing countries of Asia, Africa, and Latin America, administrative traditions are characterized by highly centralized, control-oriented management systems and institutional structures. Nation-building requirements and transfer of developed country models by international donors frequently combine to create a strong bias in favor of large bureaucracies. Public sector institutions emerge as central actors in the politics of crisis and change because of the very characteristics of developing countries, including uncertain information, poverty, pervasive state influence in the economy, and centralization of decision making. These characteristics are a result of colonial rule, the nature of state-building and nation-building activities, and structural vulnerability to international and domestic economic and political forces (Grindle and Thomas 1991, 45).

The constitutional order in Mexico consists of a federal republic with three levels of government: federal, state, and municipal. The Mexico City Metropolitan Zone (referred to in this study as Mexico City) is governed by multiple administrations, including the DF, the governments of the State of Mexico, the State of Hidalgo, and the sixteen municipalities contained within these entities, as well as numerous sectoral ministries, public enterprises, and pressure groups. The Mexican President had in effect until 1997 been also elected as governor of the DF. The mayor of the DF was appointed by the President, as were the sixteen local mayors. The National Congress was charged with legislative functions both for the nation and the DF. In 1988, an Assembly of Representatives, whose members were elected by direct secret ballot, was convened for the first time in the DF. The functions of the Assembly are ambiguous, but in practice it appeared to be acting as a watchdog on city hall expenditures and policy.

Such a highly centralized administrative structure was reinforced through political power monopolized by the ruling PRI party since the late 1930s, when the constitutional regime emergent from the 1910–1917 revolution finally consolidated the base of its party structure: a form of corporatism embracing, and increasingly controlling from above, organized labor, the rural small land-holders, and the urban petty bourgeoisie. Since 1934, presidents have been elected for a non-renewable six-year term of office.

Even before the devastating earthquake of September 1985, the administration of President Miguel de la Madrid was facing widening public resentment over its failure to meet some of its key goals (Meislin 1985, 3). The economy remained problematic despite three years of an austerity program that sharply lowered the standard of living for many Mexicans. The campaign against corruption, in the view of most Mexicans, had reached neither as wide nor as deep as had been hoped. State and local elections, in July 1985, in which some key races were widely viewed as tainted by fraud, left the impression that the Government, in parts of the country, was not strong enough either to win by legitimate means or to accept publicly a close race or a defeat.

The earthquake gave President de la Madrid a new opportunity to disprove some of the criticisms being made of him and to achieve some of his goals. The earthquake also provided some of the most difficult circumstances possible under which to do so. Many Mexicans recalled the 1972 earthquake in Managua, Nicaragua: President Anastasio Somoza Debayle's illegal appropriation of the millions of dollars sent to reconstruct the city is believed to have helped strengthen the widespread public opposition that, years later, led to his downfall. While dismissing any parallels, the government seemed anxious to prevent the growth of such public irritation in Mexico City. The government delayed plans to begin demolition of buildings in the face of a public outcry from those whose relatives, dead or alive, were still trapped under the rubble. At the same time, the Mexican government tried to quickly come up with a plan to relocate the increasingly angry and desperate people—estimated at 50,000 or more at the time—who were left homeless by the earthquake. At the Tlatelolco public housing project, which suffered some of the most severe damage, tenant groups fractured into PRI and anti-PRI factions. Its opponents viewed the PRI faction as being more interested in stifling criticism of the government than in taking care of their basic necessities (Meislin 1985, 3).

The highly centralized administrative and political structure transformed a local crisis, the earthquake in Mexico City, into a national phenomenon. This was clearly evident in the direct role played by the President, federal Ministers and institutions in rebuilding housing at the local level in Mexico City. The composition of the Junta de Gobierno (Council of Governance) of the RHP program reflects this highly centralized nature of the recovery efforts and the key role played by federal institutions:

- Jefe del Departmento del Distrito Federal (Chief of the Department of the Federal District)
- Secretario de Desarollo Urbano y Ecologia (Minister of Urban Development and Ecology, or SEDUE)
- Representative of the Secretaría de la Contraloría General de la Federación (Ministry of the Comptroller General of the Federation, or SECOGEF)
- Deputy Minister of the Secretaría de Programación y Presupuesto (Ministry of Budget and Programming, or SPP)
- Deputy Minister of the Bank of the Secretaría de Hacienda y Crédito Publico (Ministry of Finance and Public Credits, or SHyCP)
- Deputy Minister designated by the Secretaría de Gobernación (Ministry of the Interior, or SG)
- Director General of Banco Nacional de Obras (National Public Works Bank, or BANOBRAS)
- Director General of Fondo de Vivienda (National Housing Fund, or FOVI)

UNITED STATES: FEDERAL CRISIS MANAGEMENT

The conventional understanding of the political structure of the United States is that it is a grassroots democracy (Herson and Bolland 1990), with an active community involved in a bottom-up political process. However, the recovery efforts following the Los Angeles earthquake in 1994 were the opposite: a top-down approach with a lack of community initiative. The lack of community initiative in Los Angeles will be discussed later in this chapter. We will begin by examining the top-down approach in this section by focusing on the idea of crisis management by institutions of the federal government.

Immediately after a crisis occurs, such as a natural disaster, local, state, federal, and nonprofit community-based institutions respond to emergency needs for such things as food and shelter and the restoration of essential services. During the recovery phase, federal assistance is provided to help repair and rebuild homes and public facilities. The Robert T. Stafford Disaster Relief and Emergency Assistance Act was passed by Congress in 1988 and provides FEMA with the large amount of resources and authority required for large-scale crisis situations (GAO 1994).

Other federal institutions are also involved in providing assistance for crisis recovery. For example, the Federal Highway Administration provides funds for repairing roads and bridges that are part of the federal highway system, HUD may provide housing assistance funds (e.g., in the Ghost Town program), and the Department of Education may provide aid to school districts. In addition, FEMA may ask other federal agencies, such as the U.S. Army Corps of Engineers, to assist in such tasks as removing debris and inspecting damage.

Some of these federal institutions played a critical role in the successful post-earthquake recovery efforts in Los Angeles. The earthquake occurred early in the morning, and by that evening, several high-ranking leaders and institutional representatives of the U.S. Government had arrived from Washington, D.C.: U.S. Secretary of Transportation Frederico Peña, and U.S. Secretary of Housing and Urban Development Henry Cisneros along with two other senior representatives of HUD.

There are two principal reasons for this top-down, federal role in crisis recovery efforts in the United States, one is financial, the other political. Financially, given the substantial devastation caused by crises such as the 1994 Los Angeles earthquake, federal institutions are among the few public sector institutions that are able to pool the risks and garner the resources required for recovery. Politically, the executive branch (i.e., the president) and the legislative branch of the federal government (i.e., the congress) can ill afford to ignore the devastation caused by crises in their constituencies, especially politically significant ones like those in California. California has the largest population of any state in the United States, and hence a large voter base.

Mexico: Economic Safety Net

At the time the earthquake hit Mexico City, the country was in the throes of a crippling economic recession. Between 1982 and 1988, per capita domestic product fell by 11 percent (Gilbert 1993, 18). Inflation rose to unprecedented levels, rising by 99 percent in 1982 and achieving a spectacular high of 159 percent in 1987. Government policy put strong emphasis on repaying the debt, with the corollary of cutting back on government expenditure, and hence, subsidies. The effect of the recession on income levels was dramatic. In 1983 the real value of average wages fell by 23 percent, by 1988 they had fallen to 69 percent of their 1982 value. The distributional effects of the recession weighed heavily on the poor. In 1985, it was estimated that whereas the poorest 40 percent of the Mexicans received only 13 percent of total household income, the richest 20 percent received 51 percent (Gilbert 1993, 19).

Beyond the enormous cost in lives and property, the earthquake threatened to undercut efforts to revive an ailing economy. The IMF already had been preparing to suspend aid because of Mexico's failure to live up to IMF conditions for economic reforms. Deteriorating economic conditions helped spur the growing political crisis in Mexico City. With much greater intensity than before the debt crisis, urban protesters and urban social movements focused political demands on consumption and reproduction issues which had become so vital to their daily survival. When the government began to cut social expenditures and raise costs of urban services, urban social movements sprang into action. These were not minor disturbances: at one rally over the paucity of urban services, the crowds reached 300,000 (Davis 1991, 187).

The government of President Miguel de la Madrid, in power from 1982 to 1988, decided to use construction as a means of keeping the level of unemployment as low as possible. The newly nationalized banks were required to invest 3 percent of their reserves in housing construction. Despite the recession, more homes were built than ever before; more than 1 million houses were produced nationally between 1981 and 1988. Initially, Mexico City received relatively little benefit from this expansion because official policy aimed to build only 15 percent of all housing units in the country's three largest cities. The earthquake of 1985, however, substantially modified this policy. While 61,000 public housing units were built between 1983 and 1985; in the next three years the total rose to 149,000. Of this massive number, the RHP housing recovery program accounted directly for 48,749 units (Gilbert 1993, 33; RHP 1988, 109).

The fact that the RHP program was at least an attempt, however feasible, to soften the ongoing economic crisis in the city and the country is established by pronouncements in the official report of the program (RHP 1988) and separately by officials who held policy-making decisions in the program (Ebrard and Gamboa 1991). Jorge Gamboa, former Director-General Adjunct for Planning and Administration of RHP, said in an interview:

> When the earthquake happened, we [in Mexico] were at the mid-point of a strict control of fiscal spending, and President de la Madrid did not wish for the earthquake to become a catalyst for the loosening of the economy. The occasion was used to attract large amounts of international funding for housing, infrastructure, and facilities.[10]

Furthermore, Ebrard and Gamboa state that, "[i]n spite of the ongoing economic crisis, in December 1986, when construction was at is peak, 114,000 jobs had been created—61 percent unskilled labor, 25 percent skilled, 5 percent administrative staff and 9 percent professionals" (Ebrard and Gamboa 1991, 22). In terms of Mexico City's economic life, reconstruction on the same sites for the same community maintained production networks, often dating back to the beginning of the century. Small-scale enterprises in the affected neighborhoods, in shops or at home, produced a variety of goods such as shoes, clothing, toys, furniture and home appliances, as well as the repair and recycling of machines, electrical appliances, and cars (Ebrard and Gamboa 1991, 27).

Planning institutions in Mexico City also recognized the necessity of providing opportunities for those who had previously utilized their now-destroyed homes as sites for income generation. One result of this was the decision to include in the RHP plan provisions for the replacement of small stores attached to the *vecindades* that had been destroyed along with the housing. The stores that had previously existed were replaced with new 200 square foot areas that could be utilized for commercial purposes, but no new commercial space was created. Still, this constituted a small, yet significant contribution to the planning institutions' attempts to replace lost employment. The greatest contribution of the RHP to employment regeneration, however, was that the recovery program allowed the original residents to remain in the center of the city, near the majority of the sources of employment. As the plans for recovery sought to preserve, rather than alter the existing land-use pattern in Mexico City's central neighborhoods, the affected community was able to continue working or searching work, much as they had done before.

This was not the first time that housing was used as an economic and political safety net; there were precedents. For example, fearing that disgruntled citizenry might contemplate a coup in the early 1960s, and that prolonged demonstrations were sure to weaken its power base, the Mexican government moved swiftly to contain the situation. Foreign aid was solicited from the United States in 1962 for establishing a housing finance program that was funded by the international Alliance for Progress. The program had dual objectives: to channel funds from private banks into the production of housing units, and to alleviate unemployment by utilizing labor-intensive construction methods (Ward 1982).

United States: Economic Development

The critical economic issue for the City of Los Angeles and the affected communities was the near blight conditions left by the earthquake and the possibility of further economic and social decline in the ensuing months as neighbors abandoned homes, businesses closed, and the weakened housing market demonstrated no demand for either homes or apartments. As in Mexico City, the earthquake in Los Angeles represented a crisis (i.e., a natural disaster) within a crisis (i.e., an economic recession). However, in Los Angeles, the economic crisis was not severe as that in Mexico City, and it was felt much more locally, rather than nationally, as in Mexico.

Before the earthquake occurred, home prices in Los Angeles were down at an average of 20 to 30 percent. Foreclosures had risen sharply: 24,000 in Los Angeles County in 1993, compared with 12,000 at the height of the last recession in 1983. In addition to rising default rates and declining property values, there was a lingering malaise over the riots, fires, floods, layoffs, and earthquakes. The Los Angeles metropolitan area lost 524,000 real jobs from 1989 to 1994 (Meyers and Stremfel 1994, 83–95). Also, even though personal per capita income edged upward in Los Angeles in the first years of this decade—from $20,752 in 1990 to $21,434 in 1992—that increase of 3.3 percent lagged far behind the United States as a whole, where the increase was 7.7 percent. From 1992 to 1994—the year of the earthquake— the county assessor reduced by an average of 11 percent the assessment on nearly 300,000 single-family dwellings in Los Angeles—more than 15 percent of the total homes in the county. Added to 1993's 23,863 foreclosures in Los Angeles County (around 85 percent of which were single-family homes) were another 13,645 in the first half of 1994.

The United States has a tradition whereby housing is considered a tool for community economic development by virtue of its role as an investment, a form of tenure, and a location. Housing policy can therefore be a part of a creative strategy for enhancing the economic well being of individuals and communities. Housing is linked to economic development in several ways. First, as a large investment typically requiring outside financing, housing is the object through which capital is reinvested or disinvested (which was one of the dangers of the Ghost Towns) from a community.

Second, as a consumption item, investment in housing operates as a local economic stimulus. Third, as a fixed location within a larger neighborhood, housing provides or limits access to goods, services, and employment (Shlay 1995, 706).

The LAHD, like other planning institutions in the United States, considered housing to be part of an overall economic development strategy—including, to a certain extent, in the Ghost Towns. For example, in 1993, Gary Squier, the General Manager of the LAHD, reported to Mayor Bradley: "In 1993, we will continue our role as an economic stimulus in low income communities. Most of the 4,000 jobs generated by last year's project starts will come on-line this year. Our next challenge is to target that employment to residents of Los Angeles and to link contractors with inner-city job training programs" (Squier 1993, 3). An infusion of funds into the Ghost Towns was particularly crucial, then, not only in light of the economic recession at the local level, but as a possible contribution to broader strategies of economic development.

PLANNING PRACTICES

Distinctive institutional practices are particular arrangements of institution-environment relations that are expressed through routines and are relatively successful in particular contexts. One characteristic of a planning system is participant interaction among institutional actors. Participant interaction varies tremendously from one public arena to another. When high levels of interaction are maintained, participants share common information that generates common outlooks, and ways of thinking. They become more aware of the interests and activities of others. Issues of local concern, for instance, have a greater chance of being communicated to state and federal institutions. Technical and financial support from high levels of government is more likely to fit the specific needs of localities. There is more opportunity for bargaining, compromise, and adoption and implementation of acceptable planning policies for a broad range of stakeholders (Berke and Beatley 1992, 31–32).

A second characteristic of a planning system is sets of routines used to form the basis for future action. When landmark legislation is passed or a public institution adopts a particular planning innovation, precedent is established. Once that occurs, planning and its attendant policies in that arena are never quite the same. Establishing a precedent does not necessarily imply that a policy or program actually has taken a dramatic new turn, at least not in the short run. The event might or might not be small. The importance of such events lies in their precedent-setting nature. Precedents are important because people become accustomed to the new way of doing things and build new practices into their standard operating procedures. Once a precedent is established in one arena, it can be used to gradually open windows and to promote similar change in another arena that is like the first in some way. For example, passage of structural flood control legislation in the 1930s in the United States resulted in legislation for mapping flood hazards and non-structural floodplain management, dam inspection, coastal land use planning, earthquake prediction technology, and other spillover fields (Berke and Beatley 1992, 33–34).

A third characteristic is the physical proximity of those affected by particular planning policies and programs. If the supporters or opponents of a particular measure are concentrated in a geographic area and have easy access to political leaders and opinion makers, their power to influence the outcome of implementation efforts will be much greater than if they are dispersed geographically. They can also be mobilized much more quickly than can more dispersed populations. Policy makers have long displayed a particular concern for urban residents because they get information more quickly than rural inhabitants, they can be mobilized more easily, and their actions are more visible (Grindle and Thomas 1991, 145).

Mexico City: Mass Community Mobilization

The political impact of housing became clearly evident in the aftermath of the 1985 earthquake. In areas heavily affected by the tremors, tenants' organization forced substantial modifications in state housing policy. Administrators realized that in a city the size of the Mexican capital, workers cannot travel easily from the periphery to the center of the city. Cheap central housing was essential, especially when transport costs were rising. Unless there was an effective housing response, the number of social protests—including land invasions and tenant strikes—gradually may have increased.

Popular mobilization and protests in Mexico City in the aftermath of the massive earthquake destruction and the severe economic recession were enhanced by two factors associated with urban primacy. First, the concentration of national institutions and authorities in Mexico City gave local groups additional incentive to organize and protest since their mobilization garnered national as well as local political attention. Second, like many other large cities in developing countries that face social problems associated with massive urbanization, Mexico City has a history of neighborhood organization around urban development concerns (Davis 1991, 1987). Yet another factor, not necessarily associated with urban primacy, was the sudden availability of massive funding, whereby "a whole mountain of NGOs [nongovernmental organizations] appeared because there was also money coming in from Europe to finance this sort of thing" (Connolly 1996).

There was growing interest in mobilizing Mexico's civil society—nongovernmental human rights organizations, grassroots neighborhood associations, and other groups that had begun to grow up apart from the ruling political party. One of the most impressive of these groups was the Assemblea de Barrios, which was founded in 1985 to represent poor people seeking better housing. It was the devastating earthquake that had been the catalyst for the new activity. The PRI had initially failed to provide victims with food and water and clothing, and many poor people in Mexico City had discovered, that they did better on their own (Kerr 1994). Thus,

> what succeeded was the presence of community organizations in the affected neighborhoods [barrios] that existed prior to the earthquake. The organizations were strengthened by the earthquake and the pressure by the community to find solutions to the devastation of the earthquake. This pressure caused the RHP to function more quickly.[11]

The RHP program shows what can be, at least partially, achieved by mass mobilization and community participation. As urban-based opposition to the government grew stronger, the formal housing policy instruments, especially finance, acquired a new strategic political importance. As the crisis and debt sank the country into further recession, investment in house building stood out as one of the few possibilities for stimulating the economy. The Mexico City experience also shows that well-organized, large-scale protests can pressure planning institutions into taking radical action. Even if the Mexican authorities had built new homes for the poor, they would not have subsidized them. But whether this would have happened in ordinary circumstances is another question. Mexican circumstances were highly exceptional because the attention of the world's media was focused on Mexico City. Not only was there great sympathy with the people, but there was also anxiety about whether Mexico would be able to host the forthcoming World Cup football tournament. Financial support from the World Bank and developed countries helped reduce the cost of the RHP program. What the experience certainly shows is that the state is able to cope with major protests of this kind, that it can pacify demonstrators even during a recession. Ultimately, the homeless accepted what they were offered and stopped protesting, rather than pressing for demands for deeper political and structural change (Gilbert 1994, 139–142).

Los Angeles: Lack of Community Initiative

With an emphasis on individual initiative, grassroots democracy, and private property, one would expect communities in the United States to be active and willing participants in political processes, especially those that affect their housing and neighborhoods directly, such as the Ghost Town program. However, this was not the case: the community, due to a lack of financial resources and poor levels of cooperation amongst themselves, was unable to organize themselves and take the initiative in the housing recovery efforts. Most residents in the Ghost Towns, in fact abandoned their properties. This lack of community initiative may be explained by two factors: a lack of appreciation of the housing problem in the United States by most communities, and the fragmented nature of community institutions in Los Angeles.

Many Americans do not consider affordable housing, especially for lower-income groups and renters—who were most affected by the Ghost Town problems—to be a serious problem because it has ceased to touch most middle-income Americans' daily lives. For most Americans, single-family ownership of housing is the norm. Many middle-income families occupy at least three different houses during the course of a lifetime, with the dollar value and square footage per person increasing in each instance. Americans buy their first homes at age twenty-five, seek new neighborhoods when their children approach school age, move on average once while their children are of school age, keep the homestead six years after children leave for college, and ultimately move to a retirement dwelling after age sixty (Burchell and Listokin 1995, 560). This commodification of housing and constant change in housing patterns contributes to a lack of empathy for those for whom adequate and affordable housing remains a dream. In the Ghost Towns of Los Angeles, such apathy toward broader housing problems was compounded by the fact that the region was

in the midst of a recession . . . and that really crimped the style of the private community. Property values [had] dropped considerably. Most apartment owners had mortgaged their properties to the maximum, and as a result of four years of recession, they owed more on their properties than their properties were worth. They had no ability to borrow money.[12]

Another factor in the lack of community initiative and organization following the 1994 earthquake was the high cost of forming a community-based coalition in a city so geographically dispersed and socially mobile. In the past, community groups mobilized primarily with the intention of altering or stopping the redevelopment plans of the Community Redevelopment Agency (CRA). For example, the Coalition for Economic Survival defended tenants' rights and opposed CRA clearance and redevelopment strategies in the Hollywood area, while lawyers from Legal Aid advocated for the rights of extremely low-income central city residents against CRA's plans to redevelop major portions of skid row and areas south of downtown (Goetz

1993, 143). Thus, although there has been a great deal of neighborhood activism, it was essentially defensive in nature (e.g., reacting to redevelopment plans), and lacked coordination or unification into broader movements. Moreover, following the earthquake

> for the first several months, everybody was traumatized and trying to deal with their own little plot of land. And because there were so many needs and so many crises, you needed somebody, whether it be the Government or a politician . . . or the City Department to come and identify common themes.[13]

Mexico City: Co-Optation

Co-optation occurs when a leader or a group affiliates with a national institution and thereby becomes subject to its orthodoxy, rules, and routines. This is usually done because the co-opted party believes that he or she will win preferential treatment and benefit as a result of the linkage. In Mexico, co-optation is a classic strategy, an institutionalized routine, which the PRI used in giving the impression it has preferential access to resources. Covertly, for example, the national health and social security systems serve to co-opt the most powerful or organized groups in Mexican society. Thus, federal workers are catered for through the Instituto de Seguridad y Servicios Sociales de los Trabajadores al Servicio del Estado (ISSSTE); those in strategic industries enjoy their own health care facilities, as do the military. These conditions, together with the wider benefits provided by each individual social security system, have evolved in response to pressure from these more powerful groups. In the Distrito Federal, land regularization and service provision assumed importance as a means of ensuring and developing political control and support. Through the Oficina de Colonias (Office of Neighborhoods), residents were encouraged to attend political rallies and to vote for PRI in elections, and in exchange they could expect some form of government recognition for their settlement and/or the installation of minor services and occasional handouts (Ward 1990a, 167–170).

The government moved swiftly to negotiate the demands of popular groups that had mobilized independently of the PRI in the central area of Mexico City following the earthquake:

> The program became politicized very quickly. On the one hand, there were the non-governmental organizations that intervened quickly, and on the other hand, the political parties. In the central zone of the city there have been, since several years, the housing cooperative organizations and housing programs at a very local level and very well

connected to political parties, especially the PRD, the PRI, and what later became the Frente Cardenista. And then, quickly, everyone had their own clientele. For example, the PRI began with a lot of vigor and finished very badly. The PRI had their own bases in the zone. But the PRI did not deliver to its groups. The group that worked most with the people was what was to become the Frente Cardenista who had people with a solid base in the devastated neighborhoods.[14]

The authorities' response of co-opting the demands of the victims of the Mexico City the earthquake appears to have set a precedent for the policy of *concertacion* (new forms of state-society relations based on opening areas for grassroots participation). Following the mass movements led by independent organizations, the then head of SEDUE, Manuel Camacho Solis, called all groups to sign the *convenio*. In signing this agreement, the groups agreed, implicitly, to work with and not against the state. The accord therefore cleverly brought groups into line and put an end to popular protests. In this manner, the agreement is consistent with long-standing inclusionary corporatist state-society relations (Harvey 1993).

Los Angeles: Neighborhood Revitalization

In recent years, neighborhood conditions have come to be one of the most serious problems of housing quality in the United States. In 1985, for example, 40 percent of renters and 37 percent of homeowners regarded their neighborhoods as deficient in one or more respects, such as too much crime or streets requiring repairs (Marcuse 1990, 331–332). Forty-five percent of renters and 50 percent of homeowners were dissatisfied with urban services such as schools, police protection, and public transportation.

Housing credit flows—such as those enabled by the Ghost Town program—are central to neighborhood revitalization. They are essential for financial property transfers, maintaining local housing markets, sustaining property values, and supporting maintenance and refurbishment. Reinvestment is essential for maintaining the value of local housing, while disinvestment—the absence of credit from communities—works to lower property values.

Some authors consider neighborhood revitalization (i.e., neighborhood health and stability) in the United States to be community economic development (Shlay 1995). Community economic development is broadly defined as the mobilization of resources to enlarge the wealth base and economic well being of local communities. This process involves creating wealth within a community by producing net economic gains, as well as retaining wealth within a community by reducing the flow of capital and resources out of it.

Housing policy in Los Angeles is viewed as a part of a package of initiatives designed to increase wealth and build income within local communities, as housing plays a role in both creation and retention of community wealth (Shlay 1995, 705).

LEARNING FROM SIMILARITY AND DIFFERENCE

There are several implications of this comparative analysis between Mexico City and Los Angeles, and between Mexico and the United States, but also more generally for planning and policy processes in developing country versus developed country contexts. There are often important differences between developing country and developed country governments. These differences derive from the fact that organizational interests and specific groups are much more institutionalized in the developed countries, and the dispersion of power within government, particularly through active legislatures and regulatory bureaucracies, offers more formal access to interest groups. Interest groups play an identifiable and significant role in articulating citizen and organizational interests in the developed states. In developing countries, in contrast, the link between societal interests and the decision-making process is more elusive. Most important, societal interests are often likely to be represented through informal processes, such as mass protests following the 1985 Mexico City earthquake and informal networks through the ruling PRI party, rather than through more public forms of lobbying. A relatively closed decision-making process and elite-centered politics leave wide scope for pressures to be exerted on the policy-making process through informal and nonpublic channels (Grindle and Thomas 1991). Furthermore, disparate access to resources, disparate levels of economic development, and disparate social patterns easily account for strong policy-framework and policy-content differences between developing and developed societies.

The Mexico City case study illustrates an institutional environment marked by centralized and relatively closed decision making, informal processes of interest representation, and vulnerability of regimes. These factors also add to their power and simultaneously isolate them from critical information about societal preferences and tolerance for policy change. For these reasons, the preferences and belief systems that dominate key institutional actors become critical political variables in decision-making contexts. Generally, belief and value systems do not dictate policy choices; instead, they shape and color the way new information is processed. Thus, institutions tend to fit incoming information into their existing theories and images. Indeed, their theories and images play a large part in determining what they do or do not notice. Thus, not only are possible institutional responses to crisis situations shaped by existing perceptions, but the crisis itself is defined by them in terms of institutional specialization (e.g., as a housing crisis rather than an environmental crisis).

The convergence of process is what requires explanation. For all the systemic differences that are so readily apparent between developing and developed countries, commonalties of process extend to the constraints inherent in planning practices, to the freedom from those constraints that is available at certain moments ripe for innovation, and to the adventitious character of the events that produce those moments. In developing countries, as in developed countries, earlier decisions and programs (i.e., routines) form a matrix of policy into which new decisions must fit or which they must somehow transcend. Earlier commitments mark the boundaries of what seems plausible, even possible. No government writes on a clean slate. The policy formulation and implementation habits and the particular nature of each planning system shape decisions by limiting what options are considered and what decisions accepted. Policies made in an area fresh in the experience of institutions and the relevant public stand a good chance of being made in the same mold. Thus, the significance of understanding institutional routines.

A disproportionate number of policies are adopted at exceptional times, for example during times of crises, when there is a strong demand for change, times when unusual events have immobilized obstacles to new policy or drastically changed the composition of decision making bodies. At such times, organized interests are frequently ineffective. Ideas for policy become important forces, and institutional actors have a good deal of freedom to put their ideas into operation. Often, policy ideas have been in circulation before (Horowitz 1989, 205). A good many innovations are adopted during crises. In this model, innovation, even during routine times, is often the work of political entrepreneurs holding policy making positions and convictions about the direction policy should take in areas of interest to them. In the case studies, Camacho in Mexico City and Cisneros in Los Angeles, played the role of political entrepreneurs as well as institutional leaders. All of this suggests some significant autonomy for policy makers and institutions.

If we look a little more closely at the similarities enumerated earlier, we can see than they lie heavily in the realm of irregular cadences of the policy process: its stop-start quality, the extent to which it is ruled by the variable weight of a shifting complex of constraints, and the ability of participants to deflect policy, to create feedback effects, and to turn implementation into yet another policy forum (Horowitz 1989, 209). To see these institutions and conditions in tension at any given moment is also to recognize that underlying the irregular cadences of the process are the multiple permutations of such forces in tension and their changing relative importance over time.

For the developed and the developing countries, the policy process needs to be seen in terms of this changing constellation of external events (e.g., crises), and conditions (e.g., existing political-economy or planning practices), and of internal forces (e.g., institutional routines and leadership).

One of the tangible benefits of an international comparative analysis is the recognition of global linkages between such megacities as Mexico City and Los Angeles. When the 1971 San Fernando Valley earthquake occurred, local officials in Long Beach were prepared. They were aware of the problem, a solution was available in the form of recommendations made in a consulting report on retrofit, and key advocates were poised for an intensive effort to enact seismic mitigation building codes. In the city of Los Angeles, local officials were not prepared when the window opened at that point in time. Fourteen years passed before another window opened: the 1985 Mexico City earthquake. After the 1985 earthquake, the earthquake hot line run by the U.S. Geological Survey logged four times its usual number of calls from nervous residents. Officials in California said that the Mexican disaster helped speed completion of a new state disaster plan. Immediately after the earthquake, while elected officials' and the public's memory was still vivid, a stringent seismic retrofit ordinance was adopted (Berke and Beatley 1992, 36). In a sense, the Mexico City earthquake may have assisted in the reduction of devastation and loss of life in the subsequent Los Angeles earthquake of 1994.

Similarly, there are potential lessons even among the failed programs. Scenes of air pollution in Mexico City in the 1990s are reminiscent of Los Angeles in 1970s, when its levels of ozone, automobile emissions, and industrial development were roughly comparable (Fineman 1996, A11). As Los Angeles celebrated its lowest smog readings in decades, Mexico City officials have been declaring a record number of smog-emergency days—four in a row in late 1996. Ozone levels topping two-and-one-half times international norms triggered automatic bans on hundreds and thousands of automobiles and cutbacks on industrial production. Even below-emergency readings of ozone are above accepted norms almost every day, and averaged around double the highest readings in the Los Angeles metropolitan area. Los Angeles beat the worst of its ozone-driven smog with a new generation of cars equipped with catalytic converters and the mandatory use of high-quality unleaded gasoline (Fineman 1996, A11–A12). The result: just seven days of smog alerts from May through October. In Mexico City, where ozone levels exceeded international norms on all but about a dozen days in 1996, unleaded gas is sold but rarely used. And during economic crises, many drivers cannot afford either the more expensive unleaded gas or the cars that use it. Actions by planning institutions in Los Angeles in response to the air pollution crisis were appropriate to its particular context, and Mexico City needs to find responses that match its own political-economic realities.

The primary purpose of comparative policy research is not to establish the universality of relationships, but to enhance the credibility of specific predictions about specific cases and to gain useful rather than general knowledge in the short term. This is particularly relevant for megacities such as Mexico City and Los Angeles for cities are

> booming everywhere, in developing and developed countries alike . . . their growth is defying attempts to limit it . . . and . . . most important . . . the growth of cities is economically healthy and culturally beneficial . . . In the next century, the most relevant unit of economic production, social organization and knowledge generation will be the city.[15]

A common risk of conducting international comparative analyses is to expect only to learn and apply lessons from developed countries to developing countries, rather being open to the possibility of mutual learning, or even policy lessons which flow from the developing world to the developed world. In the case studies of successful crisis recovery from earthquakes in Mexico City and Los Angeles, Mexico City was more successful in leveraging limited resources toward greater effect (e.g., 48,000 housing units) than in Los Angeles (7,000 housing units).

A similar case of lessons from the developing world is made in a convincing manner by Louise Comfort, a scholar at the University of Pittsburgh who specializes in disaster response management. She compares the role of communications and community outreach in Kobe, Japan after the 1995 earthquake with Maharashtra, India following the 1993 earthquake (Glembocki 1996). Institutions in Japan had chosen a technical strategy by investing heavily in seismic safety via construction and engineering that was supposedly earthquake-proof. They did not invest in local community preparedness or in communication systems other than telephones. As a consequence, the Japanese institutions were completely overwhelmed.

The institutions in India made very different choices. In a relatively poor country, there was little funding to invest in disaster management, but there was investment made in a satellite communications system. Within four minutes of the earthquake, the local police sent a message on their handmade wireless radio from their station—a tin shed—to the district office about fifteen miles away, which then transmitted the message via satellite to the governor's office in the city of Mumbai. The response was organized within minutes, whereas in Japan there was no communication for almost the first day. The contrast is striking: Indian institutions recognized that they could make the best decisions with good communication, while the Japanese institutions believed they could somehow control the crisis primarily through earthquake engineering.

This section has offered insights from the comparative analysis in terms of the political economy, and planning practices. It has also shed light on the benefits of megacity comparisons in terms of learning across international boundaries. The final sections will suggest possible limitations of this study and close with an argument for the advantageous potential of crises, routines, institutions, and the public sector in urban planning in the broader context.

FUTURE DIRECTIONS FOR PLANNING INSTITUTIONS

There are two major aspects to the plot about institutions that dominate this book. One is understanding, which involves a study of how the planning system comprehends, changes, and maintains a relationship with its environment through its institutions. The other aspect is evaluation, which involves assessing the extent to which planning institutions contribute to a meaningful governance of the people, especially through strategies such as routines. This book has taken shape through a reciprocal relationship between empirical evidence—or events in the story—on the one hand, and theory—or the plot of the story—on the other hand, in order to construct a rich and instructive narrative of urban planning. The case studies of planning institutions' actions during crisis recovery in Mexico City and Los Angeles offer a window into broader structural issues such as the potentially beneficial roles of crises, routines, institutions, and the public sector—all of which combined constitute the main thrust of this final chapter. I will begin, however, by describing the limitations of this research and alternative explanations for the success of the RHP and Ghost Town housing recovery programs.

Limitations

This section discusses limitations of this book and its findings. The book does not purport to be an exhaustive analysis resulting in universal generalizations, but an illustrative and explanatory example of how public sector planning institutions respond successfully to sudden shocks and crisis situations. Such a universalistic analysis would require many more case studies in different political-economic contexts and during different time periods.

Since the book adopts an institutional perspective, there is an inherent institutional bias, a strong focus at the cost of other factors, on institutional actors and strategies. Thus, for example, I did not analyze the physical nature of the projects and their broader implications as a form of contemporary urban renewal in the city. The implications of the physical reconstruction for the built environment might lead to a different set of observations in terms of urban design strategies or physical rebuilding after crises.

Some of those interviewed both in Mexico City and Los Angeles did not initially agree with my proposition about the significance of institutional routines in the success of the two housing recovery programs (Stolarski 1995; Dunne 1996). However, when presented with some of the patterns of institutional policy formulation and implementation and the supporting evidence, they did agree to a certain extent with my findings. I believe such a plot, or pattern of institutional action, is implicit and often taken so much for granted that it is not always evident to the institutional representatives in a clear and explicit manner.

Perhaps the most important finding in this book is the effectiveness of routines as part of successful institutional action during crisis situations in urban planning. However, routines have several limitations. Often, standardized routine—well-established policies and programs—are applied in such a manner by planning institutions that contexts are ignored and side effects neglected. Other routines, reasonable enough in themselves, may have severe effects in combination. A public sector planning institution that utilizes routines repeatedly cannot correct its actions simply by learning from its errors. The stabilizing aspects of the public sector bureaucracy, especially the hierarchy of defined jurisdictions and the commitment to rule-governed administration, impose this cost. In such cases, routines threaten to lead to atrophy, abuse, fixation, and a danger of conservatism. Processes within planning institutions often lead individuals to orient their actions around routines even to the point where primary concern with conformity to rules and routines interferes with the achievement of purposes of the institution; for example, the frequent obsession with "proper" paperwork that beneficiaries are subjected to in most public sector housing programs (Scott 1995, 17–18).

The other alternative to routines, a crisis plan, faces its own drawbacks. No such creature as a comprehensive crisis plan or response is realistically possible. Therefore, Neal and Phillips recommend that emergency managers should anticipate, plan for, and include ad hoc emergent configurations to improve their crisis response (Neal and Phillips 1995, 335). However, the planning institution's favorite strategy, to have a plan for crises, is not always effective. Disaster plans in the United States—by virtue of both convention and the guidelines that state and federal funding agencies impose—are lengthy and dry procedural documents descended from military command models. Key officials often neglect to read the plans, and the procedures of different municipal departments drift away from a coordinated strategy when localities rely exclusively on paper planning (Karetz and Lindell 1987, 488).

In 1983 the Mexican government had engaged in a probability study of crisis situations in order to be well prepared. This study resulted in the creation of an emergency unit made up of four components: (1) a center of information and data processing, (2) field operations to be directed by the Mexican military, (3) research and development efforts, and (4) future studies. The fundamental objective of the study, and the resulting recommendations, was to maintain stability during any foreseeable crisis situation. However, a dramatic fall in crucial oil revenues to the Mexican government shortly before the earthquake caused cutbacks in the recommended crisis situation response framework and within fifteen days of the 1985 crisis in Mexico City the only parts that functioned were the operations conducted by the military.

On paper, at least, a well-conceived plan existed in the Interior and Defense ministries to rapidly mobilize security forces and other government personnel in the event of a massive earthquake. Several thousand military troops and police were, in fact, rushed to neighborhoods of greatest devastation. But most of them merely cordoned off the sites, instead of plunging ahead with excavation and rescue work. When government workers finally began digging out the victims, it was apparent that their picks and shovels were woefully inadequate (Kandell 1988, 570). Similarly, HUD accomplished its role in the successful housing recovery efforts in Los Angeles without prior existence of a comprehensive, rapid-response disaster plan, although prior experience using the CDBG and HOME programs proved extremely helpful (Galster et al. 1995).

Inevitably, the standard procedures and routines employed by any policy formulation and implementation process are considerably less differentiated than the array of problems that travels through that process. Consequently, the procedures are not necessarily well adapted to the shifting contours of those problems. Bad fit of process and problem is an ever-present possibility. When such considerations are taken into account, it is easy to see why the common result is a large measure of indecision, stalemate, and overload (Horowitz 1989, 209).

From the discussion in the preceding sections and the previous chapters, it is clear that the danger of the abusing or misusing routines occurs when institutions consider them only as ends—routines being utilized simply because they are established routines without a sense of purpose, context, or adaptability. The true success of routines derives from their utilization as means or tools that may be adopted and adapted according to needs and conditions.

The institutional perspective adopted by this book suggests that action can be seen as the application of standard operating procedures or other routines that evolve through a process of variation and selection. Duties, obligation, and roles match a set of rules to a situation by criteria of appropriateness. The duties, obligations, roles, rules, and criteria evolve through experimentation, competition, and survival. Those routines followed by institutions that survive, grow, and multiply come to dominate the pool of procedures. The model is essentially a model of evolution (March and Olsen 1989; Lin and Nugent 1995).

Bish Sanyal, who focuses on the beliefs and actions of individuals, has suggested an alternative explanation for the success of institutional action in urban planning (Sanyal 1996). Progressive planners act out of a motivation that is broader in scope and more complex in its purpose than the term self-interest conveys. For example, a concern for public welfare, a sense of social justice, a long-term view of societal trajectory, and more personal factors such as the gratification one enjoys in doing well one's share of work toward the collective good—are factors that contribute to the social construction of ethical identities of progressive planners which, in turn, guide their motivation for progressive action (Sanyal 1996, 146). In fact, Sanyal's explanation partially illustrates the extraordinary actions undertaken by planners in the RHP program in Mexico City, as described in interviews with the author:

> We spent 17 months in a small, ugly office in one of the affected neighborhoods, working 18 hours a day . . . I [Jorge Gamboa] also had good relations with the World Bank and with BANOBRAS, often obtaining loans of about $15–$20 million without paperwork because we had serious problems of cash flow . . . There were weeks and weeks on the table of Camacho, till 4 a.m. in the morning negotiating with all the leaders all kinds of conditions, for example, the salaries and the conditions that were acceptable to the World Bank.[16]

Alternative explanations also focus on the specific nature of the crisis, especially in terms of its timing and location. In this view, the effectiveness of a response also depends on the specific circumstances surrounding the particular disaster—it magnitude, location, and time of occurrence. The Los Angeles quake struck at 4:31 a.m. on a national holiday, which undoubtedly reduced losses (there was only one highway fatality, for example) and affected successful government response (Wachs and Kamel 1996, 24). In contrast, it was shortly after 7:00 a.m. and the rush hour was in full progress for the working-class population in Mexico City. Clothing factories in the city center had started up their sewing machines. Bleary-eyed laborers squeezed into buses en route to the northern industrial districts. Subways were packed with secretaries, clerks, and messengers. Public schools, functioning in two daily shifts because of crowded enrollment, had opened their doors to the morning session of students. As the earthquake took place, buildings swayed and buckled, showering pedestrians with brick and mortar, crumbling upon their foundations or exploding in fireballs. Thousands of people lay buried or worse, dead, in their ruins (Kandell 1988, 566).

The limited scope of this book does not allow a fuller, more expansive explanation of the successful housing recovery programs during crisis situations in Mexico City and Los Angeles. The main purpose of this book is to find out what works, *institutionally*, in urban planning and why; hence its focus on institutional actors and institutional strategies such as routines, which I believe to be extremely useful. Jorge Gamboa, the former Director-General Adjunct of the RHP program in Mexico City and a key policy maker, upholds this view:

> The institutional support was very important; otherwise one tends to adopt a romantic view. There was a group of opinion that it was this notion of civil society that was critical, but that is not true. It was a combination of civil society with the institutions.[17]

Institutions, Routines, and Crises in Planning

The principles underlying effective planning institutions discussed in this book offer a genuine alternative to institutions that rely exclusively on self-interested incentives or narrowly-defined efficiency. These underlying principles are a general form of social capital (i.e., common ideas or body of shared knowledge about how to design and modify institutions in an effective manner) than the specific routines used within a particular and successful institution. Although a shared knowledge of the specific routines used within an effective institution (i.e., the blueprint of that institution) is essential for its survival and adaptability over time, a knowledge of the underlying principles used in the design or evolution of those specific routines is likely to be more helpful to others facing similar problems in different circumstances. General principles may be transferable to other settings and used by many communities to design particular institutions that meet their requirements.

What, then, is the contribution of this book? It is always easier to demand recipes in the form of blueprints, for example, than to strive to attain an insight. However, it is insight into the functioning of effective planning institutions that is really needed, and is offered by this book. One example is the optimum usefulness of a trial and error strategy, based on routines, for the solving of complex problems. An institutional approach also suggests that a better understanding of the role that every planning institution perforce has to play is made possible. Therefore, the question of managing urban development is also a question of the positioning of the planning institution in a complex network of socio-cultural, technological, economic, and political factors and influences (i.e., institutional frameworks of planning as well as their mode of operation, including through informal networks).

The way routines affect institutional actions depends on very specific attributes of the services involved (e.g., housing, transportation, or land use), and on the political and economic conditions of a particular community; so, the specific routines developed in one effective institution may not work in the same way elsewhere. Thus, the blueprint may not be transferable, but the principles may be. These principles are articulated in the following sections on the potentially beneficial role of crises, routines, institutions, and more generally, the public sector, as suggested by the evidence presented in this book.

Powerful initiatives develop out of an intimate understanding of planning possibility, which has been gained by constantly reframing the problem, and by repeatedly searching for solutions through the application and modification of routines. Particular methods, learned by experience, help the planning institutions to make this journey of discovery. The great majority of planning strategies are adaptations of solutions previously used. Institutional memories are full of such customary approaches, and they know something about the situations for which they are appropriate.

As a complete planning process, incremental adaptation is useful where external changes are slow relative to the pace of environmental decision— when objectives, behaviors, technology, institutions, and settings are all relatively stable. But even in a more dynamic situation, institutions adapt previous approaches. In ordinary work, they appear everywhere, and fateful decisions are made thereby. To a large extent, stereotypes cannot be avoided; the danger lies in using them unthinkingly. The institutional routine must have some reasonable relation to the problem, and it must be possible to reach a good solution by a chain of small modifications. Recent fashions or approaches developed in different circumstances may be radically inappropriate.

Planning must be viewed as a process that tests propositions (such as routines) about the most effective means of coping with social problems, reassessing and redefining both the problems and the components of development projects as more is learned about their complexities, and about the economic, social, and political factors affecting the outcome of a proposed course of action. Complex social experiments can be partially guided but never fully controlled; thus, institutional procedures must be flexible and incremental, facilitating social interaction so that those groups most directly affected by a problem can search for and pursue mutually acceptable objectives (Rondinelli 1993, 18).

One way of coping with uncertainty, complexity, and change in megacities is to recognize that all planning projects are policy experiments, and to plan them incrementally and adaptively by disaggregating problems and formulating responses through processes of decision making that join learning with action. Such adaptive administration allows planners to perform what Wildavsky calls the basic task of policy analysis: to create problems (i.e., routinizing novelty) that institutions are able to handle with the variables under their control and in the time available (Wildavsky 1979, 15). This approach sees planning and implementation as the art of creating problems that can be solved through informed experimentation. Courses of action are shaped from lessons of past experience as well as from a more realistic understanding of current and emerging conditions.

The number and variety of alternative routines assure that one of the primary factors affecting institutional action is the process by which some of those routines, rather than others, are evoked in a particular situation. The presence of conflicting routines opens up room for individual discretion and for strategic choice (Scott 1995; March and Olsen 1989). Diversity in the planning process is beneficial. Like investors hedging against uncertainty, institutions can broaden their repertoire of routines and avoid the risks of an overly narrow approach. Furthermore, extensive institutional experience and memory promotes the knowledge of which aspects of appropriate routines to modify or even eliminate.

The importance of the risk of crises and the absence of adequate insurance mechanisms in many cities could lead planning institutions to adopt a routine production and diversification strategy. Planning institutions could further reduce their risks by making the range of routines large in size and diverse in composition by including routines that address a variety of processes, outcomes, and conditions. Institutions could also build bridges with other more powerful institutions (e.g., in terms of resources or political power) through arrangements that define, either implicitly or explicitly, mutually beneficial contracts.

The official evaluation and report of the RHP program in Mexico City recognizes the utility of institutional routines in crisis situations. The report suggests, based on the experience of housing recovery following the earthquake, that during a crisis situation time is a crucial variable, therefore it is critical to have recourse to already tested tools, techniques, and technologies—such as institutional routines—that can be adapted to the specific conditions of place, time, and nature of crisis impact (RHP 1988, 114). This does not imply that innovation is to be left out of such crisis recovery programs; rather innovations can be tested once a certain degree of stability and community confidence has been established through tangible institutional actions, as senior policy makers in Mexico City realized, "We worked with conventional construction techniques. We tried to introduce certain innovations, but we realized that during crises, innovations are not to be introduced. What is done is what people are already used to, in order to gain their confidence" (Stolarski 1995).

Similarly, within a short period following the 1994 Los Angeles earthquake, HUD devised significant new modifications to its regular programs to create three new policies for emergency relief: (1) the Section 8 Emergency Certificate Program for aiding displaced low-income renters, (2) the Mobility Program for assisting Emergency Certificate holders in successfully locating and occupying housing, and (3) the HELP Program for providing low-interest loans to owners of HUD-associated rental properties that had suffered earthquake damage. In addition, waivers were made in the well-established CDBG and HOME programs, so that they could be used more expeditiously for crisis recovery. HUD's pragmatic, problem-solving routinization of novelty, yielded widespread accolades form a variety of sources most closely involved in the recovery efforts (Galster et al. 1995, i).

The utilization of "off-the-shelf" institutional routines was indeed a familiar occurrence in Los Angeles during crisis situations:

> We were in a way psychologically prepared for the earthquake because we had just gone through a similar disaster [i.e., 1992 riots] where we had a similar result where we had entire blocks of properties destroyed. So, we had a kind of blueprint on the shelves that we could turn to in our disaster plan, and [to] what we did after the response there. And we had a lot of . . . emergency ordinances after the riots that we just kind of took off the shelf real quick, changed a few little items, and threw it back into the books in response to the earthquake. [For example, w]hat we did after the riots is we waived permitting fees, we waived a lot of requirements to get buildings built again.[18]

Planning institutions learn their way into adaptive and appropriate strategies during the heat of emergency, through a process that compresses problem definition, policy implementation and experimentation, and evaluation in a few days or weeks at best. However, the trial-and-error process of applying and modifying routines is not just a continuous process of action and reaction without direction; in fact, it is directed by a repertoire of routines and by an array of actions ordered by a combinations of a reliable process, guiding purpose or shared goals, a leader with a clear focus, and workable technologies. For example, the challenge confronting HUD in devising the

CDBG and HOME program modifications for the Los Angeles housing recovery efforts was to retain commitment to the goals of assisting low-income communities and neighborhoods while addressing in an expeditious manner the massive housing and infrastructure needs of the earthquake damaged areas.

In focusing on successful action by planning institutions in the primary case studies, I develop a different view of their role and impact than what is encountered in many studies of urban planning and policy. I believe that the analysis of concrete cases of effective planning institutions, grounded in particular political-economic contexts, and based on specific experiences in policy formulation and implementation, has allowed me to go beyond theoretical approaches that view such institutions as cogs in the wheels of large structures and systems that they have no capacity to influence or alter. Neither do my findings support approaches that consider planning institutions to be relatively powerless referees in ongoing struggles among societal interests, or those portraying them as single-minded "rent-seekers" whose every decision is dominated by the drive to maximize power. Finally, I have presented evidence to question the view that institutions and their representatives are primarily bureaucratic in-fighters in multi-layered games that lead to haphazard outcomes as some approaches suggest.

The framework is not intended to predict outcomes in terms of what choices will be made or how successfully particular actions will resolve particular planning problems. Instead, it systematizes thinking about how context influences particular situations, how circumstances shape options, how options are adapted to particular situations, and how routine characteristics affect policy in the introduction of action. Analytically, these are important sets of relationships to map out. Such a mapping can also be a way of beginning to think strategically about introducing and sustaining modifications in institutional design. Systematic thinking about interrelationships and consequences of context, circumstance, and policy characteristics therefore provides both an analytic tool for understanding the process of institutional action and a first cut at developing strategies for introducing and sustaining design for institutional effectiveness.

Although it lies within a heterogeneous tradition of literature on institutions and urban planning, this book reflects a specific perspective on institutional analysis. Within that perspective institutional actors are driven by institutional duties and roles as well as, or instead of, by calculated self-interest; policy is organized around the construction and interpretation of meaning as well as, or instead of, the making of choices; routines, rules, and forms evolve through history-dependent processes that do not reliably and quickly reach unique equilibria; the institutions of planning are not simple echoes of social forces; and the planning system is something different from, or more than, an arena for competition among rival interests.

In short, the organization of urban planning makes a difference, and institutions affect the flow of history. I have been particularly concerned with two aspects of such a view: the way in which an appreciation of the role of institutions contributes to a positive theory of urban planning, and the way in which understanding planning institutions contributes to the normative evaluation and design of them. Understanding involves a theory of how the planning system comprehends, changes, and maintains a relationship with its environment through its institutions. Evaluation involves assessing the extent to which planning institutions contribute to a meaningful governance of communities of the people, i.e., their constituencies.

Effective planning institutions are a major means for providing a city with the sustainable capacity to solve critical urban problems. Furthermore, they enhance a city's ability to marshal its own human and financial resources for urban development; and enable individuals to obtain access to the skills, resources, and services needed to increase their productivity, incomes, and well-being. The degree of effectiveness of policies and programs initiated by planning institutions is likely to depend on issues such as how institutions can organize their policy formulation and implementation activities to cope with the growing complexity, uncertainty, and change of urban development problems (Rondinelli 1993). Planning institutions need to understand that because their ability to predict and control outcomes of policy initiatives under conditions of uncertainty is limited, their methods must be better suited to recognizing and dealing with uncertainty, detecting and correcting errors on an ongoing basis, generating and using knowledge as policy experiments progress, and modifying actions as opportunities and constraints appear during implementation.

In many cases, the institutional arrangements are fixed, and the challenge is to select a strategy for planning and communication that is matched to urban conditions and community capabilities. The planner must be aware of how the performance of her plans and designs will be affected by the existing institutions, and what management changes her designs imply. She should recognize the opportunities for new institutions that can occur in creating new environments. For example, houses or land can be cooperatively owned and maintained, new schools can become community-learning opportunities, and health care in a new town can be established on a group basis. Urban environments and planning institutions possess patterns of long life, have strategic effects on the quality of human life, and those effects are magnified when the two patterns are coordinated.

These ideas are most effectively captured by the principle of idoneity; where the idoneous is what is adequate, what fully considers the conditions, what responds to the requirements, what conforms to ends and intentions, and what is appropriate to its function (Protzen 1981, 3). This principle of idoneity is inspired by a dialectical intent, where "dialectic" is not interpreted in the Hegelian sense, nor in the materialistic sense, but in its etymological sense of a method of intellectual inquiry through dialogue. What is idoneous cannot be always or necessarily known in advance. The idoneous can only be conceived of through the concrete practice of these techniques such as trying experience, exacting effort, critical discourse, and dialectical technique. "It is only as an answer to this experience and as a reward to this effort, that eventually the judgment can be formed: yes, this plan is proper to, and conforms with, the ends and intentions of those involved" (Protzen 1981, 6).

An idoneous planning institution must have the ability to learn from and adapt to the environment in which it works. This requires (1) understanding the environment in which it works (e.g., through experienced personnel, an extensive database, and the institutional memory), (2) recognizing and clarifying the objectives and intentions of those its serves (e.g., through community outreach), and of its institutional colleagues (e.g., through institutional coordination), and (3) defining ways of adapting and reconciling its environment and objectives (e.g., through rapid action and massive funding) with proposed development goals (e.g., improved conditions). This requirement is particularly critical for planning institutions because of the unfamiliarity of many professions with the diversity and complexity of conditions found in urban regions, and the rapidity and fundamental nature of the changes taking place.

Institutions express a discipline through a repertoire of routines and competencies that constrains behavior. At the same time, it is impossible to imagine a stable or competent institutional system that does not adapt to variations in the world by assigning some discretion to its participants and then protecting their latitude. As a result of the ongoing dance between the discipline of core competencies and established routines on the one hand, and latitude of adaptation to changing circumstances on the other, planning institutions are able to redirect public policy on the ground, campaign for favored policies and programs against the grain of established opinions, and reshape the ways in which preferences and collective bargains are articulated.

An appropriate strategy for designing idoneous planning institutions, then, combines external constraint with moral development (Selznick 1992, 344). This is done by establishing general standards to which an institution must adhere, and for which it can be held accountable by their constituencies, often via legislatures and courts. Principles governing the definition of mission (i.e., clear sense of vision), personnel policy, contract negotiation, fiscal responsibility, fiduciary obligation, and visibility of decisions (e.g., transparency, and participation) become part of the institutional charter. Such a charter also requires regular procedures for determining what interests are affected by the institution's major decisions; sustained consultation with constituencies and critics (e.g., stakeholders); and periodic review by competent independent auditors (e.g., monitoring and learning). Within this normative framework the planning institution makes its own decisions regarding specific objectives, internal organization, and allocation of resources.

Planning scholars have an especially significant role to play in understanding the institutional dynamics of planning and designing idoneous institutions utilizing, for example, the analytical framework described in this book because they

> can pay attention to and make comparisons among a wider range of practices than can an individual practitioner, and they can track change over time. They can also search through a range of literature and theories to develop interpretations *to account for what works and how, and what does not and why* [emphasis mine], and to draw on insights that can make planning practice more effective.[19]

In this manner, institutional analysis is helpful in comprehending key factors in the success or failure of practices and outcomes, as well as in a critical analysis of current ideas such as regional cooperation or public-private partnerships in the planning profession.

How does one begin the task of institutional design or re-design in planning? There are no standard answers to the specification of an idoneous design of planning institutions. In addition to the institutional analysis described in this book as a starting point, what can be offered are probing and exploratory questions for communities and institutions to ask themselves. For example, are the objectives of a planning institution appropriate to current urban conditions and challenges? Are the goals of efficiency and equity adequate for addressing conditions of complexity and uncertainty? How can the power of institutionalized routines be harnessed to adapt to ongoing change? In this manner, an idoneous institutional design in planning should be continually and openly accountable, making available to relevant stakeholders communities the information and arguments that lie behind decisions, the consideration of stakeholders' concerns, and perhaps, should include mechanisms for critical review and challenge on a regular basis.

The final set of broad implications from this book relate to the role of the public sector in urban planning. Contemporary criticism of public sector institutions includes their portrayal as rigid and incompetent. They are unable to adjust intelligently and rapidly to changes in the economy, demography, or mood of a city, and unable to cope with the most pressing problems of society. Contemporary literature on the public sector is filled with theories of public choice, rational choice, and rent-seeking behavior that attempt to explain, in simple and elegant ways, the familiar litany of problems: the pursuit of self-interest rather than the public interest, clientistic practices, excessive spending by government institutions, public institutions filled with poorly qualified workers, and misconceived policies and programs.

However, rather than public sector planning institutions becoming more like the private sector, we require more case studies of successful public sector institutional action grounded in specific contexts, like the ones in this book (Osborne and Gaebler 1992). The current bias of thinking in explaining the performance of planning institutions, especially in developing countries, means that these countries have few models of good government that are grounded in their own experience.

The purpose of public sector planning institutions is multi-layered, ambiguous, and complex, especially during crisis situations:

> Why do people build their dream homes on a flood plain, along a tornado alley or astride some seismic fault when normally they take great pains to protect themselves, their loved ones and their property? Could it be that they have come to see natural disasters not as capricious acts of God that they endure for personal reasons (employment, good schools, spectacular views), but as problems for governments to resolve?[20]

Public sector planning institutions cope with problems and issues that have conflicting objectives, multiple stakeholders, and intense political pressure—what Horst Rittel and Melvin Webber termed "wicked problems" (Rittel and Webber 1973). However, there are tangible benefits from the actions of these institutions. For example, "costs would be even higher [for earthquakes] but for one thing: casualty numbers have declined dramatically in the past 20 years, thanks to building codes [conceived and enforced by public sector planning institutions] that have made modern homes, workplaces and public facilities far safer" (Valery 1995, 9). The need for public sector involvement in crises is further justified by the pooling of risks and resources that are not provided by other sectors. For example, the insurance companies reported that only three out of ten homeowners affected by the Los Angeles earthquake had insurance (LAHD 1995, 15).

Since the public sector provides a framework of order on which the rest of urban planning and development is built, the importance of public sector planning institutions and their actions for urban development cannot be over-emphasized. Even the New Institutional Economics suggests that due to incomplete markets, imperfect information, transaction cost, and imperfect competition, the public sector can potentially play a major role in facilitating urban development. At the national level, Lin and Nugent cite a study that surveyed more that one hundred years of comparative development experience in forty developing countries, and found that the single most important explanatory variable is political organization and the administrative competence of public sector institutions (Lin and Nugent 1995, 2333).

For many citizens of Mexico City, especially those living the devastated neighborhoods following the 1985 earthquake, the government appeared to be engaged in a perverse effort to belittle their losses by releasing casualty and property damage figures that were far lower than estimates reported by journalists and relief workers on the scene. As a result, the public sector institutions were not given enough credit for some of their solid successes in handling the crisis: food shortages were averted; epidemics were forestalled; electricity, running water, and telephone service were restored in the affected zones within days; and most of the city continued to function even in the immediate aftermath of the cataclysm (Kandell 1988, 571). There have been charges that earthquake relief money had been misappropriated. In fact, international relief funds sent to Mexico after the disaster appear to have been well administered. U.S. officials report that around $4.7 million in assistance from the United States government was accounted for, and the U.S. coordinator for $20 to $30 million in private American disaster aid to Mexico reported that the money went where is was supposed to (Russell 1985, 58).

For some of the reasons discussed above, Comerio comes to the conclusion that the "most efficient distribution of [crisis] recovery resources is through existing housing [institutions]" (Comerio 1995, 42). In the months following the Los Angeles earthquake, the combination of pre-earthquake economic and housing conditions such as high rental vacancies, declining property values, declining rental income, high mortgage debt, and severe reduction of owner equity, made it clear that recovery would not take place without significant public sector intervention due to the scale and complexity of the crisis. Condominiums were a challenge as associations wrestled with their repair options. A single owner can file for a building permit, find a small contractor, do some work themselves, and make repair decisions quickly while they occupy the single-family home; whereas larger structures, such as multi-family apartment buildings in Los Angeles and tenement buildings in Mexico City, require more architecture and engineering design, more complex financing arrangements, longer term construction by a sophisticated contractor, and coordination between the different owners and tenants. The effort to build consensus among owners and lenders required the intervention and mediation on the part of the public sector housing institutions:

> I think we did incent [*sic*] a lot of private behavior to join us [such as with] insurance money to clear very quickly and owners to repair. You can go to [a] lender and you can say, "We know that one of the conditions in your mortgage . . . is that the owner has to keep the collateral in good repair." Call him up! Tell him to get off his butt and fix this building! You can do such things as draw deadlines, and that is what this City [of Los Angeles] did too. If you come in and talk to us and begin the application process by this date, you are going to get this level of benefit. If you wait till down here, when we are probably going to be running out of money, you are going to get a lesser level of benefit. So, you can incent [*sic*] them to do things that will create that momentum to repair in a whole neighborhood at once.[21]

In most of the Ghost Towns, it was clear that the City of Los Angeles would serve, not only as the lender of last resort, but in most cases, as the lender of first resort because of a lack of eligibility for most properties to receive funding from private—banks and insurance companies, state and federal institutions. As such, the City of Los Angeles coordinated a successful effort to garner $321 million in supplemental disaster relief funds from the U.S. Department of Housing and Urban Development to assist property owners—including those in the Ghost Towns—declined by SBA and FEMA's Individual and Family Grant Program (Comerio 1995, 43).

The discussion about the role of public sector institutions in urban planning should focus on taking those actions (e.g., planning) that maximize the benefits of public sector actions and funds (e.g., institutional routines, experience, and legitimacy), and on those circumstances that are both endogenous (e.g., extensive knowledge of constituencies) and exogenous (e.g., political pressures) to these institutions under which they are most effective. This book has made a small contribution to that discussion.

Finally, rethinking will not necessarily provide planning institutions with clear formulas for future directions, but it will prompt them to ask the right questions. Every planning institution, every routine, every program, should be confronted with these questions (Drucker 1995): "What is your mission?", "Is it still the right mission?", and "Is it still a mission worth doing?" Such constant questioning aims to reach two objectives: to understand the purpose, and to understand the morality of planning institutions and their actions. The case for unresolved contradiction and dedication to alternation among incomplete principles depends on some assumptions about the moral consequences of ethical struggle as opposed to ethical clarity. The case for struggle lies in a calculation that it forces more or less continual awareness of moral dilemmas. This maintains a stronger reconsideration of planning actions on the basis of new feelings and experiences, including the experience of guilt and doubt, than does pursuing clear formulas.

Postscript
Planning after September 11, 2001

REBUILDING THE WORLD TRADE CENTER site in New York City after the terrorist attacks of September 11, 2001 is one of the United States' largest and most closely watched urban planning projects in a generation. This challenging task is stringently testing the intricate arrangements of private, public, and nonprofit institutions involved in the undertaking.[1] A brief examination of the New York City case study offers us a more nuanced view of institutional routines than the Renovacion Habitacional Popular, Ghost Town, Hoy No Circula, or Rebuild Los Angeles programs. The rebuilding of Lower Manhattan has involved some success (e.g., in the rapid and safe cleanup of the ruins) and some failure (e.g., in developing a creative and inclusive planning process). We see that some outputs, such as community outreach and institutional coordination, are more significant in this case than in others. And the successful use of institutional routines depends on which routines are utilized, under which circumstances, and through what kind of process, as shown at the end of the postscript.

The planning project raises a number of critical questions. What is to be done with an immensely valuable piece of land that is crucial to the local economy, but also psychologically important—almost spiritual—to people in New York City and around the world? How should New York City, in thinking about what is to come, weigh the needs of its businesses and residents alongside the global statement that the recovery and rebuilding will make about the city in the twenty-first century? In the days after the attacks, an influential group of politicians and developers favored an approach involving the creation of a powerful new government institution led by the state, an institution that could cut through the normal planning process of approvals and expedite the rebuilding. However, others contended that the wounds of the crisis were so deep that priority must be given to soliciting the input of city residents and the families of the victims, even if it slowed the rebuilding process.

The New York City case study can be analyzed using the framework articulated in Chapter 2, and it offers nuanced insights into the deployment (or lack thereof) of institutional routines during periods of significant and unexpected crises. The focus of the postscript is on the first two years—from September 2001 to September 2003—of an ongoing and evolving project which will take considerable time, effort, and resources to accomplish. The New York City case study also offers a unique opportunity for truly deep and sophisticated reflection on the complex nature of planning institutions and routines, much in the same spirit as the examinations of the Renovación Habitacional Popular, Ghost Town, Hoy No Circula, and Rebuild Los Angeles programs.

CRISIS: TERRORIST ATTACKS OF SEPTEMBER 11, 2001

On September 11, 2001, two airplanes hijacked by terrorists flew into the twin 110-story towers of the World Trade Center in Lower Manhattan in New York City. A total of 2,792 people were killed, including those on the two airplanes, those who were in the two buildings, and those who raced into the buildings on a rescue mission after the first plane hit the first building. Apart from the terrible shock and the emotional blow of the attack, the economic impact was severe (Gotham Gazette 2003).

The attacks destroyed 13 million square feet of office space, damaged an additional 21 million square feet, displaced 1,100 tenants, closed 700 small businesses, and eliminated 111,500 jobs in 31 buildings (Jacquemart 2002, 5). Some 450,000 square feet of retail space were lost in the World Trade Center shopping mall. The net economic impacts were estimated at a loss of $16 billion. The area's infrastructure was also severely damaged; 11 subway stations were destroyed, damaged, or closed, and both electricity and telephone services were disrupted. One of the greatest impacts of the attack was on the transportation system. The collapse of the twin towers destroyed or disabled portions of three subway lines, including 1,900 feet of subway tunnel. The downtown Port Authority Trans Hudson (PATH) line connecting Lower Manhattan to New Jersey was disabled, and its World Trade Center station was destroyed. In addition, ferry lines were rerouted and numerous local streets in the immediate vicinity were closed either by the collapse of the buildings or to allow for debris removal.

No disaster in United States history has ever come close to the sheer numbers associated with the crisis engendered by the September 11 attacks (see Figure 7.1). The largest amount of federal disaster relief previously was the $7 billion allocated after the 1994 Los Angeles earthquake.

Figure 7.1 The devastating ruins of the World Trade Center site in Lower Manhattan after the September 11, 2001 terrorist attacks on New York City.
Source: Michael Rieger, Federal Emergency Management Agency, http://www.photolibrary.fema.gov/ photolibrary/index.jsp (accessed on August 25, 2004).

INSTITUTIONAL ACTION: LOWER MANHATTAN DEVELOPMENT CORPORATION

The formation of the Lower Manhattan Development Corporation (LMDC), a subsidiary of the State of New York's Empire State Development Corporation, was announced on November 2, 2001, two months after the tragedy and just before the New York City mayoral election. The board members were announced three weeks later on November 29, 2001 and included one African American, one downtown resident, three officials from the administration of former New York City Mayor Rudy Giuliani, one friend of U.S. President George W. Bush, four Wall Street executives, and one construction union leader. No architects, no cultural leaders, no educators, no families of 9/11 victims, no planners, no urbanists were named as board members (Marcuse 2002, 153). The LMDC was given extensive powers of eminent domain and the ability to override most local zoning and land-use regulations as was the original World Trade Center project thirty years earlier. The Port

Authority of New York and New Jersey actually owned the sixteen-acre site of the former World Trade Center. The rebuilding efforts were estimated to take ten to fifteen years, and cost a total of $7 billion (Bagli 2003, B1).

RAPID ACTION

Just weeks after the attack, Mayor Giuliani and Governor George Pataki began to imagine the rebuilding of Lower Manhattan, and they immediately saw two problems (Wyatt 2003a, B1). The first was Mark Green, the leading candidate for Mayor, a Democrat, and a man neither Republican office-holder could abide. As Mayor, he would assert significant influence over the rebuilding effort. The second was Pataki's own re-election bid the following year. Appearing to exert too much control over the rebuilding effort would leave Pataki vulnerable to charges of manipulating the city's grief to his political ends. That is why on November 2, 2001, four days before New Yorkers went to the polls to choose the Mayor and two months after the crisis began, Pataki and Giuliani announced that a new planning institution, LMDC, would direct the effort.

Almost eleven weeks after the attack, planning for the rebuilding of Lower Manhattan had stalled, as Board members of the LMDC were yet to be named three weeks after its creation. Rebuilding could not proceed until the site had been cleared and vital transportation links were repaired, which was likely to take several months. However, that did not mean that it was too early to assemble a core group of wise and creative minds to help chart the appropriate course for the project to ensure that the area would ultimately become even more robust, imaginative, and appealing that what was there before.

By January 2002, more than three months after the attack, the LMDC board had met just once; the corporation still had no staff or office of its own, and it still lacked an executive director. The chairman of the board John Whitehead knew little about the construction industry and was still being introduced to many of the important city government and civic leaders. Furthermore, actual construction of the largest portions of a rebuilt Lower Manhattan was estimated to take at least another three to five years to begin with. Litigation, insurance payments, environmental concerns, the economic trajectories, and public debate about the victims' memorial would affect the time frame as well. Given such conditions, it appears to have been more important to focus on planning an institutionalized process rather than re-constructing buildings.

A crucial component of the rebuilding is the prospective memorial for those who were killed in the attacks. However, in January 2002, four months after the attack and two months after the creation of the LMDC, Chairman

Whitehead admitted not only that they "did not know yet who will be responsible for making the decisions about what the memorial should be," but also that the "appointment of the groups [was] probably several months ahead" (cited in Wyatt 2002a, B1). These efforts contrast sharply with the process that was adopted in Oklahoma City after the April 1995 bombing of the Federal Building. The consensus for a memorial in Oklahoma was achieved largely because the various groups started communicating early. Within three months of the bombing, a 160-member advisory committee had been established and ten operating committees formed.

Seven months after the attacks, city and state officials speeded up the timetable for the rebuilding process after criticism that the planning was moving too slowly. The Port Authority and the LMDC jointly issued a request for proposals for a design of the site, including spaces for offices, a hotel, retail stores and services, and an analysis of transportation projects. A deadline of July 1, 2002 was set for initial plans, and a final proposal for the development of the site was due by September 1, 2002. Final transportation plans and an urban design for the broader Lower Manhattan area were to be completed by December 1. Teams vying to prepare the master plan had to apply by May 6, less than two weeks after the announcement (Wyatt 2002c). In addition, a schedule for the development of a memorial to the victims of the attack was to be completed by July of the same year.

The unexpectedly fast pace of the cleanup meant that decisions about what to do with the site, which had once seemed a long way off, suddenly seemed to be nearly around the corner. In March 2002, Governor Pataki and Mayor Bloomberg held a news conference during which they presented a detailed slide show of the cleaning up of the WTC site over the past six months, followed by a quick and vague discussion of the status of efforts to plan the future of the site. According to one observer (Nagourney 2002), the planning discussion ended almost as quickly as it had begun, and served as a reminder of the extent to which the cleanup effort has outpaced the LMDC's efforts to draft a master plan for what should happen with the nearly cleared land.

MASSIVE FUNDING

Funding would be a crucial factor in the planning processes following the September 11 crisis, due to the private sector interests in the form of commercial income from the WTC site, and the public sector interests in the form of large amounts of federal funding, much of it allocated even before the LMDC was fully formed. However, a set of principles for action and a preliminary blueprint for renewal released in early April 2002 did not discuss how much the proposals would cost, or how many of them could be paid for with the $21 billion that the U.S. Congress had appropriated for the city's rebuilding efforts.

The World Trade Center site generated billions of dollars. Lower Manhattan is the third largest central business district in the United States, and the World Trade Center was a key component (Helmore 2003, 3). Perhaps the most pressing constraint of the intricate sets of institutional imperatives has been the desire of the Port Authority, which owns the land, to obtain commercial development that would continue to generate more than $120 million a year in revenue from the site. Thus, the primary concept apparent in the six preliminary plans released by the Port Authority and the LMDC was the restoration of all of the commercial real estate by funneling it back onto the same site but in slightly different physical forms. The principal interests served are those of the Port Authority, the developer, Larry Silverstein, and the shopping mall developer, Westfield America, in a manner reminiscent of the urban renewal of Lower Manhattan in the 1960s.

Larry Silverstein and the Port Authority were also in a legal battle against the insurance companies that provided coverage for the WTC. Silverstein contended that he is entitled to a double payment of nearly $7 billion because two planes hit two towers in what he describes as two separate occurrences on September 11. The insurance companies claimed that the developer is due only the policy limit, about $3.5 billion, a sum that Silverstein said is not enough to rebuild the complex. In addition, Westfield America, holder of the lease for retail space at the WTC, announced in September 2003 that it was negotiating a cash settlement to pull out of its deal on the downtown complex. The company signed a nonbinding letter of intent with the Port Authority to give up its contract for $140 million (Bagli 2003, B1). Westfield had resisted efforts to create more retail at street level. While the move could have cleared the way for significant design changes sought in the rebuilding process, it raised questions about how much money would be available if there were other buyouts.

In the months after the attack, the Bush administration pledged $21.4 billion to address the crisis. The extraordinary and massive allocation of federal government funding, while less than local elected officials had petitioned for, was meant to reassure, restore, and restart emotionally and economically ravaged Lower Manhattan and New York City. More than fifteen months later, by December 2002, between $4.5 billion and $5 billion was provided, making possible early progress in providing for victims and establishing some sense of recovery for the city (Wyatt et al. 2002). Approximately $600 million was allocated to cover the costs of the monumental task of cleaning up the site, and an additional $401 million had been distributed to around 10,000 area businesses to help them continue. And $493 million in tax free bonds were approved to help finance major construction projects, including three residential complexes around Ground Zero. However, many victims' families, business executives, and community groups were both confused and angry about why, more than a year after the most serious terrorist attack on American soil, less than a quarter of the U.S. federal government's promise of massive funding had been realized, why hundreds of millions of dollars that had been transferred to officials of the City of New York had gone unclaimed, and why firm decisions had yet to be made on how additional billions of dollars were actually to be spent. By April 2002, it was clear that approximately $19 billion of the $21.5 billion President Bush had promised to New York City for the rebuilding effort was expected to be channeled through the Empire State Development Corporation (ESDC) rather than through the LMDC (Wyatt 2002c).

One of the biggest question marks in the federal government's massive funding was the $5.5 Liberty Zone tax package intended to stimulate employment and the construction of new office towers, residential buildings, and retail shops in Lower Manhattan. The $5.5 billion, which appeared to be a large amount when first announced to anxious residents in March of 2002, was actually the value over time of the tax breaks accorded to employers and construction projects that contractors and entrepreneurs might undertake, and not an infusion of cash (Wyatt et al. 2002). Furthermore, with an economic recession and ongoing job losses in the financial sector located on and near Wall Street, there was little demand for new office towers in Lower Manhattan, and in fact, there was more vacant office space in Manhattan— 46.4 million square feet—than there was office space in the entire city of San Francisco.

The distribution of funding from the U.S. Department of Housing and Urban Development had been complicated for months by the decision of the U.S. Congress to use two different institutions to deliver it. The Congress gave responsibility for $700 million in aid to the ESDC and then opted to direct $2.7 billion through the LMDC (Wyatt et al. 2002). When the ESDC requested around $800 million in additional funding to continue its grant programs and business retention efforts it had to go through the LMDC, which turned over only $350 million, and then requested a full accounting of the funding the ESDC had already handed out. As of December 2002, $1.3 billion of the $2.7 billion given to the LMDC still remained unspent and unallocated. This money was coveted by a number of people including Mayor Bloomberg, who had his own ambitious plan to build housing, revitalize business districts, and improve transportation.

The crisis also focused attention on Lower Manhattan and prompted the government to offer financial incentives for people to move in. The exodus of downtown neighbors following the attacks was so dramatic that by December 2001, some 25 percent of all rental apartments below Chambers

Street were vacant (Herman 2003). In response, landlords slashed rents, and the LMDC promised $280 million in grants to people who would commit to living in the area below Canal and Delancey streets for two years—including tenants who already lived there.

In May of 2002, a revised housing aid plan by the LMDC increased to $1,750 the amount available to residents in the area which extended north from Canal Street to Delancey or Kenmare streets and east from Lafayette Street to the East River (Wyatt 2002d, B4). The new benefit was similar to that already proposed for Manhattan residents who lived below Canal Street. Households with at least one child under the age of eighteen that had committed to remain in the area for at least one year would receive a $750 family bonus. In addition, as previously proposed, a $1,000 grant per household was available to residents who had been living in the area on September 11, 2001. The proposed revision was included in a $300 million assistance plan for people and businesses affected by the terrorist attack. In July 2003, the U.S. Secretary of Housing and Urban Development Mel Martinez, Governor Pataki, and Mayor Bloomberg announced that the LMDC would allocate $50 million in HUD funding, including surplus from the LMDC Residential Grant Program, for an affordable-housing initiative (LMDC 2003d). The grant is intended to fund approximately 300 affordable units for moderate to middle-income working families in the income range of approximately $50,000 to $85,000. By September 2003, more than 40,000 people had applied and more than $180 million in grants had been approved. Some 50 percent of those who applied for residential grants were not living in the area prior to September 11.

Unlike the post-crisis case studies discussed thus far, the massive funding for the rebuilding of Lower Manhattan was—at least in theory—generous and forthcoming. However, it soon became clear that President Bush's commitment of $21 billion for the rebuilding effort was largely a symbolic, and indeed political, gesture. An example is the $5.5 billion for the so-called Liberty Zone, which was a series of multi-year concessions from the payment of taxes rather than the massive infusion of funding that it initially appeared to be. Furthermore, the funding was dominated by narrow private interests rather than a sense of a larger common interest in the future of the area. Such private interests included the $120 million in annual commercial revenue generated by the WTC site, and the minimum $3.5 billion that the lease holding developer would receive in insurance compensation.

IMPROVED CONDITIONS

The rebuilding of the World Trade Center area was supposed to be an once-in-a-lifetime opportunity for some of the brightest architects, urban designers, and planners an to come up with breathtaking innovations and urban solutions to enhance the quality of Lower Manhattan's built environment. "The real challenge is to overcome the constraints and to recognize that the plans should be geared to the future, not the past," said Mitchell Moss, Director of the Taub Urban Research Center at New York University (cited in Bagli 2002, B1). "This is a once-in-a-century opportunity to rebuild Lower Manhattan with new transportation, housing, and open spaces, as well as creative commercial development."

The designers and planners envisioning the future of the site had to grapple with a latticework of financial considerations and commercial development objectives, which resulted in some remarkable similarities for the six preliminary site plans commissioned by the LMDC. A major reason is that all six proposals started not with blank slates and visionary ideas, but rather with a set of parameters: a relatively dense eleven million square feet of office space (which is the equivalent of five Empire State Buildings), 600,000 square feet of retail space, and an 800-room hotel (Bagli 2002, B1). Some of the proposals included a museum or cultural institutions, but none included the multi-family housing that is essential for creating a vibrant neighborhood all day and all week. With nearly 20 percent of Lower Manhattan office space vacant and little demand for new skyscrapers, community groups advocated greater emphasis on residential and cultural development.

The design community clearly defined improved conditions solely on design criteria. For example, Robert Ivy, editor of the magazine *Architectural Record*, said that the architecture community is "concerned that the [developer] Larry Silverstein not have too heavy a hand in influencing what was a powerful vision [of the architects]" (cited in Grimes 2003, 20). However if one examines the architectural history of New York City closely, one finds that developers with commercial interests at heart built the city's most beloved buildings, such as the Empire State Building and Rockefeller Center.

Surprised by the negative response of communities and mindful of upcoming elections, city and state officials began to look for alternative planning approaches. By August of 2002, talk had begun about properties surrounding the WTC site. For example, New York City offered to trade the land it owned under La Guardia and Kennedy airports, for which the Port Authority paid a substantial rent due to further increase, in exchange for the WTC site. This would have brought Ground Zero and its rebuilding under city control and gotten the Port Authority out of planning and development in Lower Manhattan and back to transportation and infrastructure facilities, where its role is more appropriate (Huxtable 2002).

The LMDC rebuilding plans, as of September 2003, included a regional transport network of trains, buses, ferries, and routes connecting the city's airports as well as a broader vision to transform Lower Manhattan into a lively community served by new cultural institutions and public spaces. Plans extended far beyond the footprint of the World Trade Center, with parks, tree-lined avenues, pedestrian walkways, and 3,000 new housing units (Murray 2003, 1).

After September 11, New Yorkers were surprised to discover new view corridors that had been blocked for decades by the World Trade Center. Suddenly, they could see the Winter Garden from Broadway, and Battery Park City no longer seemed so isolated. There was a tremendous opportunity to rebuild Lower Manhattan into a more attractive and humane neighborhood. Furthermore, before September 11, Lower Manhattan had one of the highest densities of any business district in the world, and one of the highest proportions of transit users, with about 85 percent of commuters arriving by transit (Jacquemart 2002, 9). Even though the two towers were 110 stories tall, the WTC site was built at a floor-area ratio (FAR) of only fourteen, less than the average FAR of sixteen for Midtown Manhattan. That means it would be possible to provide the same floor area at a much lower height, thus further improving physical conditions in the area.

The role of the private sector in improving conditions is both central and ambiguous. Even though Whitehead claimed that the LMDC would work with the private sector to determine a market-driven response, the fact of the matter is that the movement of the office market was away from Lower Manhattan and toward Brooklyn and New Jersey (Marcuse 2002, 155–156). Thus, questions linger over whether Lower Manhattan can ever draw back all the businesses it housed before the terrorist attacks. Many companies have already relocated to other parts of the metropolitan region, and for security reasons, few would now contemplate putting all their operations in one building. Empire Blue Cross and Blue Shield, the health insurance provider that had 3,000 employees in its World Trade Center headquarters, has relocated its primary facilities to Brooklyn, as has the Bank of New York and the back offices of the New York Stock Exchange (Murray 2003, 1). What is clear is that the private sector (e.g., developers, banks, corporations) had been heavily involved in the building of the World Trade Center and is doing so again, but not by working through the market; rather it is pursuing its interests through the public sphere.

Due to the symbolic significance of the rebuilding of the World Trade Center site and its surroundings, improved conditions, along with community outreach, is an output particularly worthy of attention. In this case, the non-physical aspects (i.e., the planning process) are more important than the physical aspects (i.e., the planning product). Thus, greater effort needed to be bestowed upon how the recovery was to be planned, including mechanisms for collective and deep reflection, dialogue and debate, and a carefully considered process of city re-imagining and re-building. The LMDC began with an approach of essentially replacing lost office space, while housing advocates, planners, and community groups pursued ideas of truly improved conditions that included affordable housing units and mixed land uses. A key point of such improved conditions was to renegotiate the lease with the developer so that it would not become the driving force leading to simply replacing lost commercial opportunities. Similarly, widening the pool of designers and planners was one step in the creation of a larger variety of rebuilding strategies.

COMMUNITY OUTREACH

Community outreach in the LMDC can be seen in the degree of community representation on the board, mechanisms of public input, and the degree of transparency in the actual design and planning process of the WTC site. An urban planning scholar, Peter Marcuse, has noted that the board sounds more like the kind of heavyweight body that views itself as having unlimited authority to get things done, in the style of the Robert Moses era, than a diverse, thoughtful, deliberating body guiding a city through a democratic process to elucidate its own general interest (Marcuse 2002, 154).

From the beginning, it was clear that Governor Pataki would control the endeavor, for he appointed seven of the corporation's initial eleven board members, including the chairman, and the board became a subsidiary of Empire State Development Corporation, the state's economic development institution, run by one of the Governor's closest allies, Charles Gargano. Reflecting the overwhelming importance of the financial industry in the minds of the governor and the mayor, the board is heavy with representatives from Wall Street, including John Whitehead, age 79—a reflection of conservative (rather than creative) thinking in the LMDC leadership. Chief among other members is Richard Grasso, former chairman of the New York Stock Exchange, appointed to the LMDC by Mayor Giuliani. Grasso's presence was considered vital to the status of Lower Manhattan as the nation's financial capital. Pataki appointed two other financial industry representatives, such as Frank Zarb, the former chairman of NASDAQ, and Deborah Wright, the chief executive of the Federal Savings Bank in Harlem. Pataki also appointed Ed Malloy, president of the Building Construction Trade Council of Greater New York. The LMDC was expected to solicit investment by private entities in the rebuilding effort, including union pension plans.

The original board was notably light on representatives of small businesses, among those hardest hit by the economic stagnation that has settled much over Lower Manhattan after September 11, 2001 (Wyatt 2001). The original board had only one representative (Madelyn Wils, chairperson of Community Board 1) of the downtown residents, small businesses, and cultural institutions that were most affected by the attack's economic fallout. Also lacking direct representation were many of the neighborhoods below Houston Street that were not in the area immediately surrounding the WTC, including Chinatown, SoHo, and parts of Little Italy.

In early April 2002, Mayor Bloomberg appointed four additional members to the LMDC board, bringing the number of mayoral appointees to eight. The new members would significantly change the ethnic makeup of the board, which had been criticized by City Council members for including only one member of a minority group and two women. The new appointees were Sally Hernandez-Pinero, an attorney who had been Deputy Mayor for Economic Development under former Mayor David Dinkins; Billie Tsien, a principal of the architecture firm Tod Williams, Billie Tsien and Associates; E. Stanley O'Neal, president and chief operating officer of Merrill Lynch; and Carl Weisbrod, president of the Alliance for Downtown New York, a business improvement organization. Hernandez-Pinero is Hispanic, Tsien is an Asian American, and O'Neal is an African American. As in the Rebuild Los Angeles case study, which too involved belated appointments of women and ethnic minority board members, it is unclear at best whether such token diversity has any effect at all on genuine community outreach.

The primary public input mechanism of the LMDC is a General Advisory Council, which was supposed to seek input from a wider array of community groups, business owners, and other stakeholders in the future of Lower Manhattan, and to make recommendations to the board based on that input. However, less than 20 percent of those who lost their jobs as a direct result of the terrorist attack lived in Manhattan, and many of those who lost their lives or their jobs were immigrants, who have not been represented. At the very least this is a regional project concerning the entire New York City metropolitan area (rather than just Lower Manhattan); from a broader perspective, this is in fact a project of global significance. Yet the General Advisory Council's outreach remains limited to the most vested stakeholders in the immediate area.

Moreover, some Lower Manhattan residents who had already been active in efforts to help shape the rebuilding plans said that the advisory committee suffered from the some of the flaws of the LMDC itself. "When I look at it from a neighborhood standpoint, the people who are working most directly with the neighborhood don't appear to have prominent positions on the list," said Beverly Willis, a co-chairwoman of the Rebuilding Downtown, Our Town, a group of residents, small business people, civic groups, and other interested in the rebuilding effort (cited in Wyatt 2002, B3). Furthermore, as late as April 2002, seven months after the attack, the process involving the victims' families in the memorial was unclear. "I have concerns about the memorial process," said Amanda Burden, chairwoman of the City

Planning commission (cited in Wyatt 2002c, B1). "Right now, the family members have no clear idea of what the process is, so their anxieties and concerns are totally understandable."

In a manner reminiscent of RLA, the LMDC had established, by September 2003, a cumbersome set of institutional arrangements as public input mechanisms in order to address criticism of a lack of genuine community outreach. Thus, in addition to the now sixteen-member board of directors, the LMDC had nine Advisory Councils, including a General Advisory Council, a Families Advisory Council, a Residents Council, and a Restaurants, Retailers and Small Business Advisory Council. Once again, though, one finds a significant presence of the private sector in the Development Advisory Council (e.g., large developers such as Tishman Speyer Properties), the Financial Services Advisory Council (e.g., multinational banks such as Credit Suisse First Boston), and the Professional Firms Advisory Council (e.g., international consulting firms such as Deloitte and Touche). A study of the minutes of the meetings of the Advisory Councils reveals a range of community participation, from the cursory in the General Advisory to the more engaging in the Residents Council (LMDC 2003a).

A key point in the design process was in late September 2002, when the LMDC announced the selection of six planning and design teams to study the future of the WTC site. The six teams spanned a range of generations, nationalities, and architectural points of view. The six teams were: (1) The THINK team, consisting of Frederic Schwartz and Rafael Viñoly of New York, and Shigeru Ban of Tokyo; (2) United Architects, a group of younger and more experimental designers including Greg Lynn, Ben van Berkel of UN Studio and Reiser Umemoto; (3) Sir Norman Foster of Great Britain; (4) a team of some of the most well-known American architects including Richard Meier, Peter Eisenman, Charles Gwathmey, and Steven Holl; (5) Skidmore, Owings and Merrill the large corporate architecture, urban design and planning; and (6) Daniel Libeskind, the Polish American architect.

To address the perceived shortcomings of the six early proposals, the LMDC called for some of the world's "star" architects to think in grandiose terms about the future of the site. In December 2002, nine plans from seven groups of architects were unveiled. The competition was soon whittled down to Libeskind and the team known as THINK. Both design proposals contained primarily public space and public functions, with room for office buildings, retails stores, and other commercial development around the edges of the site. The THINK project proposed a pair of steel latticework towers, each more than 1,600 feet tall and containing cultural facilities such as museums. Libeskind's project centered around what would be the tallest structure in the world and office buildings with crystalline forms and slicing angles. The part of Libeskind's project that attracted the most attention was

Figure 7.2 The selected design for the World Trade Center site by Daniel Libeskind.
Source: ©Jock Pottle/Esto, March 2003.

the exposed slurry wall of concrete that formed the foundation of the original twin towers, nicknamed the "bathtub" (see Figure 7.2).[2]

In the end, Libeskind's project was selected. However, more significant than the design is the process by which it was selected and the question of who the actual clients are. The two teams approached the final weeks of the competition in very different ways, which had a significant bearing on their fortunes. The THINK team spent nearly all its time working on the elaborate engineering of its cultural towers. Libeskind, meanwhile, spent several days cloistered with the Port Authority officials working to satisfy their desires for underground parking and mechanical systems.

Due to the enormous symbolic, economic, and historic significance of this site, the role of the lead architect is a challenging one. The role of the lead architect of the rebuilding project, Daniel Libeskind, is complicated by the fact that eight million New Yorkers are actually his clients, in that all New Yorkers see him as working for them. Libeskind himself is somewhat delusional about his relationship to his "clients," including the supposed transparency of the process: "And you have to remember that this design was selected . . . not in a boardroom by some elite backroom dealers. It was done in a transparent process with all the citizens of New York and 50 million people voting on the Internet. My responsibility is to that great constituency" (Libeskind cited in Helmore, 3). In fact, the final decision was made by Governor Pataki, who overturned the jury's decision to award the project to another team of designers, called THINK, led by Rafael Viñoly.

The day before the architects made their final pitches, a committee of LMDC directors recommended that THINK team's design be chosen, and one committee member told the *New York Times*, "We don't expect anyone to overrule us" (cited in Wyatt 2003b, 4). Aides say that comment incensed Pataki and caused him to favor Libeskind. Mayor Bloomberg also favored the Libeskind plan. Hours before a committee of officials from the Port Authority, the LMDC, the Governor, and the Mayor's offices were supposed to meet to choose a winner, the decision was already sealed.

In contrast to what happened with the LMDC, greater transparency in the design process can yield surprising results. The city of San Francisco rebuilt the Embarcadero district after the 1989 earthquake with a wide-open democratic process, and the result is a creative rejuvenation of a once-moribund waterfront. A committee in an open design competition that was rife with debate selected the moving and stunning design of the Vietnam Veterans Memorial in Washington.

Given the significance of this planning project, community outreach is one of the most crucial—and complicated—outputs of the LMDC. Ever since the community forums organized by the Civic Alliance with nearly 5,000 citizens and described later in this chapter, the officials at the LMDC have congratulated themselves for what came of that experiment in civics: Acting on the public's rejection of the original six plans, they went back to the drawing board, and the architect Daniel Libeskind emerged with a winning design. "It was the aggressive outreach to a broader public that resulted in the consensus behind this plan," crowed Governor Pataki (cited in Wyatt

2003b, 4). But for all the talk of groundbreaking public participation, government officials who have guided the planning with a firm hand have made many significant decisions out of public view. For example, the story of the evolution of the design by Libeskind turns less on the will of the public than on the political imperatives of Pataki, who was running for re-election in autumn 2002. The 2002 version of the rebuilding plan attempted to satisfy several constituencies: the victims' families, who wanted significant space for a memorial; neighborhood residents and architects, who wanted to breakup the sixteen-acre superblock; and the Port Authority, that wanted to keep receiving $120 million in annual rents from the site. However, a key aspect of satisfying these constituencies was to fulfill another goal: muting any significant controversy over the Ground Zero rebuilding project that could disrupt Pataki's re-election campaign. The new thrust in the rebuilding process came after Governor Pataki's re-election, since he then had less reason to worry that his decisions about the rebuilding could hurt him politically, according to state officials (Wyatt 2003b, 49). The lack of community outreach also depended on financial considerations.

Much like the output of massive funding, community outreach has been somewhat of a game between appearances and on-the-ground reality. The appointment of the LMDC board demonstrated not only that governor of New York state was in charge, but also that in his mind political and financial interests came first. The Advisory Councils were an afterthought, and two years into the project, did not show much promise in mobilizing or even incorporating community concerns. Similarly, the design process and funding mechanisms reinforce the dominance of private business interests in the rebuilding process.

INSTITUTIONAL COORDINATION

The institutional coordination of the LMDC is notable for its exclusion of local planning institutions, as well as the dominance of state government institutions, such as the Port Authority and ESDC, even though LMDC Chairman Whitehead suggested that the LMDC was not beholden to them. Furthermore, LMDC case study reveals a key aspect of institutional coordination: power relations. In the power struggles over the rebuilding, Pataki engineered predominance over New York City's civic leadership. It has been Pataki, and not Bloomberg, who controls appointments to the nominally independent LMDC (Helmore 2003). The governor also has been the one to set the first hard deadlines for the list of rebuilding projects, largely overriding the Bloomberg.

At a news conference in March 2002, Pataki and Bloomberg tried to end confusion about precisely who had the final authority over what happens at the site, which was stirred by the convoluted structure of the LMDC, and the conflicting lines of authority under the mayor, the governor, and the site's owners, the Port Authority of New York and New Jersey. "At the end of the day, the Mayor and the Governor are responsible, and we're proud to have responsibility," the governor said while the mayor enthusiastically nodded in agreement (cited in Nagourney 2002, B1). However, the LMDC remained a subsidiary of the Empire State Development Corporation and thus remained an agency of the State of New York, notwithstanding the mayor's appointees.

The planning process spawned intense rivalries over which institution was in fact in charge of the rebuilding effort. Those rivalries were most evident in April 2002 when the LMDC issued a request for proposals for an urban planner to complete designs for the site and the surrounding areas. Within days the request was withdrawn after Port Authority officials objected, saying that they were not adequately consulted (Wyatt 2002c). A few days later, the Port Authority issued its own call for plans. Although it was similar to the earlier one and was issued in cooperation with the LMDC, it made clear that the Port Authority was driving the plans for the site. The rivalries between the two institutions became enough of an issue that they agreed to a memorandum of understanding laying out details of how they would work together: the LMDC would basically solicit input from the public and from government institutions about the process and take the lead role in planning for a memorial, while the Port Authority would have more of a say over the WTC site.

Further tension surfaced over what appears to be separate planning efforts at the two agencies. In August 2002, when the LMDC conducted a news conference to announce it would hire several new teams of architects to draw up more innovative plans for the WTC site, executives from the Port Authority were absent. The next month, just days before the new teams were selected, the Port Authority hired its own architectural firm, Ehrenkrantz Eckstut & Kuhn, as an in-house consultant on the site.

The success of the rebuilding process and the end result depend on the LMDC and the Port Authority overcoming their obvious mutual distrust (Wyatt 2002e, 49). This distrust was much in evidence at a meeting in October 2002, when a task force of state, White House, and Port Authority officials met to hammer out the detailed instructions to be given to the seven architecture and planning groups. Since the public rejection in July of the initial plans for the WTC site, officials from other agencies had pressed the Port Authority to loosen its demands that all of the 11 million square feet of commercial space destroyed on September 11 be restored. At the October 2002 meeting, Joseph Seymour, the executive director of the Port Authority, finally agreed to allow the architects to place anywhere from 6.5 million to

10 million square feet of office space on the site, as long as the remainder was on other parcels of land nearby. Wary that the Port Authority would renege on its promise, Roland Betts, a LMDC director who heads that institution's site planning committee, hastily scribbled an outline of the terms on a piece of scrap paper and passed it around for each of the eight people present to sign, according to four people who were at the meeting (Wyatt 2002e, 49). The gesture evoked nervous laughter, but it continued to grate on Port Authority officials.

Even if the Port Authority played a less conspicuous role, the City of New York's choices about recovery and rebuilding would still be constrained by decisions made in the state capital, Albany. The chair is the designee of Pataki of the State of New York and John C. Whitehead, former co-chair and senior partner of the Wall Street investment firm, Goldman Sachs. Since 1999, he has donated $51,000 to the state Republican Committee and the maximum amount allowed under the law, $30,700, to Governor Pataki (Marcuse 2002, 154). Pataki also made a majority of the sixteen appointments to the board of the LMDC and thus has had a large say in how federal recovery funds—such as $2.7 billion in Community Development Block Grant funds—are spent. The governor's loyalties are further reflected in the fact that, a year after the attack, all three of the New York State's sponsored housing construction deals financed for Lower Manhattan by federal recovery funds have been dedicated to luxury rental housing.

INSTITUTIONAL ROUTINES

The New York case study is indeed a messy one. As of September 2003, there were ongoing battles between Silverstein and the families of the victims, and between Silverstein and Libeskind. The battles were over what will be built and when, as Silverstein, several victims' organizations, insurance companies, state government, and city officials are involved. Silverstein would like more office space than provided in Libeskind's design, and has criticized the design as impractical. Silverstein demoted the architect from being the chief designer to a collaborating architect, and appointed another architect, David Childs, to be the lead designer of the project's centerpiece, the Freedom Tower. Several lawsuits were ongoing or expected. How effective could institutionalized routines possibly be in such a fluid situation? The LMDC chose not to follow such familiar and tested precedents appropriately adapted to changing circumstances. Routines were not only available, but also effectively applied by other institutions involved in the post-September 11 crisis recovery efforts.

Three examples will serve to illustrate the usefulness of routines, including the potential use of established New York City and New York State planning procedures and community outreach practices. From the perspective of a broader planning process and more diverse development, the more active involvement of the City of New York would have been welcome. A city-guided process would most likely be subjected to the Uniform Land Use Review Procedure mandated by the city charter, and thus redevelopment would probably also be more open and participatory under the city's supervision than under the LMDC (Wolf-Powers 2002).

Initially, the LMDC and the Port Authority failed to identify potential development sites beyond Ground Zero, including land, buildings, roads or rights of way owned or controlled by state and public agencies, and opportunities for linkage, trades, or air-rights zoning transfers, among others (Huxtable 2002). Such institutionalized routines are available, but both the Empire State Development Corporation (ESDC)—the parent corporation of the LMDC—and the Port Authority have even stronger planning and development tools. For example, they can override local zoning completely, issue bonds to finance construction, and use the power of eminent domain to condemn and purchase land. These routines open the door to much more creative and broader planning possibilities than have yet been presented.

In January 2002, two months after the chairman of the LMDC declared that a memorial to those lost in September 11 would be its main priority, the groups of victims' families had barely begun to speak to each other. LMDC officials had made public statements that the views of victims' families, downtown residents and others would be considered in planning the memorial, yet the corporation had not made public any set of formalized practices for making a decision, and other public sector planning institutions appeared to be steering clear of such a critical issue. Absent any set of institutionalized practices, hundreds of people in roughly a dozen ad hoc groups had started gathering in small numbers and discussing plans for a memorial. "We can't just go on as we are saying people should put out whatever designs they want and hopefully one of them will resonate with someone," said Frederic Bell (cited in Wyatt 2002a, B1), executive director of the New York chapter of the American Institute of Architects and a member of New York New Visions, a coalition of architecture, planning, and design groups which was hoping to influence the rebuilding of Lower Manhattan. "Some formalized process [i.e., institutionalized practice] needs to be put together, and it should happen immediately [i.e., rapid action]."

As described in previous chapters, the relative effectiveness of routines also depends on issues of institutional legitimacy, specialization, and fit. The institutional legitimacy of the LMDC was jeopardized from the onset by a board of Directors dominated by corporate executives and only one community representative, and by the political tug-of-war between the city and the state. One method of establishing legitimacy over time would have been to make the planning as informed, democratic and transparent as possible. An effective example of this is the Civic Alliance to Rebuild Downtown New York.

The Civic Alliance is a coalition of more than eighty-five civic, business, environmental, community, university, and labor groups seeking to develop consensus strategies for recovery and rebuilding in Lower Manhattan. The Civic Alliance was convened by the non-profit Regional Plan Association in partnership with three educational institutions: the Wagner Graduate School of Public Service at New York University, the Milano Graduate School at New School University, and the Center for Community and Environmental Development at Pratt Institute.

The Civic Alliance's Listening to the City forum brought more than 4,300 people to the Javits Convention Center in July 2002, another 200 participated in a second forum later that month, and more than 800 took part in the two-week online Internet dialogue that followed (Civic Alliance 2002, 2). Contrary to the claims of the LMDC (LMDC 2003c), this was not an LMDC event; rather, the LMDC was one of fifteen underwriters of the event, and LMDC members were present as observers to listen to the discussions of the participants. Participants in these community forums were asked to give their thoughts about six preliminary concepts for the WTC site a few days after the designs were unveiled.

Many criticized the plans as too dull and too commercial. The participants also called on planning institutions to seek ways of rebuilding not only the actual WTC site, but also the neighborhoods around it, including the need to make much-needed housing and transportation infrastructure improvements. A key recommendation that emerged from the forums was that every effort be made to cancel the current lease for the site, so that planning decisions would not be governed by its primarily commercial requirements. An important goal of Listening to the City was to use new technologies (e.g., video conferencing and the Internet) to make it possible for a broad cross-section of the region to help set priorities for Lower Manhattan and surrounding areas. The public's involvement has had an impact: it is partially responsible for the LMDC's decision to scrap the six original plans for the World Trade Center site and start afresh.

An example of successful institutional specialization was the cleanup process for the site after the attacks. The cleanup work turned out to be much quicker, less expensive and safer than expected. The estimated cost was revised to a low of $600 million, after early estimates of as high as $200 billion (Nagourney 2002, B1). The task of removing over 1.5 million ton of debris from the World Trade Center site was immense, as it involved over 3 million man-hours of labor and over 100,000 truckloads (Gotham Gazette

2003). The cost of cleaning up was estimated to be up to a staggering $7 billion, but ended up costing much less: $750 million. During the course of the six-month cleanup project, all of the subway stations, except four, had reopened, and office workers were returning to the area at an unexpectedly fast clip.

Despite the many problems discovered in the cleanup operations, including instances of looting by firefighters, police, and construction workers, the dismantling of the WTC ruins was a success, according to the most detailed account of the operation (Langewiesche 2002). Within a few months, the complicated and painstaking task of identifying the remains of nearly 1,300 of the dead had been accomplished, and just as importantly, no one was killed in the cleanup operation, despite the enormous dangers to be found in the ruins. One-and-a-half-million tons of the ruins were extracted from the sixteen acres of the site, and sent on a twenty-six-mile journey to the Fresh Kills Landfill for sorting, final inspection, and burial. The success of the operation was due to a planning institution of the City of New York, the Department of Design and Construction, because of its equipment, its connections, and most of all the initiative shown by its leadership, especially commissioner Kenneth Holden. The paradox of this successful operation is that while the World Trade Center's monolithic presence visibly represented, at some level, the command and control ideals of 1960s planning and urban renewal, the cleanup, on the other hand had an unruly but productive free-flowing quality in which people of different classes and backgrounds had the opportunity to step in and make contributions as individuals, but within a clear mandate.

The challenges faced by the LMDC were more multi-faceted in terms of institutional specialization. The LMDC would have to sift through numerous suggestions about how to build not only on the WTC site, but also adjacent areas affected by the attack. It would have to work closely with the Port Authority, which owned the site, and Larry Silverstein, who owned the lease and was bound to receive a substantial insurance payment. The LMDC would have to serve as an advocate for federal assistance and would be asked to devise strategies for coaxing business and residents back to the area. A memorial to the WTC victims would have to be designed, most likely with extensive community input, especially from the emotionally charged victims' families. Such an agenda was large and complex, with pressure to show some sort of a tangible result in a short period of time.[3]

The multi-faceted nature of the crisis suggested several recovery strategies, including the creation of multiple specializations within one planning institution (e.g., economic development, housing finance, physical planning, regional transportation), or extensive institutional coordination (e.g., at the city, state, and federal levels, and with community groups). Instead, the LMDC chose to adopt a more single-minded path of primarily replacing lost commercial space and income.

The issue of institutional fit best illustrates the dances that effective planning institutions engage in—between a set of established and familiar routines on the one hand and a set of unexpected and changing circumstances on the other. Effective fit depends on extensive knowledge of current conditions, a trial-and-error approach of testing and modifying familiar strategies, or a combination of the two. The LMDC chose none of these options. Even though the crisis of September 11 was vast in scope and unique in nature, one strong basis for effective planning is to have a sophisticated understanding of the situation. For example, a wealth of information was available—and could have been put to use—from local planning institutions involved in past and current studies of the area. If there were an attempt at such an in-depth understanding of existing conditions, and an effort to devise a truly creative program (rather than simply replacing what existed on the WTC site) the outcomes would be different and much better than expected.

Recovery from this crisis involves bringing back some sense of normalcy in the short term, ensuring that infrastructure including transportation and communications systems are working. Simultaneously, it involves establishing a deliberate and thoughtful process based primarily on those routines promoting democracy, inclusivity, and creativity. Such a process would foster hard and deep thinking about what kind of city New York would like to become, how best to remember the dead, and how best to address the multi-faceted needs of downtown residents. Such a process could transform the crisis into a true turning point, not simply by freezing a moment in time with a memorial, not simply by arrogantly rebuilding bigger and better, and not simply by bending to market forces and performing legalistic maneuvers. Ultimately, the city will be best served if decision makers view the crisis as a unique opportunity and an open-ended experiment for broadly defined planning institutions and planning processes.

Appendix
Research Methodology and Interview Questions

BASED ON AN INTERROGATIVE PROCESS OF CRITICAL THINKING, the research methodology adopted for this study is a combination of case study, narrative, and comparative research strategies, which are described in the following sections. Institutional theories and the analytical framework outlined in the preceding chapters guided the gathering of data and empirical evidence, which subsequently influenced the analytical framework. Thus, the evidence also contains a bias and a limitation because it is from an institutional perspective; that is, the research methodology attempts to discover insights by applying some of the ideas of institutional literature. The units of analysis were the outputs of the recovery programs. From these short-term institutional results, I worked backwards asking "how?" and "why?" questions about the institutional routines (i.e., established arrangements, policies, programs, and practices) that the outputs were based upon.

The overall research design consists of comparative case studies, which investigate the nature of housing policies and institutional activities before and after the earthquakes of 1985 in Mexico City and 1994 in Los Angeles. Such a comparative analysis allows for understanding two phenomena: in what manner housing policies shifted, if at all, in response to crisis situations, and the differences and similarities in such shifts in two different contexts. The elements of the research design include research questions, research propositions, units of analysis, logic linking data to propositions, and criteria for interpreting findings (Yin 1994).

The logic linking the collected data to the research propositions is essentially based on pattern matching. This informed and focused data collection method consisted of primary data (e.g., open-ended interviews, site visits, and census data gathering), and secondary data (e.g., newspaper accounts, journal articles, and scholarly books). The criteria for interpreting findings is based on an inquiry about how well the findings match with the analytical framework, limitations, insights, policy implications, and alternative or complementary explanations. The data analysis and the interpretation of findings were conducted through an analytical framework primarily, of institutional analysis, and secondarily, of crisis situations as policy analysis and institutional effectiveness.

The type of data analyzed from Mexico City and Los Angeles includes census data on socio-economic profiles, types, and quantities of housing; official housing policy documents of public sector institutions at the local, regional, and national levels; taped interviews with institutional representatives and researchers; newspaper accounts of the earthquakes and the housing recovery programs; journal articles on earthquake recovery and the housing programs; slides and photographs of the housing projects and their surrounding neighborhoods; and books on the political-economy of the two cities.

CASE STUDIES

The fundamental research methodology applied in gathering evidence for each housing recovery program in Mexico City and Los Angeles was the case study approach: that is, a "how?" and "why?" question was asked about a relatively contemporary set of events over which the investigator had little or no control. The evidence-gathering methodology tried to illustrate an institutional action or set of actions: why they were taken, how they were implemented, and with what short-term results (i.e., outputs). The case studies are unusual (e.g., successful urban planning), and of general public interest (e.g., institutional actions during crises) in both theoretical and policy terms. These case studies serve to illustrate the analytical framework of institutional action during crisis situations, but do not go as far as to represent universal generalizations. While the gathering of data and evidence was based on the "how?" and "why?" questions that characterize the case study method, the presentation and structuring of this evidence follows a narrative and comparative format.

The final explanation of this study is a result of a series of iterations: making an initial theoretical statement or an initial proposition about policy or social behavior; comparing the findings of an initial case against such a statement or proposition; revising the statement or proposition; comparing other details of the case against the revision; and again revising the statement or proposition. This iterative process began with a month-long research trip to Mexico in 1993, followed by ongoing research in Los Angeles, another field research trip to Mexico City in the summer of 1995, fieldwork in Los Angeles, and a final research trip to Mexico City in the summer of 1996.

Additional fieldwork was conducted in both cities in 1999. Such a back-and-forth fieldwork process between the two case studies over a period of three years enabled a gradual building of an explanation; similar to the process of refining a set of ideas, in which an important aspect is again to entertain other plausible or rival explanations.

The case study database contains the following elements: notes, documents, tabular materials, and narratives. The notes take a variety of forms (e.g., handwritten in a notebook, on the margins of photocopied journal articles, and on computer diskettes) are a result of my interviews, observations, and document analysis. The notes are divided into the major subjects—as outlined in the chapters of the study—in a fairly logical and obvious manner so as to be accessible to other interested researchers. Many documents relevant to the case studies were collected during the course of the study and are listed by chapter in the bibliography. Tabular materials collected for the research include census data from Mexico and Los Angeles and other quantitative data relating specifically to the recovery programs (e.g., amounts of money spent and number of housing units rebuilt) obtained from official government documents.

There has been a conscious attempt on my part to ensure that the case studies presented in this study are significant, complete, display sufficient evidence, and are composed in an engaging manner. In doing a field study, for instance, the evidence presented should convince the reader that the investigator has indeed been in the field, has acted thoughtfully while there, and has become steeped in the issues about the case. For example, for the Los Angeles case study, I lived in the city for three years; I have personal friends in several planning institutions such as the Los Angeles Housing Department, the Community Redevelopment Agency, and the Southern California Council of Governments; I was a member of the executive board of the Los Angeles chapter of the American Planning Association; and I conducted field research on an ongoing basis through site visits to different housing projects, interviews with several housing officials and local researchers, and archival research at the city hall. For the Mexico City case study, I learned Spanish, undertook three, three- to four-week fieldwork trips to Mexico City, immersed myself in Mexican art and architecture, and conducted site visits to housing projects, interviews with housing officials and researchers at local universities, and archival research at libraries.

NARRATIVE

Finally, I have attempted to compose the case studies in an engaging manner, that is, presenting the evidence as clearly as possible and with the enthusiasm that I experienced during the fieldwork. I searched for two critical elements:

structure, in terms of a plot that organizes the relationships in each case study; and meaning, in terms of an idea or lesson that the reader can come away with from each case study. The most effective format for such a presentation, organized around plot and meaning, is a narrative.

A narrative is a story with a beginning, middle, and end, and stories "describe an action that begins, continues over a well-defined period of time, and finally draws to a definite close" (Cronon 1992, 1367). The most important element of a narrative is its structure or plot; "by plot we mean a structure of relationships by which the events contained in the account are endowed with a meaning by being identified as parts of an integrated whole" (White 1987, 9). The second most important element of a narrative is meaning, which helps us make sense of the narrative: "the demand for closure in the . . . story . . . is a demand . . . for moral meaning, a demand that sequences of real events be assessed as to their significance as elements of a moral drama" (White 1987, 21).

The significance of narratives, or stories, is threefold. First, it is basic to cultural beliefs: "we force our stories on a world that doesn't fit them" (Cronon 1992, 1368). Second, it is a fundamental way of organizing experience because "we inhabit an endlessly storied world" (Martin Heidegger cited in Cronon 1992, 1368). Third, we have a natural impulse to narrate: "narrative might well be considered a solution to a problem of general human concern, namely the problem of how to translate knowing into telling" (White 1987,1).

Social scientists are quite skeptical of the narrative format because of its supposed lack of rigor, highly subjective nature, and limited applicability. However, there exist various criteria for judging the validity and usefulness of narratives: depth of explanation and thoroughness of details, breadth of scope, simplicity of the story which reveals useful insights, inclusiveness of different voices and events, coherence through tight linkages in text, based on scholarly tradition while simultaneously pushing its boundaries, and lucid and engaging reading. Furthermore, one could pay attention to the significance of the narrative in terms of the importance of plot, scene, and character; beginnings, middles, and ends; the rhetoric of storytelling; and the different agendas of narrators and readers.

Narrative is among our most powerful ways of encountering the world, judging our actions within it, and learning to care about its many meanings. For example, narratives contain beginnings, middles, and ends; much like the case studies, in which the crises (i.e., earthquakes) constitute the beginning, the institutional actions over a period of time (i.e., program formation) constitute the middle, and the successful outputs (i.e., program implementation) constitute the ends. Similarly, narratives possess a plot that represents the explanations or theories that make the case studies meaningful, and are thus the most critical elements of this study. In the two case studies of post-earthquake housing recovery programs in Mexico City and Los Angeles, the plot (i.e., the explanation or theory) would provide meaning to a series of institutional actions by addressing the question: In what ways and for what reasons were these programs successful? In this manner, narratives are also a powerful tool for policy analysis (Krieger 1981; Roe 1994), because they relate a succession of events, help us understand patterns of decision making, highlight the roles of important actors and provide meaning to such events, decisions, and actors. The plots or theories that structure such narratives are also a way of organizing urban planning experiences in comparative analyses of similar crisis situations, but in different political-economic contexts.

COMPARATIVE ANALYSIS

To compare is a common way of thinking. Nothing is more natural than to consider people, ideas, or institutions in relation to other people, ideas, or institutions (Dogan and Pelassy 1990, 3). We gain knowledge through references. By enlarging the field of observation, the comparativist searches for rules and tries to bring to light the general causes of social phenomena. In general, it seems more sensible to concentrate on similar rather than total dissimilar phenomena or processes. The principal reason for making a comparison is to shed light on how some common process produces different kinds of results in different places, or to examine why different processes produce similar results: looking first at what the two case studies have in common, then at the major differences among them, and finally, at the common processes (applied in variable degrees) which have led to the wide and very real differences which we now find.

International comparisons require articulated conceptual frameworks. Comparisons are significant if we want to find out whether planning issues in a particular political-economic context such as in Mexico or the United States are unique or common to other societies, and to determine the validity of sweeping generalizations. Such comparisons involve a number of tasks: identifying underlying patterns and explanations, specifying particular similarities and differences, and understanding the effect of the underlying institutional framework—for example, in this study, the structure and role of public sector planning institutions in the provision of housing services.

Comparisons also help us to better understand particular housing issues, for example in the United States, and to determine if those issues are more or less serious than in other societies. The policy relevance of comparison emerges from a study of the effects of different housing policies on different contexts, that is, to understand what works under what conditions. This might involve similar problems but different approaches, for example to the limited availability of housing finance, the reduction in affordable rental housing stock, or housing reconstruction after natural disasters.

Over and above the policy relevance of comparative analysis, familiarity with different contexts is important in an increasingly interconnected and interdependent world. The Habitat II Conference of June 1996 in Istanbul, Turkey built upon the momentum of two decades of consciousness-raising about the global interconnectedness of our lives through flows of capital, culture, and ideas. Globalization became a central theme of the late twentieth century. It is a concept that was borne out of the seemingly global expansion of market capitalism. One aspect of this urban discourse is the recognition of globally competitive cities and regions such as New York, Tokyo, London, Mexico City, and Los Angeles, all of which nourish innovative, entrepreneurial, and cultural activities across national boundaries.

From the literature on comparative research (Dogan and Pelassy 1990; Oyen 1990), the critical question is *how* we compare rather than *what* we compare. For example, in this study, the analytical framework for comparison is based on the following elements: institutional analysis; crisis situations as occasions for policy analysis and test cases for institutional effectiveness; the case study and narrative research methodologies; and the "how?" and "why?" research questions.

Furthermore, this comparative analysis was guided by a number of principles, such as the notion of functional equivalence, and the articulation and aggregation of interests. Functional equivalence implies that one should not be mislead by superficial data and labels, and suggests that one ask questions such as: By what institutional structures are particular types of planning policies transmitted? Such questions warn us of situations in which the same role may be played by different institutions in various countries. For example, in Mexico political actors and considerations largely influence urban planning decisions and policies, while in the United States private sector actors and considerations largely influence urban planning decisions.

A special case of comparative analysis is between a developing country context, such as Mexico, and a developed country context, such as the United States. On the one hand, it is clear that the systemic frameworks of policy—the institutions, participants, resources, the role of the state—all vary as they do between developing and developed countries in general. The same is true for the scope of policy activity, the configuration of issues, and the actual content of policy. On the other hand, the institutional decision making process—the constraints, the ripe moments that produce innovation, the tendency for policy to have unanticipated consequences—appears to display regularities that transcend the categories of developing or developed country (Horowitz 1989).

The following are the elements of a comparative analytical framework utilizing institutional analysis for a better understanding of urban planning: institutional arrangements, policies, programs, and practices. An institutional arrangement refers to the relationships of institutions vertically (e.g., between housing institutions at the international, national, regional, and local levels) and horizontally (e.g., between housing institutions at the local level in the private, nonprofit, and public sectors). Such arrangements provide an understanding of the basic structure or form of decision making; the relationships among formal decision makers as well as outside groups; the content of power which attempts to identify individual decision makers, their status, their values, and their perception of the public interest; and the operation of power that focuses on the style and techniques of influence—how policies are politically executed.

The second element of the analytical framework for comparison consists of the policies that characterize planning institutions in each context. This includes a study of typical planning policies or strategies and refers to predominant themes, impetuses and inspirations. For example, characteristic planning policies in Mexico might include programs and projects that enhance political support from labor unions in Mexico City, or promoting private sector profit and investment in the United States.

The third element, institutional programs, reflects the rules of the game in planning systems which vary considerably as priorities and dominant concepts vary. This involves an analysis of specific programs—such as the two case studies—in order to determine the decision-making rationalities, which may be socially constructed and culturally relative. Analysis of programs also point to characteristics of planning institutions that include degrees of activity specialization and growth patterns of institutions (e.g., evolutionary versus discontinuous).

The final element of the comparative analytical framework consists of the types of planning practices that characterize different institutions. Planning practices are ways of organizing, controlling, and directing planning institutions. These practices reflect successful forms of planning behavior for achieving goals. Examples would include the degrees of personal authority, the relative importance of formal procedures (e.g., institutional routines), and different administrative styles (e.g., directive versus facilitative). A history and preponderance of such practices often evolves into local planning traditions, which in turn provide an understanding of long-term trends; for example, the use or absence of tools such as master plans or legal ordinances or funding mechanisms such as low-interest loans or subsidies.

RESEARCH PROCESS

A number of data and information collection methods were utilized, including open-ended interviews with institutional representatives, community members, and academic scholars. I also analyzed available records, including institutional memos, policy documents, consultant reports, scholarly research, and newspaper accounts. Finally, I visited the sites of the programs in Mexico City and Los Angeles to note the condition of the housing and to record it on color slides.

One key element of the research methodology consisted of interviews with institutional representatives in Mexico City and Los Angeles. The interviews were open-ended, geared to letting the interviewee tell her or his story and enabling me to see how others define a specific policy problem, identify, and assess its alternatives. However, the interviews were not exhaustive, contained respondent biases, and it was not always easy to analyze and interpret the answers. Thus, they were utilized, not as a primary source of information, but to confirm information obtained from other sources and to obtain behind-the-scenes information not presented in official documents. A total of twelve taped, forty-five-minute, interviews were conducted with public officials, research scholars, and community representatives in Mexico City and Los Angeles. In addition, I had several informal conversations (which involved note-taking) with other relevant observers.

The second key element of the research methodology was the analysis of available records and data such as official documents, consultant reports, and statistical records. Much of this information was quantitative, contained familiar measures, and came from independent sources such as consultants and third parties. However, the data was often limited and had to be analyzed in each context. For example, the rebuilding of one hundred housing units has a very different connotation in Mexico City than in Los Angeles in terms of funding sources, administrative procedures, political pressures, and community involvement.

Prior to beginning fieldwork, it was critical to identify the institutional issues that emerged during the two housing recovery programs. With this intention in mind, I analyzed a number of documents, published and unpublished, official, and from the media. This analysis was used to develop Mexico City and Los Angeles interview instruments and to identify interview respondents. I also identified interview respondents through personal contacts, prominent individuals in newspaper accounts, and requesting initial interview respondents to provide names and contacts of other key individuals and institutions. Although the field interview instruments contained a set of structured questions that were asked of all interview respondents, they were open-ended enough to allow for more informal or focused discussion, as and when the situation warranted. The interview questions for both the Mexico City fieldwork (in Spanish) and the Los Angeles fieldwork are presented in the last section of this Appendix. My interview strategy was to conduct in-person interviews with representatives from the principal institutional actors involved in the two programs. I also collected, reviewed, and analyzed official documents and administrative records in order to gain insights into institutional action (i.e., policy formulation and implementation) and the factors that shaped the housing recovery efforts. One of the main objectives of this research process was to obtain relevant information, identify key issues, modify the analytical framework accordingly, and to verify the relevant information using a variety of primary and secondary sources.

In summary, my research involved a multiple methodology, qualitative approach to gather theoretical explanations and empirical evidence about the planning institutions' actions in housing recovery following the Mexico City and Los Angeles earthquakes. Structured and recorded interviews with institutional representatives at both the policy formulation and implementation levels, informal conversations with informed observers in the community and in academia, analyses of official documents, site visits, personal observations documented in slides and photographs, consultants' evaluations, newspaper and magazine accounts, and other studies published in books and journals comprised my sources of information. I conducted nine extensive in-person interviews with key institutional representatives in Mexico City and Los Angeles in 1995. Follow-up interviews were completed by August 1996. I visited the sites of housing projects undertaken by the two programs, RHP and Ghost Town, in 1995 and 1996. I undertook a content analysis of earthquake and housing recovery related accounts in newspapers and magazines such as *La Jornada, El Excelsior,* the *Los Angeles Times,* the *New York Times,* and *Time* magazine. I conducted a detailed analysis of official documents such as the expropriation decree passed by the DDF in Mexico City in 1985, and motions passed by the Los Angeles City Council in 1994. Finally, I conducted a secondary analysis of official documents from institutions involved in the housing programs, such as the RHP agency and the LAHD; and subsequent consultant evaluations, including those by the Urban Institute in Washington, D.C. and the Center for Environmental Design Research in Berkeley, California.

The comparative nature of the study allowed for a back-and-forth movement between field work in Mexico City and in Los Angeles. The first trip to Mexico City was in the summer of 1993, for other research that eventually served as a background to the current study. In the summer of 1995, I talked to representatives of the LAHD and collected official reports and documents. This fieldwork helped focus and shape a field trip to Mexico

City soon after, during which I conducted several interviews, collected official documents, and obtained newspaper accounts. The Mexico City trip, in turn, informed the next phase of fieldwork in Los Angeles, including further interviews, documents, and newspaper accounts. The final field trip to Mexico City for the RHP case study in the summer of 1996 was a follow-up to find missing information and intensive visits to the sites.

Research on the secondary case studies, representing unsuccessful institutional actions in planning, began in 1998 with the collection of data, newspaper accounts, and existing research on recovery efforts following the 1989 Mexico City air pollution crisis and the 1992 Los Angeles riots. These two case studies were selected as counter-points—that is, perceived to be failures—to the primary case studies, which were examples of successful institutional actions in planning. Furthermore, the case studies broadened the sense of "crisis," rather than the narrow notions of earthquake or natural disaster recovery that the primary case studies appeared to convey, because these were clearly crises generated by human actions. Finally, the two secondary case studies were situated in Mexico City and Los Angeles rather than other megacities in order to obtain some degree of control of the political-economic contexts.

From materials (e.g., magazine articles, newspaper accounts, official reports, journal articles, and books) gathered on Mexico City air pollution and the Los Angeles riots, I identified key institutional actors in recovery programs and their roles. I also identified sources of primary material (e.g., archives, officials, community activists) via telephone calls to scholars in Mexico City and Los Angeles. Fieldwork in Mexico City and Los Angeles in July and August of 1999 consisted of interviews, archival research, alternative sources of primary information, and site visits, to riot-affected areas in Los Angeles where RLA had attempted to create economic development projects

INTERVIEW QUESTIONS

The interview questions for the case studies were first tested in Los Angeles with acquaintances in the LAHD in June of 1995. Based on these tests, the questions were modified, adapted to the Mexico City case study, and translated into Spanish immediately thereafter. The questions were tried in Mexico City during the field trip in July and August of 1995, and were modified slightly, depending on the position and perspective of each respondent. For example, they were made more specific about particular housing institutions, such as FONHAPO, or particular housing programs that a respondent might be involved in directly.

Subsequent to the Mexico City experience, the questions were once again modified and adapted to the Los Angeles case study for use during the fieldwork in March of 1996. By now the principal questions were clearly established, with minor modifications in Los Angeles being made in a similar fashion to that of Mexico City, as stated above. Thus, questions were more specific and pointed about particular institutions, when talking to officials in LAHD or HUD, for example. These questions were asked in July and August of 1996. The final fieldwork trip to Mexico City occurred in August of 1996, by which stage the follow-up questions were extremely clear and focused. The second set of questions for the counterpoint case studies of unsuccessful institutional actions in planning were developed and asked in July and August of 1999. In conclusion, the back-and-forth comparative research methodology between Mexico City and Los Angeles proved to be extremely productive in terms of learning from the research and interview process in each context, and then applying those lessons to the other context. The questions listed below are the basic and generic questions, modified somewhat depending on the person being interviewed and the amount of information already collected prior to the interview.

Primary Mexico City Case Study Questions: RHP

1. ¿Cuándo fue el primer concepto del programa de Renovación Habitacional Popular, y de parte de quien—fue una de una persona o de una institución?
2. ¿Quienes fueron los actores institucionales más importantes en este programa, y porque—hay razones económicas, políticas, sociales, o históricas en la participación de actores institucionales particulares y no de otros en el programa?
3. ¿Piensa usted que el programa (RHP) fue un éxito, y porqué? ¿Puede usted darme algunas razones y factores específicos?
4. ¿Hubo elementos, por una parte, idénticos, y por otra parte, diferentes, en este programa que en programas y políticas de vivienda normales? ¿Puede usted mencionar ejemplos concretos como mecanismos o criterios de financiamiento, diseños de casas, formas de construcción, o otros trámites?
5. ¿Cuál es el papel normal de FONHAPO en el provisión de vivienda de interés social, y cual es la diferencia con su papel en el programa de Renovación Habitacional Popular después del sismo de 1985?
6. ¿Cuáles son los relaciones institucionales entre FONHAPO y a) El Banco Mundial, y b) BANOBRAS a nivel de la canalización de fondos, y a nivel de la influencia sobre la política de vivienda?
7. ¿Cómo ve usted el programa Renovación Habitacional Popular en la perspectiva más grande de la política de vivienda en la ciudad de México? ¿Porque no es posible para otros programas de vivienda de interés social de ser tan exitosos? ¿Y hay impactos o lecciones de largo plazo del programa, y de que tipo?

8. ¿Usted puede sugerir otras cosas importantes que yo debería estudiar, a parte de estas preguntas, para mi investigación?

9. ¿Quiero visitar y sacar fotos de algunos de estos proyectos—puede usted recomendar algunos, y tiene usted un mapa de estos sitios?

10. ¿Hay documentos para consultar o las personas con quien yo pueda hablar para saber más detalles?

Primary Los Angeles Case Study Questions: Ghost Town Program

1. How does the Ghost Town recovery program compare with other housing recovery programs following the 1994 earthquake? How does it compare in terms of rapidity of action, scale of intervention, political importance, and so forth? (What are some of the factors that make it unique or different from other housing programs?

2. Do you think the Ghost Town program has been successful so far, or not really? In what ways has it been a success, and in what ways has been less successful? What are the reasons why it has been a success, or a failure? (For example, individual actors, institutional structures, institutional capabilities, political pressure, or a combination of circumstances?)

3. What did the earthquake bring forth or enable, in terms of housing programs, that would not have normally happened? What might be the long-term impact of the Ghost Town program, for example, in terms of neighborhood recovery, housing market, and housing policies and programs?

4. When was the Ghost Town phenomenon first identified as a major public policy problem and by whom?

5. Who are the principal institutional actors involved in the Ghost Town recovery effort? (At the city level? State? Federal? At the community or neighborhood level? And in the private sector?)

6. Were there existing funding programs, established strategies of intervention, institutional experience, and tried-and-tested policies that are being used to shape and implement the Ghost Town recovery program? If so, which ones? Could you mention a few examples of these?

7. Were there new funding sources, ad-hoc strategies, and other types of new or exceptional mechanisms that were used in the Ghost Town recovery—things which had not really been tried before? If so, which ones were these? Could you mention a few examples?

8. What role did the community play in the Ghost Town neighborhoods? (For example, the individual homeowners, tenants' associations, neighborhood associations, community groups, or special interest groups?)

9. Could you suggest any particular aspects or elements of the post-earth-quake housing recovery in general, and the Ghost Town program in particular, that I should look at more closely for my research?
10. Could you also suggest the names of people I should interview, or documents I should look at for my research?

Secondary Mexico City Case Study Questions: HNC

1. ¿Cuándo fue el primero concepto del programa Hoy No Circula y de parte de quien?
2. ¿Quienes son los actores institucionales más importantes en este programa?
3. ¿Piensa usted que el programa Hoy No Circula es un éxito o un fracaso, y porque?
4. ¿Hay antecedentes del programa en México o en otros países?
5. ¿Hay impactos o lecciones de largo plazo del programa Hoy No Circula, y de que tipo?
6. ¿Hay documentos para consultar, o las personas con quien yo pueda hablar para saber más detalles?

Secondary Los Angeles Case Study Questions: RLA

1. What were the effective versus the ineffective recovery efforts following the 1992 Los Angeles riots?
2. Why were some recovery efforts more effective than others?
3. How do we know (for example, via specific measures or indicators) when some efforts are actually effective, especially given the complexity of the problems being addressed?
4. Were there any precedents for recovery efforts such as RLA?
5. What are the lessons of these recovery efforts for the future?

Notes

Chapter 1

1. Selznick, *The Moral Commonwealth: Social Theory and the Promise of Community* (Berkeley: University of California Press, 1992), 76.
2. Due to its proximity and trade relationship with the United States, and recent technological and economic development, Mexico is often only marginally viewed as representing the developing countries of Asia, Africa, and Latin America, yet no single country could possibly represent the variety of socio-political structures and historical experiences of developing countries. Mexico has in common with many of these developing countries a high rate of industrialization, urbanization, and increased literacy and education. Before the revolution, Mexican government and politics were essentially extractive and exploitative resting uneasily on a society made up essentially of kinsmen, villagers, and ethnic and status groups. In recent decades, however, the Mexican Revolution has deeply affected the social and political structure and has stimulated modern and democratic aspirations and expectations (Almond and Verba, *The Civic Culture: Political Attitudes and Democracy in Five Nations* (Newbury, CA: Sage, 1989, 38). Such a rapid pace and large scale of political-economic change is representative of many developing countries and their largest cities.
3. Friedrich cited in Butler and Pick, *Mexico Megacity* (Boulder, CO: Westview Press, 1997), 174.
4. Davis, *Journal of Urban Affairs*, 1994, 295.
5. Rieff, *Los Angeles: Capital of the Third World* (New York: Touchstone, 1991), 78.
6. Davis, *City of Quartz: Excavating the Future in Los Angeles* (New York: Vintage Books, 1990), 7.
7. Hall, *The World Cities* (New York: St. Martin's Press, 1984), 214.
8. Ibid., 251–252.

Chapter 2

1. Selznick, *The Moral Commonwealth: Social Theory and the Promise of Community*, 233–234.
2. March and Olsen, *Rediscovering Institutions: The Organizational Basis of Politics* (New York: The Free Press, 1989), 38.
3. Knight, *Institutions and Social Conflict* (Cambridge: Cambridge University Press, 1992), 25.
4. March and Olsen, 48.
5. Friedmann, *Planning in the Public Domain: From Knowledge to Action* (Princeton, NJ: Princeton University Press, 1987), 47.
6. Gamboa, interview with the author, 1995.
7. Hurtado, interview with the author, 1996.

Chapter 3

1. Kandell, *La Capital: The Biography of Mexico City* (New York: Random House, 1988), 559.
2. Stolarski, interview with the author, 1995.

3. Of the four programs coordinated by the Ministry of Urban Development and Ecology (Secretaria de Desarrollo Urbano y Ecologia, or SEDUE) and the Mexico City government (DDF), two had a direct impact in the housing production and improvement of substandard and deteriorated dwellings—Renovación Habitacional Popular, and Fase II.
4. Hurtado, interview with the author, 1996.
5. Connolly, Housing in the State of Mexico in *Housing Policy in Developing Countries* (London: Routledge, 1990), 27.
6. Different housing modules were proposed for different economic groups. For example, Type 1 housing was designed for those earning 2–2.8 times the minimum salary and paying 15 percent interest; Type 2 for those earning 3.2–4.2 times the minimum salary and paying 19 percent interest; Type 3 for those 4.3–6.2 times the minimum salary and paying 25 percent interest; and Type 4 for those earning 6.3–7.5 times the minimum salary at 30 percent interest. When inflation was between 60–100 percent annually, this represented a substantial subsidy for homebuyers (Ward, *Mexico City: The Production and Reproduction of an Urban Environment*, 1990a, 429).
7. Connolly, interview with the author, 1996.
8. Ibid.
9. Stolarski, interview with the author, 1995.

Chapter 4

1. Adler, After the Quake, *Newsweek*, 1994, 27.
2. Markman, Still Shaken: A Resilient Los Angeles Seeks to Retrieve Its Future, *Los Angeles Times*, January 15, 1995, U1.
3. Zeidman, interview with the author, 1996.
4. Galster et al., Documentation of LA Earthquake Disaster Housing Assistance Policies and Procedures (Washington, DC: The Urban Institute,1995), 79.
5. Gruel, interview with the author, 1996.
6. Smith, Developing an International Political Economy Approach and The Logic of Historical-Structural Analysis. In *Third World Cities In Global Perspective: The Political Economy of Uneven Urbanization*, 1996.
7. Gruel, 1996.
8. Smith, 1996.
9. Zeidman, 1996.
10. Gruel, 1996.

Chapter 5

1. Fineman, No Breather from Crisis in Mexico City, *Los Angeles Times*, November 12, 1996, A1-A11.
2. Baldassare 1994, 2
3. Humberto Bravo of the Universidad Nacional Autonoma de México cited in Preston, The City That Can't Fix the Air, *New York Times*, February 4, 1993, E4.
4. Rico, interview with the author, 1999.
5. The main air pollutants in Mexico City are ozone (O_3), particulate matter (PM), nitrogen oxides (NOx), sulphur oxides (SO_3), carbon monoxide (CO), and lead (Pb). Ground-level ozone is the major component of smog. While ozone in the upper atmosphere occurs naturally and protects life on earth from harmful ultraviolet radiation, ozone at ground level is a noxious pollutant. Ground-level ozone is not directly emitted, but is formed by the reaction of oxides of nitrogen (NOx) and volatile organic compounds (VOC) in the presence of sunlight. Ozone is a severe irritant, responsible for choking, coughing, and stinging eyes associated with smog. Ozone damages lung tissue, aggravates respiratory disease, and makes people more susceptible to respiratory infections. Owing to the latitude and altitude of Mexico City, ultraviolet rays are more intense and stimulate ozone formation (from Garza 1996, 316).

   Particulate matter (PM) is the term used for a mixture of solid particles and liquid droplets found in the air. PM can be emitted directly by a source or formed in the atmosphere by the transformation of gaseous emissions such as sulfur dioxide (SO_2), oxides of nitrogen (NO_x), and volatile organic compounds (VOC). Fine particles, under 2.5 microns in diameter ($PM_{2.5}$), result from fuel combustion from motor vehicles and other sources, as well as transformation of gaseous emissions. Coarse particles under 10 microns in diameter (PM_{10}) generally consist of windblown dust, and are released from materials handling, agriculture, and crushing and grinding operations. Particulate matter irritates the membranes of the respiratory system, caused increased respiratory symptoms and disease, decreased lung function, alterations of the body's defense systems, and premature mortality. The combustion of petroleum products is primarily responsible for the production of nitrogen dioxide (NO_2). Sulphur oxides (SO_x) are emitted when fuels containing sulphur, such as diesel oil and diesel, are used. The main component is sulphur dioxide (SO_2), a colorless gas that reacts with a variety of air particles and drops of water to form sulphates, aerosols, and acid rain. Carbon monoxide (CO) is a colorless, odorless and tasteless gas somewhat lighter than air, produced mainly by incomplete combustion of gasoline in motor vehicles. The incomplete burning of carbon in fuels produces CO, including gasoline. High concentrations of CO occur along roadsides in heavy traffic, particularly at major intersections, and in enclosed areas, such as garages and poorly ventilated tunnels. Health effects of CO include dizziness, headaches, fatigue, visual impairment, reduced work capacity, reduced manual dexterity, and poor learning ability. Peak CO concentrations typically occur during the colder months of the year when CO vehicular emissions are greater and night-time inversion conditions are more frequent, as in Mexico City (from FHA 1999).

The presence of lead (Pb) particles in the environment is caused basically by leaded gasoline fuel, although it is also produced by paint manufacturing and foundry processes. The main source of lead exposure in Mexico City is through inhalation of lead in ambient air, which results largely from combustion of leaded gasoline in motor vehicles (from Onursal and Gautam 1997, 132).

6. The 1993 public opinion survey was based on a sample of 380 residents of the DF using a stratified random cluster sample. The sample was representative of the residents of the DF who are aged 18 years or older. Sampling error was 5% or less. The sample of 30 city council members (or 'representates', was drawn by selecting names from the directory of the Asamblea de Representates del Distrito Federal.

7. Cited by the Ad Hoc Committee 1992, Summary of Public Hearing Held on July 30, 19

8. Cited by the Ad Hoc Committee 1992, Summary of Public Hearing Held on July 30, 19

9. Eibenschutz 1999

Chapter 6

1. Connolly, interview with the author, 1996.
2. Gruel, interview with the author, 1996.
3. Stolarski, interview with the author, 1995.
4. Gruel, 1996.
5. Stolarski, 1995.
6. Gruel, 1996
7. Zeidman, interview with the author, 1996.
8. Gruel, 1996.
9. Smith, 1996.
10. Gamboa, interview with the author, 1995.
11. Eibenschutz, interview with the author, 1995.
12. Smith, interview with the author, 1996.
13. Gruel, 1996.
14. Stolarski, 1995.
15. Parker and Yeo, Turn Up the Lights: A Survey of Cities. *The Economist*, July 29, 1995, 1.
16. Gamboa, 1995.
17. Gamboa, 1995.
18. Smith, 1996.
19. Innes, Viewpoint: Challenge and Creativity in Postmodern Planning, *Town Planning Review*, 1998, vi.

20. Valery, Earthquake Engineering: Survey, *The Economist*, April 22, 1995, 11.
21. Zeidman, 1996.

Postscript

1. The significance of the recovery efforts following the September 11, 2001 terrorist attacks on the twin towers of the World Trade Center for urban planning is sadly ironical. The hijackers of the two aircraft code-named the World Trade Center the "Faculty of Urban Planning." *New York Times*, 2002, A26.
2. Goldberger, 2003, 81
3. In some ways, the entire city has suffered devastating consequences as a result of the September 11th attacks. This is most true with respect to job loss. The five occupations in which the greatest numbers of 9/11-related layoffs occurred were waiters and waitresses, janitors, retail salespersons, food preparation workers, and cashiers. An estimated 60 percent of the 79,000 workers laid off earned less than $11 per hour, and it is certain that the vast majority of them did not live in Lower Manhattan (Wolf-Powers, GothamGazette.com, 2002).

Bibliography

Ad Hoc Committee on Recovery and Revitalization, Los Angeles City Council. (1992). Report of the ad hoc committee on recovery and revitalization to the Los Angeles city council. October 29.

Adler, Jerry. (1994). After the quake. *Newsweek*, January 31: 25–33.

Alarcon, Richard. (1994). Motion. Los Angeles city council. May 20.

Alchian, Armen and Demsetz, Harold. (1972). Production, information costs, and economic organization. *American Economic Review*, 62 (December): 777–795.

Allen, Elizabeth. (1994). Political responses to flood disaster: The example of Rio de Janeiro. In *Disasters, development and environment*, ed. Ann Varley, 99–108. Chichester: John Wiley and Sons.

Almond, Gabriel and Sidney Verba. (1989). *The civic culture: Political attitudes and democracy in five nations*. Newbury Park, CA: Sage Publications.

Alterman, Rachelle. (1995). Can planning help in time of crisis? Planners' response to Israel's recent wave of mass immigration. *Journal of the American Planning Association*, 61, 2, (Spring): 156–177.

Álvarez, José Rogelio, ed. (1994). Contaminación ambiental. In *Enciclopedia de México*, ed. J. R. Alvarez, 1803–1806. Mexico City: Enciclopedia de México.

Assaad, Ragui. (1996). Formalizing the informal? The transformation of Cairo's refuse collection system. *Journal of Planning Education and Research*, 16: 115–126.

Azuela, Antonio. (1987). De inquilinos a propietarios: Derecho y política en el program de Renovación Habitacional Popular. *Estudios Demograficas y Urbanos*, 2, 1 (January–April): 53–73.

Badshah, Akhtar. (1996). NGO and community partnerships for integrated area development. In *Our urban future: New paradigms for equity and sustainability*, 40–64. London: Zed Books.

Bagli, Charles. (2002). Six plans for ground zero share striking similarities. *New York Times*, July 11.

Bagli, Charles. (2003). Retail operator at trade center is pulling out of the deal. *New York Times*, September 16, B1.

Baldassare, Mark, ed. 1994. *The Los Angeles riots: Lessons for the urban future*. Bolder, CO: Westview Press.

Battle-Bey, Marva Smith. (Executive Director of the Vermont Slauson Economic Development Corporation). (1999). Interview with the author, July 22, Los Angeles. Written notes.

Bell, Brenda. (1999). The liquid earth. *The Atlantic Monthly*, 283, 1 (January): 58–72.

Bendikat, Elfi. (1996). Qualitative historical research on municipal policies. In *Cross-national research methods in the social sciences*, eds. Linda Hantrais and Steen Mangen, 129–137. London: Pinter.

Berger, Peter and Thomas Luckmann. (1966). *The social construction of reality: A treatise in the sociology of knowledge*. New York: Doubleday.

Berke, Philip. (1998). Environmental hazards: Hurricanes. In *The encyclopedia of housing*, ed. Willem van Vliet, 154–156. Thousand Oaks, CA: Sage.

Berke, Philip and Timothy Beatley. (1992). *Planning for earthquakes: Risk, politics, and policy*. Baltimore: The Johns Hopkins University Press.

Bernardi, Ernani. (1988). Testimony. Submitted to the Joint Hearing of the House and Senate Housing Subcommittees on a New National Housing Policy. National Housing Policy Conference and Public Hearing, Los Angeles. April 7: 187–191.

Bernson, Hal. (Councilman from the 12th District of Los Angeles). (1996). Interview with the author, August 2, Los Angeles. Tape recording.

Bolan, Richard. (1996). Planning and institutional design. In *Explorations in planning theory,* eds. Seymour Mandelbaum, Luigi Mazza, and Robert Burchell, 497–513. New Brunswick: Center of Urban Policy Research, Rutgers, The State University of New Jersey.

Bolin, Robert and Lois Stanford. (1991). Shelter, housing and recovery: A comparison of U.S. disasters. *Disasters,* 15, 1 (March): 24–34.

Bryson, John and Barbara Crosby. (1996). Planning and the design and use of forums, arenas, and courts. In *Explorations in planning theory,* eds. Seymour Mandelbaum, Luigi Mazza, and Robert Burchell, 462–482. New Brunswick: Center of Urban Policy Research, Rutgers: The State University of New Jersey.

Buchanan, James. (1980). Rent seeking and profit seeking. In *Toward a theory of the rent-seeking society,* ed. James Buchanan, Robert Tollison, and Gordon Tullock. College Station: Texas A & M University Press.

Burby, Raymond with Timothy Beatley, Philip Berke, Robert Deyle, Steven French, David Godschalk, Edward Kaiser, Jack Kartez, Peter May, Robert Olshansky, Robert Paterson, and Rutherford Platt. (1999). Unleashing the power of planning to create disaster-resistant communities. *Journal of the American Planning Association,* 63, 3 (Summer): 247–258.

Burchell, Robert and David Listokin. (1995). Influences on United States housing policy. *Housing Policy Debate,* 6, 3: 559–617.

Butler, Edgar and James Pick. (1997). *Mexico megacity.* Bolder, CO: Westview Press.

Caiden, Naomi and Aaron Wildavsky. (1974). *Planning and budgeting in poor countries.* New York: Wiley.

Campbell, Tim and David Wilk. (1986). Plans and plan-making in the valley of Mexico: The evolution of a planning process, 1970–1985. *Third World Planning Review,* 8, 4: 287–313.

Catanese, Anthony and James Snyder, eds. (1988). *Urban planning.* New York: McGraw-Hill.

Chesire, Paul, Ana Furtado, and Stefano Magrini. (1996). Quantitative Comparisons on European Cities and Regions. In *Cross-national research methods in the social eciences,* eds. Linda Hantrais and Steen Mangen, 39–50. London: Pinter.

Christensen, Karen. (1985). Coping with uncertainty in planning. *Journal of the American Planning Association,* 51, 1 (Autumn): 63–73.

Christensen, Karen. (1993). Teaching savvy. *Journal of Planning Education and Research,* 12, 3 (Spring): 202–212.

Civic Alliance to Rebuild Downtown New York. (2002). Listening to the city: Report of proceedings. New York: Civic Alliance to Rebuild Downtown New York.

Coase, Ronald. (1937). The nature of the firm. *Economica,* 3 (November): 386–405.

Cohen, Michael. (1996). The hypothesis of urban convergence: Are cities in the north and south becoming more alike in an age of globalization? In *Preparing for the urban future: Global pressures and local forces,* ed. Michael Cohen, Blair Ruble, Joseph Tulchin, and Allison Garland, 25–38. Washington, DC: The Woodrow Wilson Center Press.

Comerio, Mary. (1995). Los Angeles housing losses. Report prepared for the California Governor's Office of Emergency Services. Berkeley: Center for Environmental Design Research. August.

Comerio, Mary. (1998). *Disaster hits home: New policy for urban housing recovery.* Berkeley: University of California Press.

Comerio, Mary, John Landis, and Yodan Rofe. (1994). Post-disaster residential rebuilding. Working paper 608. Study for California Governor's Office of Emergency Services. Berkeley: Institute of Urban and Regional Development, University of California at Berkeley. February.

Committee on Banking, Housing, and Urban Affairs, U.S. Congress. (1993). Hearing: The state of urban America. Washington, D.C: U.S. Government Printing Office. April 28.

Connolly, Priscilla. (1987). La política habitacional después de los sismos. *Estudios Demograficos y Urbanos,* 2, 1 (January–April): 101–120.

Connolly, Priscilla. (1990). Housing and the state in Mexico. In *Housing policy in developing countries,* ed. Gil Shidlo, 5–32. London: Routledge.

Connolly, Priscilla. (1993). "The go-between": CENVI, a habitat NGO in Mexico City. *Environment and Urbanization,* 5, 1 (April): 68–90.

Connolly, Priscilla. (Collaborator at the Center for Housing and Urban Studies (CENVI), Mexico City, and professor of sociology in the Autonomous Metropolitan University–Azcapotzalco Unit, Mexico City). (1996). Interview with the author August 13, Mexico City. Tape recording.

Connolly, Priscilla. (1999). Mexico City: Our common future? *Environment and Urbanization*, 11 (1): 53–78. April.

Corwin, Ronald. (1987). *The organization-society nexus: A critical review of models and metaphors*. New York: Greenwood Press.

Cronon, William. (1992). A place for stories: Nature, history, and narrative. *Journal of American History*, 78, 4 (March): 1347–1376.

Cuny, Frederick. (1983). Disasters and development. New York: Oxford University Press.

Davis, Diane. (1991). Urban fiscal crisis and political change in Mexico City: From global origins to local effects. *Journal of Urban Affairs*, 13, 2: 175–199.

Davis, Diane. (1994). *Urban leviathan: Mexico City in the twentieth century*. Philadelphia: Temple University Press.

Davis, Mike. (1990). *City of quartz: Excavating the future in Los Angeles*. New York: Vintage Books.

Davis, Mike. (1998). *Ecology of fear: Los Angeles and the imagination of disaster*. New York: Metropolitan Books.

DDF (Departmamento de Distrito Federal). (1985). Decreto por el que se apreueba el Programa Emergente de Renovación Habitacional Popular del Distrito Federal. In *Diario oficial: Organo del gobierno constitutional de los Estados Unidos Mexicanos*, 392, 30 (October 14): 7–10.

Dear, Michael, Eric Schockman, and Greg Hise. (1996). *Rethinking Los Angeles*. Thousand Oaks, CA: Sage.

DiMaggio, Paul and Walter Powell. (1991). Introduction. In *The new institutionalism in organizational analysis,* eds. Walter Powell and Paul DiMaggio, 1–38. Chicago: University of Chicago Press.

Dirección General de Prevención y Control de la Contaminación (DGPCC). (1999). *Informe de Actividades 1998*. Mexico City: Secretaría del Medio Ambiente del Gobierno del Distrito Federal.

Dogan, Mattei. (1994). Use and Misuse of Statistics in Comparative Research. In *Comparing nations: Concepts, strategies, substance*, eds. Mattei Dogan and Ali Kazancigil, 35–71. Oxford: Basil Blackwell.

Dogan, Mattei and Dominique Pelassy. (1990). *How to Compare Nations: Strategies in Comparative Politics*. 2nd ed.. Chatham, MA: Chatham House Publishers.

Douglas, Mary. (1986). *How institutions think*. Syracuse: Syracuse University Press.

Dowall, David and David Wilk. (1989). Population growth, land development and housing in Mexico City. Working paper 502. Berkeley: University of California at Berkeley.

Dowding, Keith. (1994). The compatibility of behaviouralism, rational choice and 'new institutionalism'. *Journal of Theoretical Politics*, 6, 1: 105–117.

Drucker, Peter. (1995). Really reinventing government. *The Atlantic*, 275, 2 (February): 49–58.

Dunne, Maya. (Director of Planning and Policy, Los Angeles Housing Department (LAHD), Los Angeles). (1996). Interview with the author July 11, Los Angeles. Written notes.

Earthquake Ghost Town Task Force. (1994). Plan to address crime and vandalism problems at earthquake "Ghost Towns." Memorandum to the Ad Hoc Committee on Earthquake Recovery. City of Los Angeles. June 20.

Earthquake Ghost Town Task Force. (1996). Status of earthquake Ghost Town recovery and security. Memorandum to the Ad Hoc Committee on Earthquake Recovery. City of Los Angeles. June 4.

Ebrard, Marcelo and Jorge Gamboa. (1991). Reconstruction in central Mexico City after the 1985 earthquakes. *Ekistics*, 58, 346/347 (January/February–March/April): 18–27.

Economist, The. (1996). Cultural Explanations,. 341, 7991: 23–26. November 9.

Economist, The. (1997). Rebuilding the ruins, 343, 8014: 26. April 26.

Eggertsson, Thrainn. (1990). *Economic behavior and institutions*. New York: Cambridge University Press.

Eibenschutz, Roberto. (Former Director-General of the National Fund for Popular Housing (FONHAPO), Mexico City, and former Sub-Secretary in the Ministry of Urban Development and Ecology (SEDUE), Mexico City). (1995). Interview with the author, July 25, Mexico City. Tape recording.

Eibenschutz, Roberto. (Secretary of Urban Development and Housing, Government of Mexico City). (1999). Interview with the author, August 26, Mexico City. Tape recording.

Elazar, Daniel. (1966). *American federalism: A view from the states.* New York: Crowell.

Eskeland, Gunnar. (1992). Attaching air pollution in Mexico City. *Finance and Development,* 29 (4): 28–30. December.

Eskeland, Gunnar, and Tarhan Feyzioglu. (1995). The 'Day Without A Car' in Mexico. World Bank Policy Research Working Paper 1554. December. Washington, DC, The World Bank.

Ethington, Philip and Eileen McDonagh. (1995a). The common space of social science inquiry. *Polity,* 28, 1 (Fall): 85–90.

Ethington, Philip and Eileen McDonagh. (1995b). The eclectic center of the new institutionalism: Axes of analysis in comparative perspective. *Social Science History,* 19, 4 (Winter): 467–477.

Evans, Hugh. (1983). *Planning and decision making: Implementing an integrated approach to development in the Potosi region of Bolivia.* Ph.D. dissertation. Cambridge: Massachusetts Institute of Technology.

Ezcura, Exequiel and Marisa Mazari-Hiriart. (1996). Are megacities viable? A cautionary tale from Mexico City. *Environment,* 38 (1): 6–35. January / February.

Faludi, Andreas. (1970). The planning environment and the meaning of "planning." *Regional Studies,* 4, 1: 1–9.

Federal Highway Administration (FHA). (1999). *Transportation Air Quality: Selected Facts and Figures.* Report. Washington, DC: U.S. Department of Transportation. January.

Feldman, Paul. (1994). 2 years after riots, private sector proves no panacea. *Los Angeles Times,* April 29.

Feldman, Paul. (1995). RLA board chairman to stay through 1995. *Los Angeles Times,* May 24.

Fineman, Mark. (1996). No breather from crisis in Mexico City. *Los Angeles Times,* November 12, A1–A12.

Flanigan, James. (1996). Rebuilding L.A., one neighborhood business at a time. *Los Angeles Times,* October 30.

Friedmann, John. (1987). *Planning in the public domain: From knowledge to action.* Princeton, NJ: Princeton University Press.

Friedmann, John. (1998). The Common Good: Assessing the Performance of Cities. In *City, space + globalization: An international perspective,* ed. Hemalata Dandekar, 15–22. Ann Arbor: College of Architecture + Urban Planning, University of Michigan.

Fulton, William. (1991). *Guide to California planning.* Point Arena, CA: Solano Books.

Fulton, William. (1993). In Los Angeles, the healing begins. *Planning,* 59, 1: 21–28. January.

Galster, George, Carla Herbig, Joshua Silver, and Maria Valera. (1995). Documentation of LA earthquake disaster housing assistance policies and procedures. Report prepared for the U.S. Department of Housing and Urban Development. Washington, DC: The Urban Institute. March 1.

Gamboa, Jorge. (Former Adjunct Director-General of the program for the Renovation of Popular Housing, Mexico City, and President of the Society of Mexican Architects, Mexico City). (1995). Interview with the author, July 31, Mexico City. Tape recording.

GAO (U.S. General Accounting Office). (1994). Los Angeles earthquake: Opinions of officials on federal impediments to rebuilding. Report to the Congress, Washington, D.C. June.

Garza, Gustavo. (1996). Uncontrolled air pollution in Mexico City. *Cities,* 13 (5): 315–328.

Giddens, Anthony. (1979). *A central problem in social theory: Action, structure and contradiction in social analysis.* Berkeley: University of California Press.

Giddens, Anthony. (1984). *The constitutions of society: Outline of the theory of structuration.* Berkeley: University of California Press.

Giddens, Anthony. (1985). *The nation-state and violence.* Berkeley: University of California Press.

Gilbert, Alan. (1992). Third World cities: Housing, infrastructure and servicing. *Urban Studies,* 29, 3/4: 435–460.

Gilbert, Alan. (1993). *In search of a home: Rental and shared housing in Latin America.* Tucson: The University of Arizona Press.

Gilbert, Alan. (1994). *The Latin American city.* London: The Latin American Bureau.

Gilbert, Alan and Ann Varley. (1991). *Landlord and tenant: Housing the poor in urban Mexico.* London: Routledge.

Gillman, Howard. (1996). More and less than strategy: Some advantages to interpretive institutionalism in the analysis of judicial politics. Paper. Los Angeles: University of Southern California. Photocopy.

Glembocki, Vicki. (1996). Flirting with disaster. *Pitt Magazine.* September. Pittsburgh: University of Pittsburgh. http://www.univ-relations.pitt.edu/pittmag/sep96/disasterh.html (accessed October 9, 2002).

Goetz, Edward. (1993). *Shelter burden: Local politics and progressive housing policy.* Philadelphia: Temple University Press.

Goldberger, Paul. (2003). Eyes on the prize: The amazing design competition for the World Trade Center site. *The New Yorker,* March 10: 78–82.

Goldfied, David. (1988). The future of the metropolitan region. In *Two centuries of American planning,* ed. Daniel Schaffer, 303–322. Baltimore: The Johns Hopkins University Press.

Gordon, Larry. (1995). Peter Elias. In "Special quake report: One year later." *Los Angeles Times,* January 15.

Gordon, Larry. (1996). Expiring RLA seeks heir to carry on task. *Los Angeles Times,* September 7.

Gotham Gazette. (2003). Rebuilding at a glance. http://www.gothamgazette.com/rebuilding_nyc/at_a_glance.shtml (accessed on September 9).

Greene, Fernando. (Architect of RHP housing projects and Professor at the Universidad Nacional Autonoma de Mexico). (1995). Interview with the author, August 2, Mexico City. Written notes.

Grindle, Merilee and John Thomas. (1991). *Public choices and policy change: The political economy of reform in developing countries.* Baltimore: The Johns Hopkins University Press.

Grigsby, Eugene. (1993). Rebuilding Los Angeles: One year later. *National Civic Review,* 82, 4 (Fall): 348–353.

Grimes, Christopher. (2003). Contrasting visions could cloud the picture at Ground Zero. *Financial Times,* September 8.

Gruel, Wendy. (Southern California Representative, U.S. Department of Housing and Urban Development, Los Angeles). (1996). Interview with the author, March 21, Los Angeles. Tape recording.

Hall, Peter. (1984). *The world cities.* 3rd ed. New York: St. Martin's Press.

Hamilton, Rabinovitz and Alschuler, Inc. (1994). The 1994 Los Angeles rental housing study: Summary. Los Angeles: City of Los Angeles Housing Department, Rent Stabilization Division. December. Photocopied.

Hamza, Mohamed and Roger Zetter. (1998). Structural adjustment, urban systems, and disaster vulnerability in developing countries. *Cities,* 15, 4: 291–299.

Harrison, Michael. (1994). *Diagnosing organizations: Methods, models, and processes.* Thousand Oaks, CA: Sage.

Harsman, Bjorn and John Quigley, eds. (1991). *Housing markets and housing institutions: An international comparison.* Boston: Kluwer Academic Publishers.

Harvey, Neil, ed. (1993). *Mexico: Dilemmas of transition.* London: Institute of Latin American Studies.

Hayashi, Chikio, Tatsuzo Suzuki and Masamichi Sasaki. (1992). *Data analysis for comparative social research: International perspectives.* Amsterdam: North-Holland.

Healey, Patsy. (1997). *Collaborative planning: Shaping places in fragmented societies.* Vancouver: University of British Columbia Press.

Healey, Patsy. (1998). Collaborative planning in a stakeholder society. *Town Planning Review,* 69, 1 (January): 1–21.

Healey, Patsy. (1999). Institutionalist analysis, communicative planning, and shaping places. *Journal of Planning Education and Research,* 19, 2: 111–121.

Helmore, Edward. (2003). New York's challenge: Manhattan transformation. *The Observer,* September 14.

Herson, Lawrence and John Bolland. (1990). *The urban web: Politics, policy, and theory.* Chicago: Nelson-Hall Publishers.

Herman, Eric. (2003). Coming home to a new downtown. *The New York Daily News.* September 8. http://www.gothamgazette.com/rebuilding_nyc/news/sept03.shtml (accessed September 9).

Hirschman, Albert. (1958). *The strategy of economic development.* New Haven: Yale University Press.

Hirschman, Albert. (1967). *Development projects observed.* Washington, DC: The Brookings Institution.

Hirschman, Albert. (1970). *Exit, voice and loyalty: Responses to decline in firms, organizations and states.* Cambridge: Harvard University Press.

Hong, Peter. (1995a). Central city repairs picking up. In "Special quake report: One year later." *Los Angeles Times*, January 15.

Hong, Peter. (1995b). Alvin Martin. In "Special quake report: One year later." *Los Angeles Times*, January 15.

Horowitz, Donald. (1989). Is there a third-world policy process? *Policy Sciences,* 22 (November): 197–212.

Howe, Con. (Director of Planning of Los Angeles). (1999). Interview with the author, July 21, Los Angeles. Written notes.

HUD (U.S. Department of Housing and Urban Development), Office of Policy Development and Research. (1994). *Early observations on HUD's Los Angeles (Northridge) earthquake disaster response.* Washington, DC. March 7.

HUD (U.S. Department of Housing and Urban Development), Office of Policy Development and Research. (1995a). *Preparing for the big one: Saving Lives through earthquake mitigation in Los Angeles, California.* Washington, DC, January 17.

HUD (U.S. Department of Housing and Urban Development), Office of Policy Development and Research. (1995b). CDBG: Making a difference in America's communities. *Recent Research Results,* August: 1–3.

HUD (U.S. Department of Housing and Urban Development), Office of Policy Development and Research. (1996). HOME helps low-income households, says evaluation. *Recent Research Results,* May: 4.

Hurtado, German. (Local community leader and founder of the Unified Coordination of Earthquake Victims (CUD), Mexico City). (1996). Interview with the author, August 20, Mexico City. Tape recording.

Huxtable, Ada Louise. (2002). 'Downtown' is more than ground zero. *Wall Street Journal,* August 7.

Inam, Aseem. (1994). Values of modern planning institutions. Paper presented at the 36th Annual Association of Collegiate Schools of Planning Conference, Phoenix, Arizona.

Inam, Aseem. (1994). Rebuilding our inner cities: Making planning relevant. *Dispatch,* 25, 4 (April/May): 1–4.

Inam, Aseem. (1995). Judging institutions in urban planning and development. Paper presented at the 3rd Annual Interdisciplinary Students of Organizations Conference, Chapel Hill, North Carolina.

Inam, Aseem. (1995). Housing policy in Mexico City: Institutional change and crisis situations. Paper presented at the 37th Annual Association of Collegiate Schools of Planning Conference, Detroit, Michigan.

Inam, Aseem. (1996). Institutional analysis and urban planning: A case study in post-earthquake housing recovery in Los Angeles. Paper presented at the Association of Collegiate Schools of Planning/Association of European Schools of Planning Joint Congress, Toronto, Canada.

Inam, Aseem. (1997). Routinizing novelty: Housing institutions and crisis recovery. Paper presented at the conference on Housing in the 21st Century, International Sociological Association, Alexandria, Virginia.

Inam, Aseem. (1999). Institutions, Routines, and Crises: Post-Earthquake Housing Recovery in Mexico City and Los Angeles. *Cities,* 16 (6): 391–407.

INEGI (Instituto Nacional de Estadistica, Geografica e Informatica). (1992a). *Ciudad de Mexico (Area Metropolitana): Resultados Definitivos: Tabulados Basicos: XI Censo General de*

Poblacion y Vivienda, 1990. Aguascalientes: Instituto Nacional de Estadistica, Geografia e Informatica.

INEGI (Instituto Nacional de Estadistica, Geografica e Informatica). (1992b). *Anuario Estadistico de los Estados Mexicanos: Edicion 1991.* Aguascalientes: Instituto Nacional de Estadistica, Geografia e Informatica.

Innes, Judith. (1998). Viewpoint: Challenge and creativity in postmodern planning. *Town Planning Review,* 69, 2 (April): v–ix.

Innes, Judith and D. Booher. (1999). Consensus-building as role playing and bricolage: Toward a theory of collaborative planning. *Journal of the American Planning Association,* 67, 1: 9–26.

Instituto Nacional de Estadística Geografía e Informática (INEGI). (1999). *Estadísticas del Medio Ambiente Federal y Zona Metropolitana 1999.* Mexico City: Instituto Nacional de Estadística Geografía e Informática.

Jacquemart, Georges. (2002). Getting Lower Manhattan moving again. *Planning,* 68, 9 (September): 4–9.

Jencks, Charles. (1993). *Heteropolis: Los Angeles, the riots and the strange beauty of hetero-architecture.* London: Academy Editions.

Johnson, William. (1989). *The politics of urban planning.* New York: Paragon House.

Kandell, Jonathan. (1988). *La capital: The biography of Mexico City.* New York: Random House.

Karetz, Jack. (1984). Crisis response planning: Toward a contingent analysis. *Journal of the American Planning Association,* 50, 1 (Winter): 9–21.

Karetz, Jack and Michael Lindell. (1987). Planning for uncertainty: The case of local disaster planning. *Journal of the American Planning Association,* 53, 4 (Autumn): 487–498.

Karetz, Jack and Michael Lindell. (1990). Adaptive planning for community disaster response. In *Cities and disaster,* ed. Richard Sylves and William Waugh, 5–31.

Keating, Michael. (1991). *Comparative urban politics: Power and the city in the United States, Canada, Britain and France.* Aldershot, UK: Edward Elgar Publishing.

Keil, Roger. (1998). *Los Angeles: Globalization, urbanization and social struggles.* Chichester: John Wiley and Sons.

Kerr, Sarah. (1994). The mystery of Mexican politics. *New York Review of Books,* 41, 19 (November 17): 29–34.

King, Anthony. (1990). World Cities, Colonial Cities: Connections and Comparisons. In *Global Cities: Post-Imperialism and the Internationalization of London,* 33–52. London: Routledge.

King, Jr., Martin Luther. (1998). Pilgrimage to Nonviolence. In *The autobiography of Martin Luther King, Jr.,* ed. Clayborne Carson, 121–134. New York: Warner Books.

Kloppenberg, James. (1995). Institutionalism, rational choice, and historical analysis. *Polity,* 28, 1 (Fall): 125–128.

Knight, Jack. (1992). *Institutions and social conflict.* Cambridge: Cambridge University Press.

Krieger, Martin. (1981). *Advice and planning.* Philadelphia: Temple University Press.

Krueger, Anne. (1974). The political economy of the rent-seeking society. *American Economic Review,* 64, 3 (June): 291–303.

LAHD (Los Angeles Housing Department). (1994). *Earthquake recovery: Housing update,* 1, 2, August.

LAHD (Los Angeles Housing Department). (1995). Los Angeles Housing Department report on the earthquake recovery program and prioritization plan per the Alarcon/Hernandez motion (C.F. 95-0073). Committee transmittal to Mayor Richard Riordan. Photocopied. November 20.

LAHD (Los Angeles Housing Department). (1996). Rebuilding communities after the 1994 Northridge earthquake: Year two recovery report. Los Angeles: Los Angeles Housing Department. Photocopied. January 17.

Lane, Jan-Erik. (1993). *The public sector: Concepts, models and approaches.* London: Sage.

Langewiesche, William. (1998). The lessons of ValuJet 592. *The Atlantic Monthly,* 281, 3 (March): 81–98.

Langewiesche, William. (2002). *American ground: Unbuilding the world trade center.* New York: North Point Press.

Larson, Tom. (1998). An economic view of south central Los Angeles. *Cities,* 15, 3: 193–208.

Leavitt, Jacqueline. (1996). Los Angeles neighborhoods respond to civil unrest: Is planning an adequate tool? In *Revitalizing urban neighborhoods*, ed. W. Dennis Keating, Norman Krumholz, and Philip Star, 112–130. Lawrence: University Press of Kansas.

Lezama, José Luis. (1997). El problema del aire en el valle de México: Crítica al la política gubernamental 1979–1996. *Estudios Demográficos y Urbanos*, 12 (3): 427–472. September–December.

Lezama, José Luis. (Professor in the Center for Demographic Studies and Urban Development of El Colegio de México, and Editor of the journal *Estudios Demográficos y Urbanos*). (1999). Interview with the author, August 25, Mexico City. Tape recording.

Lin, Justin and Jeffrey Nugent. (1995). Institutions and economic development. In *Handbook of development economics*, volume 3A, eds. Jere Behrman and T.N. Srinivasan, 2301–2370. Amsterdam: Elsevier Science B.V.

Linden, Eugene. (1993). Megacities. *Time*, 141, 2 (January 11): 28–38.

Litvin, Daniel. (1998). Development and the environment: Living dangerously. *The Economist*, 346 (8060): S8. March 21.

LMDC (Lower Manhattan Development Corporation). (2003a). Advisory councils. http://www.renewnyc.org/AboutUs/Advisory/index.shtml (accessed September 18).

LMDC (Lower Manhattan Development Corporation). (2003b). LMDC Board of Directors. http://www.renewnyc.org/AboutUs/board.shtml (accessed September 18).

LMDC (Lower Manhattan Development Corporation). (2003c). Process and framework. http://www.renewnyc.org/plan_des_dev/default.asp (accessed September 18).

LMDC (Lower Manhattan Development Corporation). (2003d). Secretary Martinez, Governor Pataki, and Mayor Bloomberg announce $50 million program for affordable housing in Lower Manhattan. http://www.renewnyc.org/News/DisplayStory.asp?id=73 (accessed September 18).

Los Angeles Times. (1992). Understanding the riots.

Lynch, Kevin. (1981). *Good city form*. Cambridge: The MIT Press.

Lynch, Kevin. (1990). City and regional planning. In *City sense and city design: Writings and projects of Kevin Lynch*, eds. Tridib Banerjee and Michael Southworth, 535–562. Cambridge: The MIT Press.

Lynch, Kevin and Gary Hack. (1984). *Site Planning*. 3rd ed. Cambridge: The MIT Press.

Malik, F. and G. Probst. (1984). Evolutionary management. In *Self-organization and management of social systems: Insights, promises, doubts, and questions*, eds. H. Ulrich and G. J. B. Probst, 105–120. Berlin: Springer-Verlag.

Mandelbaum, Seymour. (1985). The institutional focus of planning theory. *Journal of Planning Education and Research*, 5, 1 (Autumn): 3–9.

Mandelbaum, Seymour, Luigi Mazza and Robert Burchell, eds. (1996). *Explorations in planning theory*. New Brunswick, NJ: Center for Urban Policy Research.

Manuel, Louise. (Local Initiatives Service Corporation). (1999). Interview with the author, July 21, Los Angeles. Written notes.

March, James. (1988). *Decisions and organizations*. Oxford: Basil Blackwell Ltd.

March, James and Johan Olsen. (1984). The new institutionalism: Organizational factors in political life. *The American Political Science Review*, 78, 3: 734–749.

March, James and Johan Olsen. (1989). *Rediscovering institutions: The organizational basis of politics*. New York: The Free Press.

Marcuse, Peter. (1990). United States of America. In *International handbook of housing policies and practices*, ed. Willem van Vliet, 327–376. New York: Greenwood Press.

Marcuse, Peter. (2002). What kind of planning after September 11? The market, the stakeholders, consensus—or . . . ? In *After the world trade center*, eds. Michael Sorkin and Sharon Zukin, 153–161. New York: Routledge.

Markman, Jon. (1995). Still shaken: A resilient Los Angeles seeks to retrieve its future. In "Special quake report: One year later." *Los Angeles Times*, January 15.

Martin, Hugo. (1994). Loans to rebuild quake 'Ghost Towns' OKd. *Los Angeles Times*, July 23.

Martin, Hugo. (1995). 99% of 'Ghost Town' owners get quake aid. *Los Angeles Times*, November 22.

McGeary, Johanna. (1999). Buried alive. *Time*, 154, 9 (August 30): 26–31.

McGreevy, Patrick. (1999). Five years later, valley showing strong recovery signs. *Los Angeles Times*, January 15.

Meislin, Richard. (1985). After the quakes: Political rumblings. *New York Times*, October 4.

Meyers, Laura and Michael Stremfel. (1994). What's your house worth now? *Los Angeles Magazine*, 39, 9 (September): 83–95.

Mitchell, James, ed. (1999). *Crucibles of hazard: Mega-cities and disasters in transition.* Tokyo: United Nations University Press.

Mitroff, Ian. (1983). *Stakeholders of the organizational mind: Toward a new view of organizational policy making.* San Francisco: Josey-Bass.

Moe, Terry. (1984). The new economics of organization. *American Journal of Political Science*, 28, 4: 739–777.

Molina, Luisa, and Mario Molina, eds. (2002). *Air quality in the Mexico megacity: An integrated assessment.* Dordecht, Netherlands: Kluwer Academic Publishers.

Moos, A. I. and Michael Dear. (1986a). Structuration theory in urban analysis: 1. Theoretical exegesis. *Environment and Planning A*, 18, 231–252.

Moos, A. I. and Michael Dear. (1986b). Structuration theory in urban analysis: 2. Empirical application. *Environment and Planning A*, 18, 351–373.

Mumme, Stephen. (1991). Clearing the air: Environmental reform in Mexico. *Environment*, 33, 10: 6–30. December.

Murray, Sarah. (2003). Redevelopment, after the drama. *Financial Times*, May 27.

Mydans, Seth. (1994). Months after the quake, ghost towns in the city of angels. *New York Times*, August 10.

Myrdal, Gunnar. (1968). *Asian drama: An inquiry into the poverty of nations.* New York: The Twentieth Century Fund.

Nabli, Mustapha and Jeffrey Nugent, eds. (1989). *The new institutional economics and development: Theory and applications to Tunisia.* Amsterdam: North Holland.

Nagourney, Adam. (2002). Ground zero: The site. *New York Times*, March 7.

Nasr, Joseph. (1996). Beirut / Berlin: Choices in Planning for the Suture of Two Divided Cities. *Journal of Planning Education and Research,* 16 (1): 27–40. Fall.

National Geographic Society. (1999). *National geographic atlas of the world*, 7th ed. Washington, DC: National Geographic Society.

Neal, David and Brenda Phillips. (1995). Effective emergency management: Reconsidering the bureaucratic approach. *Disasters* 19, 4 (December): 327–337.

New York Times. 2002. More than an academic exercise. September 24, A26.

Niskanen, William. (1971). *Bureaucracy and representative government.* Chicago: Aldine.

NIST (National Institute of Standards and Technology). (1994). Performance of HUD-assisted properties during the January 17, 1994 Los Angeles earthquake. Report prepared for U.S. Department of Housing and Urban Development. Washington, DC: Office of Policy Development and Research. August.

North, Douglass. (1986). Institutions and economic growth: An historical introduction. Paper prepared for the Conference on the Role of Institutions in Economic Development. Ithaca, NY: Cornell University.

North, Douglass. (1990). *Institutions, institutional change and economic performance.* New York: Cambridge University Press.

North, Douglass. (1992). Transaction costs, institutions, and economic performance. Occasional papers number 30. San Francisco: International Center for Economic Growth.

North, Douglass. (1994). Economic performance through time. *The American Economic Review,* 84, 3, June, 359–368.

O'Riordan, Patrick. (1994). Planning for disaster. *Administration*, 41, 4: 411–432.

Oden, Clyde. (Chief Executive Officer of WATTS Health Systems Incorporated). (1999). Interview with the author, 20 July, Los Angeles. Written notes.

Onursal, Bekir and Surhid Gautam. (1997). *Vehicular air pollution: Experiences from seven Latin American urban centers.* World Bank Technical Paper No. 373. Washington, DC: The World Bank.

Opper, Jan. (Senior Program Officer in the Office of Block Grants of the U.S. Department of Housing and Urban Development). (1996). Telephone interview with the author, August 2. Written notes.

Organization for Economic Co-operation and Development (OECD). (1996) *Towards clean transport: Fuel-efficient and clean motor vehicles.* Washington, DC: OECD Publications and Information Center.

Osborne, David and Ted Gaebler. (1992). *Reinventing government: How the entrepreneurial spirit is transforming the public sector.* Reading, MA: Addison-Wesley.

Ostrom, Elinor. (1986). An agenda for the study of institutions. *Public Choice,* 48: 3–25.

Ostrom, Elinor. (1991). Rational choice theory and institutional analysis: Toward complementarity. *American Political Science Review,* 85, 1 (March): 237–243.

Ostrom, Elinor, Larry Schroeder, and Susan Wynne. (1993). *Institutional incentives and sustainable development: Infrastructure policies in perspective.* Boulder, CO: Westview Press.

Oyen, Else, ed. (1990). *Comparative methodology: Theory and practice in international social research.* London: Sage.

Palm, Risa. (1998). Urban earthquake hazards: The impacts of culture on perceived risk and response in the USA and Japan. *Applied Geography,* 18, 1: 35–46.

Pantelic, Jelena. (1998). Housing after disasters. In *The encyclopedia of housing,* ed. Willem van Vliet, 253–254. Thousand Oaks, CA: Sage.

Parker, John and George Yeo. (1995). Turn up the lights: A survey of cities. *The Economist,* 336, 7925 (July 29): 1–18.

Perlman, Janice. (1990). A dual strategy for deliberate social change in cities. *Cities,* 7, 1 (February): 3–15.

Perló, Manuel. (1991). Housing policy and its implications on the real estate market in central Mexico City. Paper presented at the IX Encuentro de la Red Nacional de Investigacion Urbana, México D.F. (October). Photocopied.

Perrow, Charles. (1984). *Normal accidents: Living with high-risk technologies.* New York: Basic Books.

Pezzoli, Keith. (1987). The urban land problem and popular sector housing development in Mexico City. *Environment and Development,* 19, 3: 371–397.

Picciotto, Robert. (1994). Visibility and disappointment: The new role of development evaluation. In *Rethinking the development experience: Essays provoked by the work of Albert O. Hirschman,* eds. Lloyd Rodwin and Donald Schon, 210–230. Washington, DC: The Brookings Institution.

Pick, James and Edgar Butler. (1997). *Mexico megacity.* Boulder, CO: Westview Press.

Preston, Julia. (1996). The city that can't fix the air. *New York Times,* February 4, E4.

Protzen, Jean-Pierre. (1981). Reflections on the fable of the caliph, the ten architects, and the philosopher. *Journal of Architectural Education,* 34 (Summer): 2–8.

Pugh, Cedric. (1994). Housing policy development in developing countries: The World Bank and internationalization, 1972–93. *Cities,* 11, 3: 159–180.

Regalado, James. (1994). Community coalition-building. In *The Los Angeles riots: Lessons for the urban future,* ed. Mark Baldassare, 205–235. Boulder, CO: Westview Press.

Renwick, Lucille. (1994). Ghost town. In "City Times." *Los Angeles Times,* October 2.

RHP (Renovación Habitacional Popular). (1988). *Memoria de la reconstrucción.* Mexico City: Renovación Habitacional Popular. Photocopied.

Rico, Ernesto. (Director General of the Secretariat of the Environment, Government of Mexico City). (1999). Interview with the author, August 26, Mexico City. Tape recording.

Riding, Alan. (1986). A year after quake, Mexico City is on the mend. *New York Times,* September 20.

Rieff, David. (1991). *Los Angeles: Capital of the third world.* New York: Touchstone.

Rittel, Horst and Melvin Webber. (1973). Dilemmas in a general theory of planning. *Policy Sciences,* 4, 155–169.

River, Carla. (1993). City's riot recovery process is confused, ineffectual, report concludes. *Los Angeles Times,* April 29.

RLA. (1997). Rebuilding LA's urban communities: A final report from RLA. Santa Monica, CA: Milken Institute.

Roe, Emery. (1994). *Narrative policy analysis: Theory and practice.* Durham, NC: Duke University Press.

Rohter, Larry. (1987). Mexico quake victims try to forget. *New York Times,* September 21.

Rojas, Martinez Rosalba. (1997). Salud y medio ambiente. In *Problemas emergentes de la zona Metropolitana de lad Ciudad de México,* eds. M. Castillo and S. Reyes. Mexico City: Universidad Nacional Autónoma de México.

Rondinelli, Dennis. (1993). *Development projects as policy experiments: An adaptive approach to development administration,* 2nd ed. London: Routledge.

Rosen, Christine. (1986). *The limits of power: Great fires and the process of city growth in America*. Cambridge: Cambridge University Press.

Russell, George. (1985). Trouble after an earlier disaster. *Time*, November 25.

Ruttan, V. M. and Y. Hayami. (1984). Toward a Theory of Induced Institutional Innovation. *Journal of Development Studies*, 20 (July): 203–223.

Said, Edward. (1993). Introduction. In *Culture and imperialism*, xi–xxviii. New York: Alfred Knopf.

Sager, Tore. (1999a). Positive theory of planning based on institutionally-enriched social choice. Paper presented at the 41st Annual Conference of the Association of Collegiate Schools of Planning, Chicago.

Sager, Tore. (1999b). Manipulation in planning: The social choice perspective. *Journal of Planning Education and Research*, 19, 2: 123–134.

Sanyal, Bishwapriya. (1996). Meaning, not interest: Motivation for progressive planning. In *Explorations in planning theory*, eds. Seymour Mandelbaum, Luigi Mazza, and Robert Burchell, 134–150. New Brunswick: Center of Urban Policy Research, Rutgers, The State University of New Jersey.

Sartori, Giovanni. (1994). Compare Why and How: Comparing, Miscomparing and the Comparative Method. In *Comparing nations: Concepts, strategies, substance*, eds. by Mattei Dogan and Ali Kazancigil, 14–34. Oxford: Basil Blackwell Ltd.

Savitch, H. V. (1988). *Post-industrial cities: Politics and planning in New York, Paris, and London*. Princeton, NJ: Princeton University Press.

SCEPP (Southern California Earthquake Preparedness Project), Governor's Office of Emergency Services, State of California. (1991). Earthquake recovery and reconstruction planning guidelines for local governments. Sacramento: State of California.

Schneekloth, Lynda and Robert Shibley. (1995). *Placemaking: The art and practice of building communities*. New York: John Wiley and Sons.

Schön, Donald. (1983). *The reflective practitioner: How professionals think in action*. New York: Basic Books.

Schotter, Andrew. (1981). *The economic theory of social institutions*. New York: Cambridge University Press.

Scott, W. Richard. (1995). *Institutions and organizations*. Thousand Oaks, CA: Sage.

Self, Peter. (1982). *Planning the urban region: A comparative study of policies and organizations*. University AL: Alabama Press.

Selznick, Philip. (1992). *The moral commonwealth: Social theory and the promise of community*. Berkeley: University of California Press.

Shlay, Anne. (1993). Shaping place: Institutions and metropolitan development patterns. *Journal of Urban Affairs*, 15, 5: 387–404.

Shlay, Anne. (1995). Housing in the broader context in the United States. *Housing policy debate*, 6, 3: 695–720.

Simon, Richard and Myron Levin. (1995). Nearly a year after quake, U.S. aid exceeds $5 billion. *Los Angeles Times*, January 8: A1–A24.

Skidmore, Thomas and Peter Smith. (1992). *Modern Latin America*, 3d ed. New York: Oxford University Press.

Skowronek, Stephen. (1995). Order and change, *Polity*, 28, 1 (Fall): 91–96.

Smith, David. (1996). Developing an international political economy approach and the logic of historical-structural analysis. In *Third world cities in global perspective: The political economy of uneven urbanization*, 9–25 and 39–46. Boulder, CO: Westview Press.

Smith, Doug. (1994). Cisneros, Riordan tour 'Ghost Towns.' *Los Angeles Times*, August 5.

Smith, Greig. (Chief Deputy to Councilman Hal Bernson in the 12th District of Los Angeles). (1996). Interview with the author, July 12, Los Angeles. Tape recording.

Solo, Tova-Maria. (1991). Rebuilding the tenements: Issues in El Salvador's earthquake reconstruction program. *Journal of the American Planning Association*, 57, 3 (Summer): 300–312.

SPP (Secretaria de Programación y Presupuesto). (1983). *Plan nacional de desarrollo: Mandato popular y mi compromiso constitucional 1983–88*. Mexico City: Secretaria de Programación y Presupuesto.

Squier, Gary. (1992). Letter from Los Angeles to the honorable Tom Bradley, Mayor, City of Los Angeles, January 14. Housing Preservation and Production Department, Los Angeles. Photocopied.

Squier, Gary. (1993). Letter from Los Angeles to the honorable Tom Bradley, Mayor, City of Los Angeles, January 20. Housing Preservation and Production Department, Los Angeles. Photocopied.

Stanfield, Rochelle. (1994). For some, the waiting is nothing new. *National Journal*, 26, 7 (February 12).

Steedman, Scott. (1995). Megacities: The unacceptable risk of natural disaster. *Built Environment*, 21, 2/3: 89–93.

Stockton, William. (1986). Long wait ending for Mexico quake victims. *New York Times*, August 3.

Stolarski, Noemi. (Formerly in the Coordination of Investigation and Integration of the Document of the Renovation of Popular Housing (RHP) program, Mexico City, and formerly in the National Fund for Popular Housing (FONHAPO), Mexico City). (1995). Interview with the author, August 1. Tape recording.

Sullivan, William. (1995). Institutions as the infrastructure of democracy. In *New communitarian thinking: Persons, virtues, institutions, and communities,* ed. Amitai Etzioni, 170–180. Charlottesville: University Press of Virginia.

Sylves, Richard and Thomas Pavlak. (1990). The Big Apple and disaster planning: How New York City manages major emergencies. *In Cities and disaster: North American studies in emergency management,* eds. Richard Sylves and William Waugh, 185–219. Springfield, IL: Thomas Books.

Tendler, Judith and Sara Freedheim. (1994). Bringing Hirschman back in: A case of bad government turned good. In *Rethinking the development experience: Essays provoked by the work of Albert Hirschman,* eds. Lloyd Rodwin and Don Schon, 176–209. Washington, DC: The Brookings Institution.

Thornley, Andy. (1998). Institutional change and London's urban policy agenda. *The Annals of Regional Science*, 32, 1: 162–183.

Tullock, Gordon. (1965). *The politics of bureaucracy.* Washington, DC: Public Affairs Press.

UN (United Nations). (1991). Population growth and policies in mega-cities: Mexico City. Population policy paper no. 32. New York: United Nations.

Uphoff, Norman. (1986). *Local institutional development: An analytical sourcebook with cases.* West Hartford, CT: Kumarian Press.

Urrutia, Alonso. (1996). Pedirá la ARDF una prórroga en la verficación de vehículos. *La Jornada,* February 21. http://www.jornada.unam.mx/1996/feb96/960221/cirucla.html (accessed on November 19, 2001).

U.S. Department of Commerce. Bureau of the Census. (1992). *1990 Census of Population and Housing: Summary Social, Economic, and Housing Characteristics: United States (1990 CPH-5-1).* Washington, DC: U.S. Government Printing Office.

Valery, Nicholas. (1995). Earthquake engineering. Survey. *The Economist,* 335, 7911 (April 22): 3–12.

Van den Berghe, Pierre. (1978). *Race and racism: A comparative perspective.* 2nd ed. New York: John Wiley and Sons.

Wachs, Martin and Nabil Kamel. (1996). Decision-making after disasters: Responding to the Northridge earthquake. *Access,* 1, 8 (Spring): 24–29.

Walters, Donna. (1993). Rebuild L.A.'s Kinsey busy polishing agency's image. *Los Angeles Times,* April 28.

Ward, Peter, ed. (1982). *Self-help housing: A critique.* London: Mansell Publishing Ltd.

Ward, Peter. (1990a). *Mexico City: The production and reproduction of an urban environment.* Boston: G. K. Hall.

Ward, Peter. (1990b). Mexico. In *The international handbook of housing policies and practices,* ed. Willem van Vliet, 407–436. New York: Greenwood Press.

Weise, Julie. (2001). City continues effort to improve environment. *The News,* October 29.

White, Hayden. (1987). *The content of the form: Narrative discourse and historical representation.* Baltimore: The Johns Hopkins University Press.

Whittow, John. (1995). Disaster impact and the built environment. *Built Environment,* 21, 2/3: 81–88.

Wildavsky, Aaron. (1979). *Speaking truth to power: The art and craft of policy analysis.* Boston: Little, Brown.

Williamson, Oliver. (1975). *Markets and hierarchies: Analysis and antitrust implications.* New York: Free Press.

Wirth, Clifford. (1997). Transportation policy in Mexico City: The politics and impacts of privatization. *Urban Affairs Review,* 33 (2): 155–181. November.

Wolf-Powers, Laura. (2002). 9/11/01–02: The swap, the lease, the Governor, the Olympics, the rest of the city. New York: GothamGazette.com. http://www.gothamgazette.com/landuse/91102.html (accessed October 10, 2002).

Woodall, Pam. (1994). The Global Economy (survey following p. 70). *The Economist,* 333 (7883): 3–38. October 1st.

World Bank. (1992). *Housing: Enabling markets to work.* Policy paper. Washington, DC: The World Bank.

World Health Organization (WHO) and United Nations Environment Program (UNEP). (1992). *Urban air pollution in megacities of the world.* Cambridge MA: Blackwell Reference.

Wyatt, Edward. (2001). A nation challenged: Rebuilding. *New York Times,* November 30.

Wyatt, Edward. (2002a). Ground Zero: Planning. *New York Times,* January 26.

Wyatt, Edward. (2002b). Panel of politicians is to advise in rebuilding. *New York Times,* February 1.

Wyatt, Edward. (2002c). Trade center plans are speeded up after criticism. *New York Times,* April 24.

Wyatt, Edward. (2002d). Downtown families eligible for more housing aid. *New York Times,* May 15.

Wyatt, Edward. (2002e). Planners vow to cooperate in rebuilding. *New York Times,* December 1.

Wyatt, Edward. (2003a). From political calculation, a sweeping vision of Ground Zero rose. *New York Times,* March 3.

Wyatt, Edward. (2003b). Trade center design shaped by politics more than by public. *The International Herald Tribune,* September 12.

Wyatt, Edward, David Chen, Charles Bagli, and Raymond Hernandez. (2002). After 9/11, parcels of money, and dismay. *New York Times,* December 30.

Yin, Robert. (1994). *Case study research: Design and methods,* 2nd edition. Thousand Oaks, CA: Sage.

Zahariadis, Nikolaos. (1997). Theoretical Notes on Method and Substance. In *Theory, Case, and Method in Comparative Politics,* 1–46. Fort Worth, TX: Harcourt Brace College Publishers.

Zearley, Thomas. (1993). Creating an enabling environment for housing: Recent reforms in Mexico. *Housing Policy Debate,* 4, 2: 239–249.

Zeidman, Barbara. (Former Assistant General Manager of the Los Angeles Housing Department (LAHD), Los Angeles). (1996). Interview with the author, July 15, Los Angeles. Tape recording.

Zepeda, Pedro and Alejandro Mohar. (1993). *Vivienda para pobladores de bajos ingresos: Políticas e instituciones.* Mexico City: El Nacional.

Zucker, Lynne. (1983). Organizations as institutions. In *Research in the sociology of organizations,* ed. Samuel Bachrach, 1–47. Greenwich, CT: Jai Press.

Index